SHONEN JUMP ADVANCED Manga Edition

Claymore

クレイモア

Vol. 1
Silver-eyed Slayer

Story and Art by **Norihiro Yagi**

Claymore

クレイモア

Vol. 1

ONTENTS

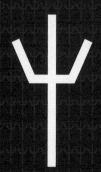

Scene 1: The Silver-Eyed Slayer

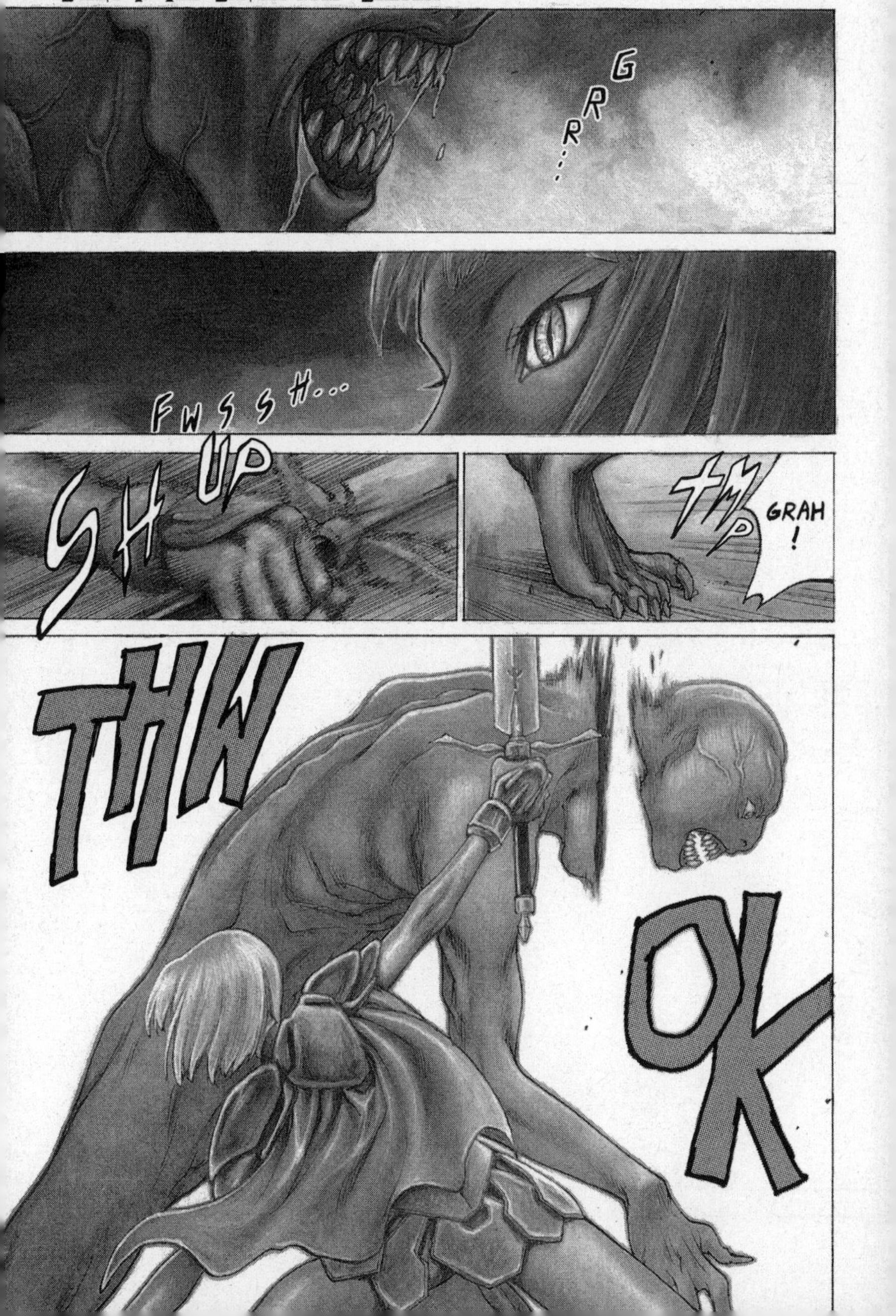
GRR...
FWSSH...
TMP
GRAH!
SHUP
THWOK

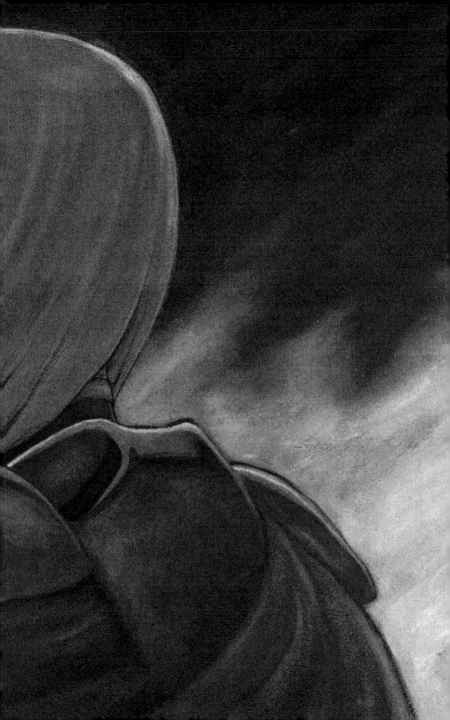

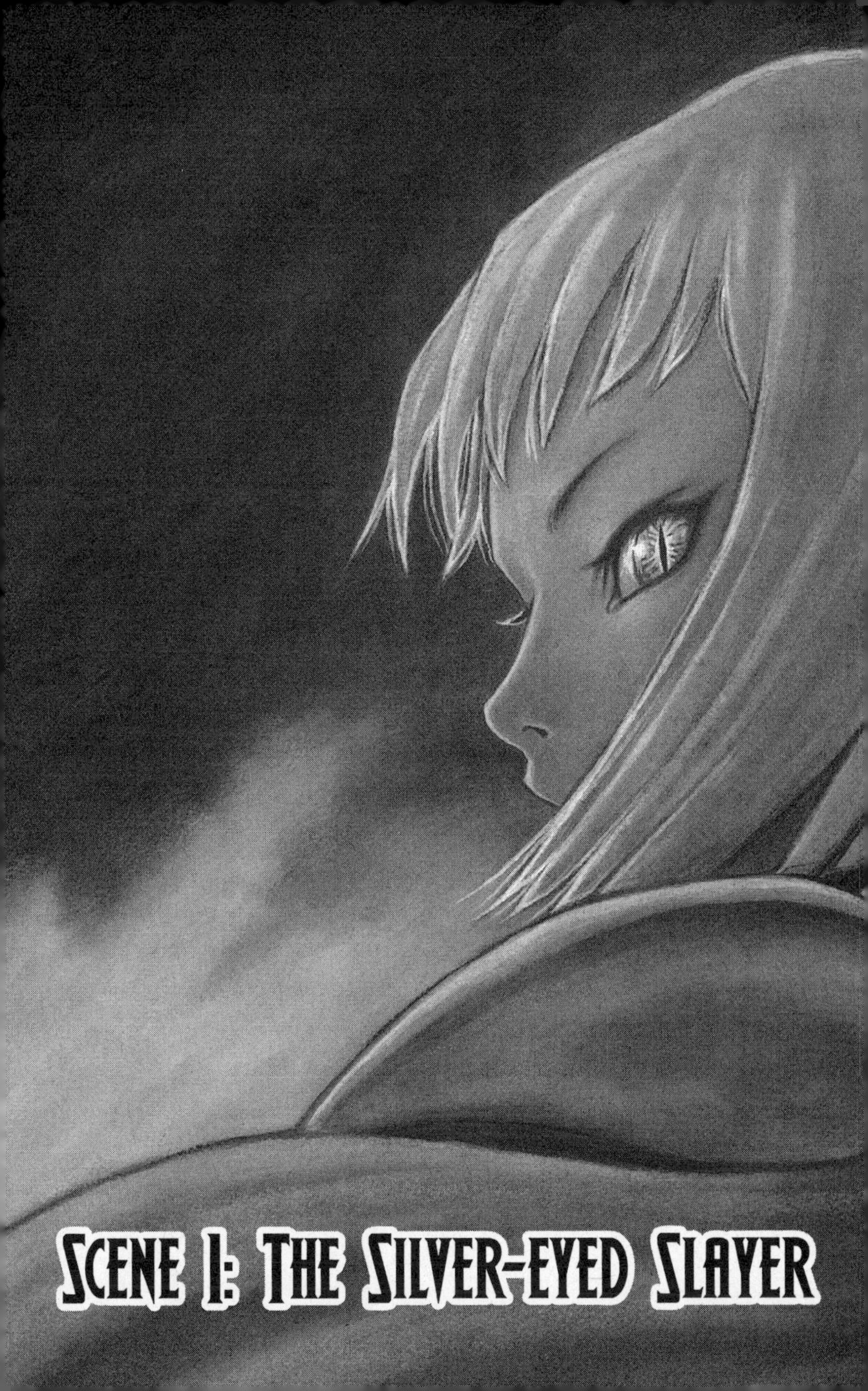

Scene 1: The Silver-eyed Slayer

READ THIS WAY

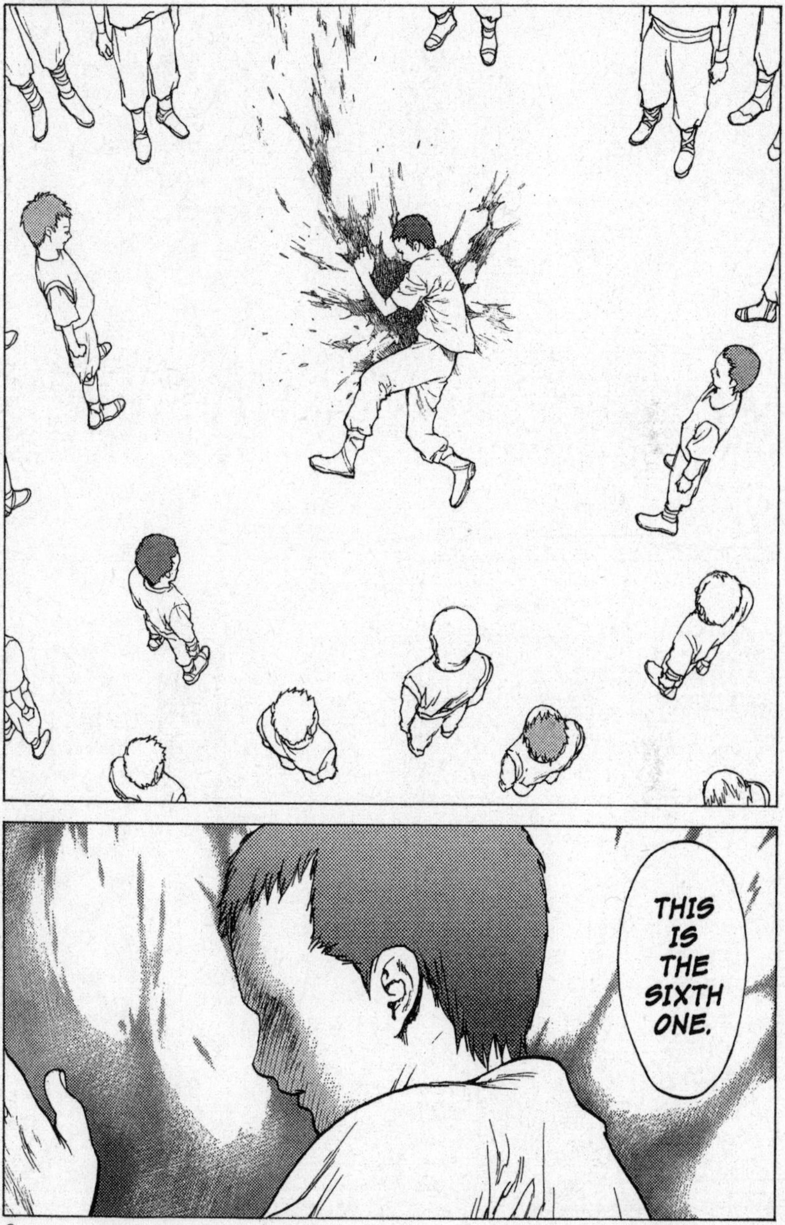
THIS IS THE SIXTH ONE.

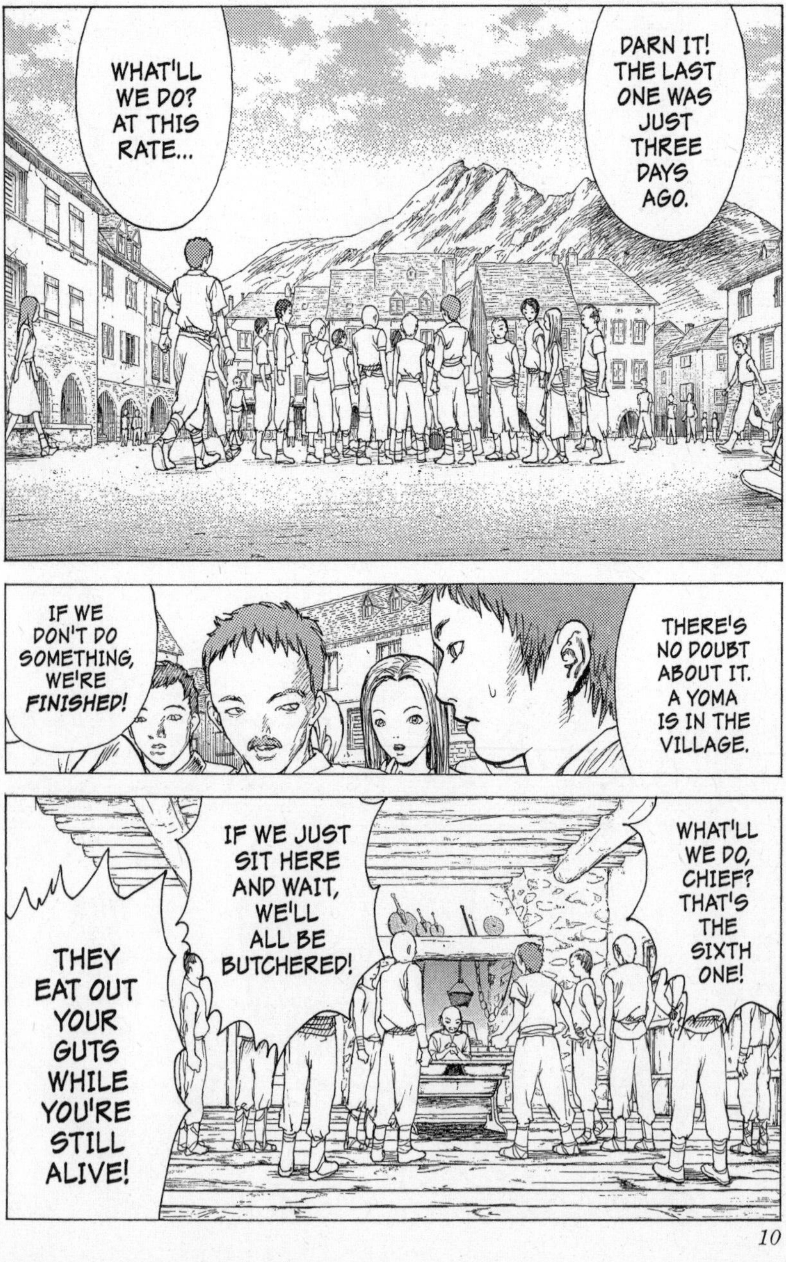
DARN IT! THE LAST ONE WAS JUST THREE DAYS AGO.
WHAT'LL WE DO? AT THIS RATE...
THERE'S NO DOUBT ABOUT IT. A YOMA IS IN THE VILLAGE.
IF WE DON'T DO SOMETHING, WE'RE *FINISHED!*
WHAT'LL WE DO, CHIEF? THAT'S THE SIXTH ONE!
IF WE JUST SIT HERE AND WAIT, WE'LL ALL BE BUTCHERED!
THEY EAT OUT YOUR GUTS WHILE YOU'RE STILL ALIVE!

READ THIS WAY

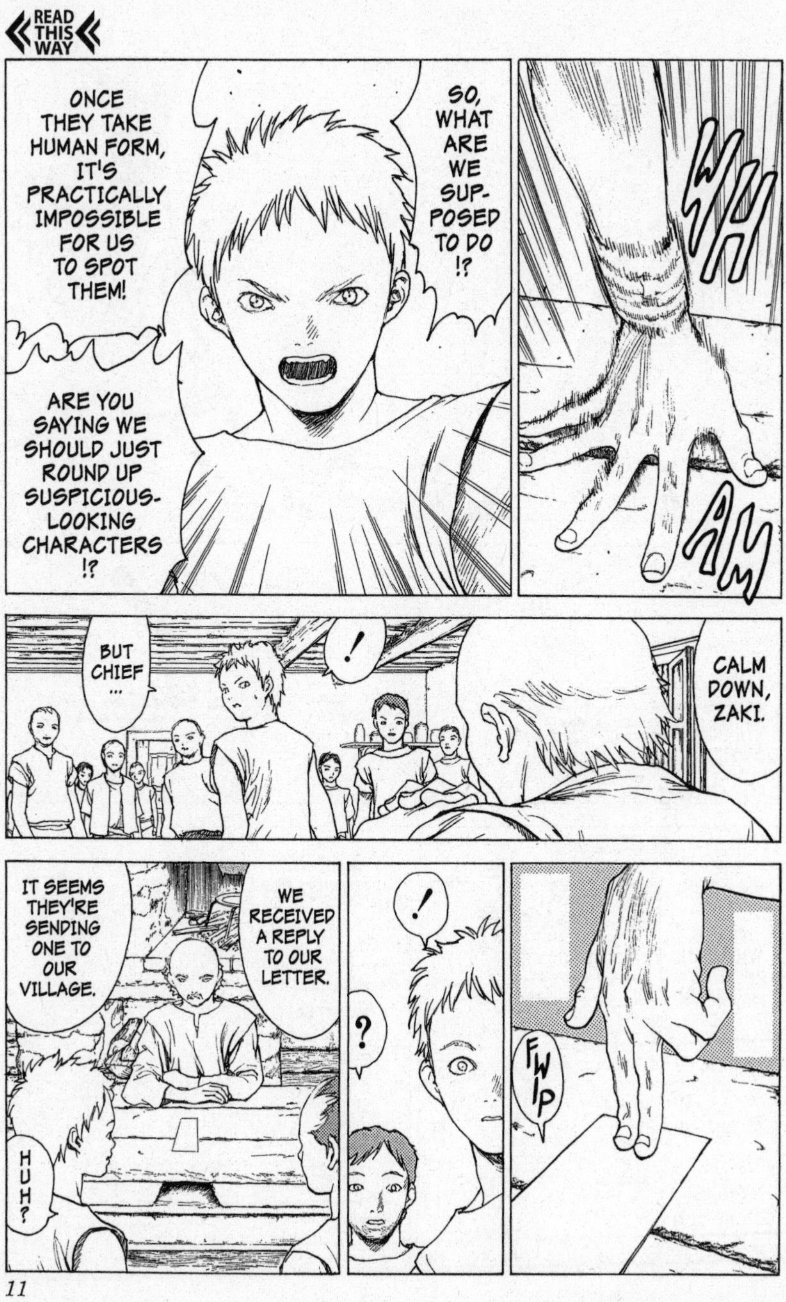
WHAM
SO, WHAT ARE WE SUP-POSED TO DO !?
ONCE THEY TAKE HUMAN FORM, IT'S PRACTICALLY IMPOSSIBLE FOR US TO SPOT THEM!
ARE YOU SAYING WE SHOULD JUST ROUND UP SUSPICIOUS-LOOKING CHARACTERS !?
CALM DOWN, ZAKI.
!
BUT CHIEF ...
FWIP
!
?
WE RECEIVED A REPLY TO OUR LETTER.
IT SEEMS THEY'RE SENDING ONE TO OUR VILLAGE.
HUH?

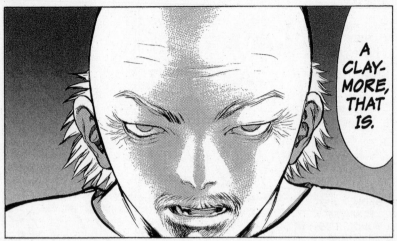

A CLAY-MORE, THAT IS.
!
GASP
A...A CLAY-MORE?
ARE YOU SERIOUS?
YOU WANT TO HIRE ONE OF THEM?
YES.
WE HAVE NO CHOICE.
THEY ARE THE ONLY ONES WHO CAN DETECT A MONSTER IN HUMAN FORM.

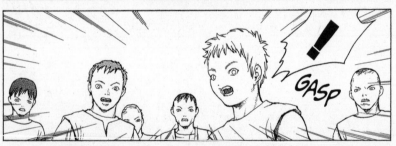

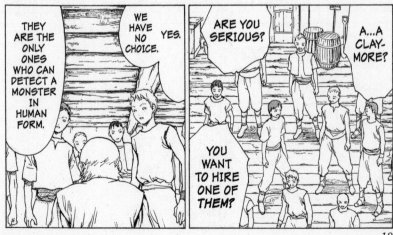

READ THIS WAY

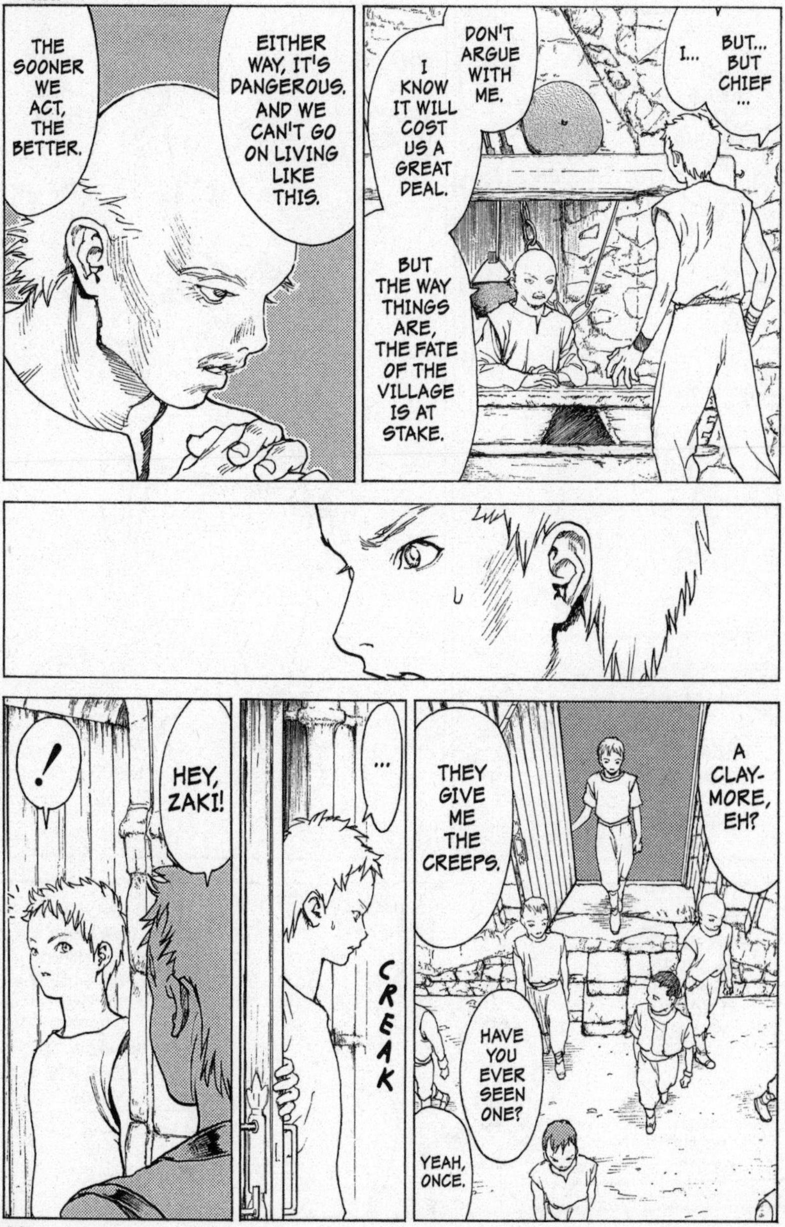
BUT... BUT CHIEF ...
I...
DON'T ARGUE WITH ME.
I KNOW IT WILL COST US A GREAT DEAL.
BUT THE WAY THINGS ARE, THE FATE OF THE VILLAGE IS AT STAKE.
EITHER WAY, IT'S DANGEROUS. AND WE CAN'T GO ON LIVING LIKE THIS.
THE SOONER WE ACT, THE BETTER.
A CLAYMORE, EH?
THEY GIVE ME THE CREEPS.
HAVE YOU EVER SEEN ONE?
YEAH, ONCE.
...
CREAK
HEY, ZAKI!
!

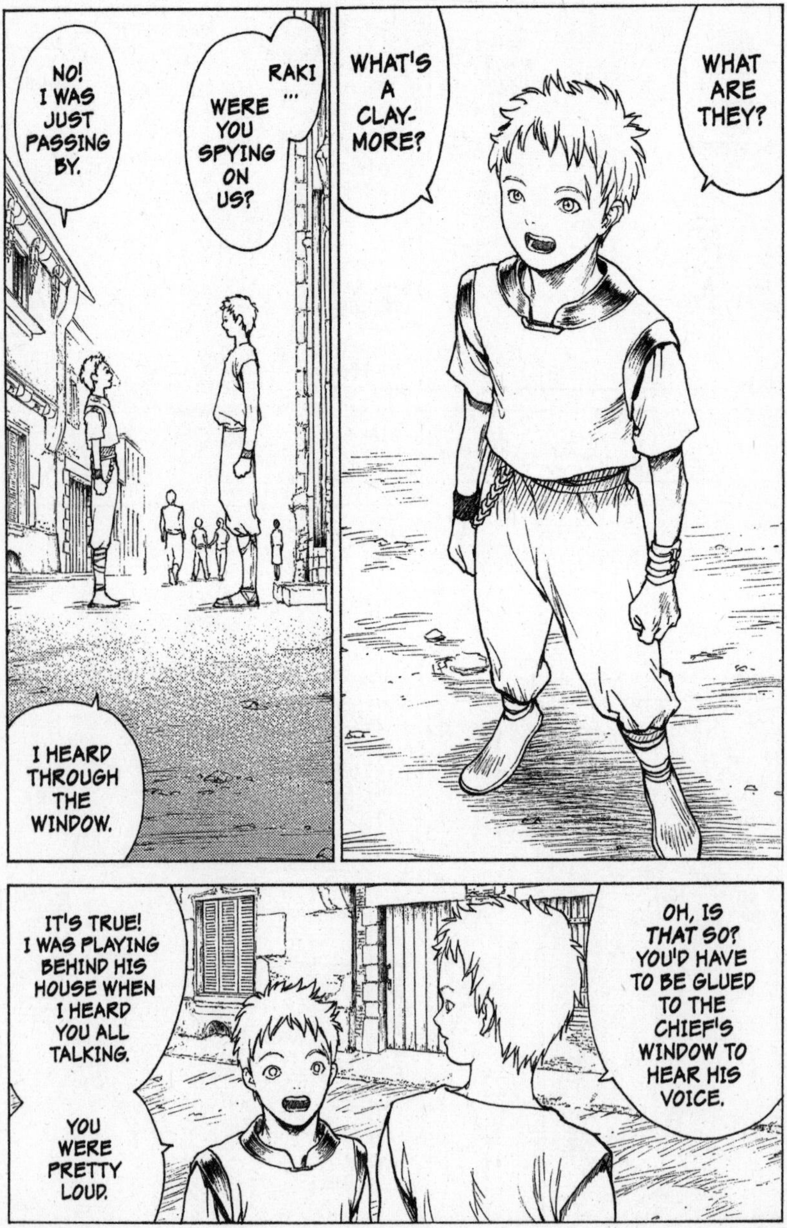
WHAT ARE THEY?
WHAT'S A CLAY-MORE?
RAKI ... WERE YOU SPYING ON US?
NO! I WAS JUST PASSING BY.
I HEARD THROUGH THE WINDOW.
OH, IS THAT SO? YOU'D HAVE TO BE GLUED TO THE CHIEF'S WINDOW TO HEAR HIS VOICE.
IT'S TRUE! I WAS PLAYING BEHIND HIS HOUSE WHEN I HEARD YOU ALL TALKING.
YOU WERE PRETTY LOUD.

READ THIS WAY

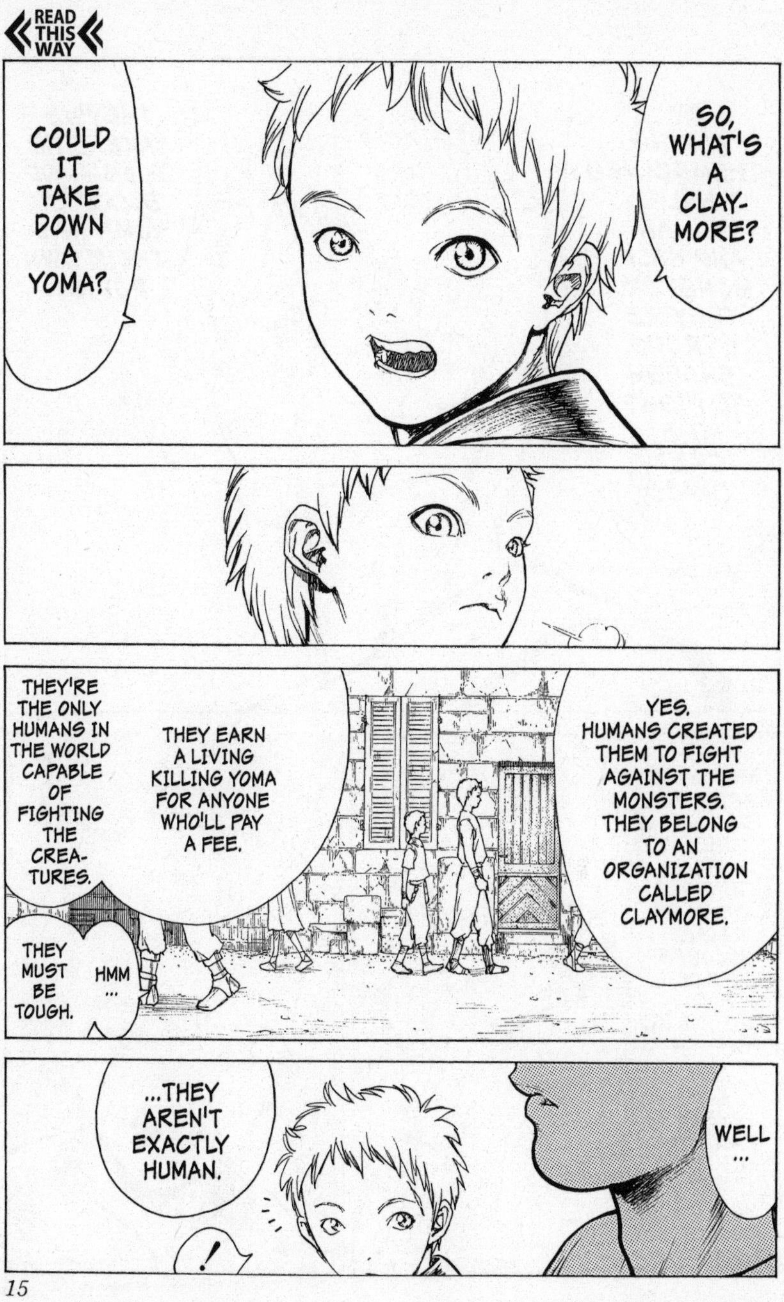
SO, WHAT'S A CLAYMORE?
COULD IT TAKE DOWN A YOMA?
YES. HUMANS CREATED THEM TO FIGHT AGAINST THE MONSTERS. THEY BELONG TO AN ORGANIZATION CALLED CLAYMORE.
THEY EARN A LIVING KILLING YOMA FOR ANYONE WHO'LL PAY A FEE.
THEY'RE THE ONLY HUMANS IN THE WORLD CAPABLE OF FIGHTING THE CREATURES.
HMM ...
THEY MUST BE TOUGH.
WELL ...
...THEY AREN'T EXACTLY HUMAN.
!

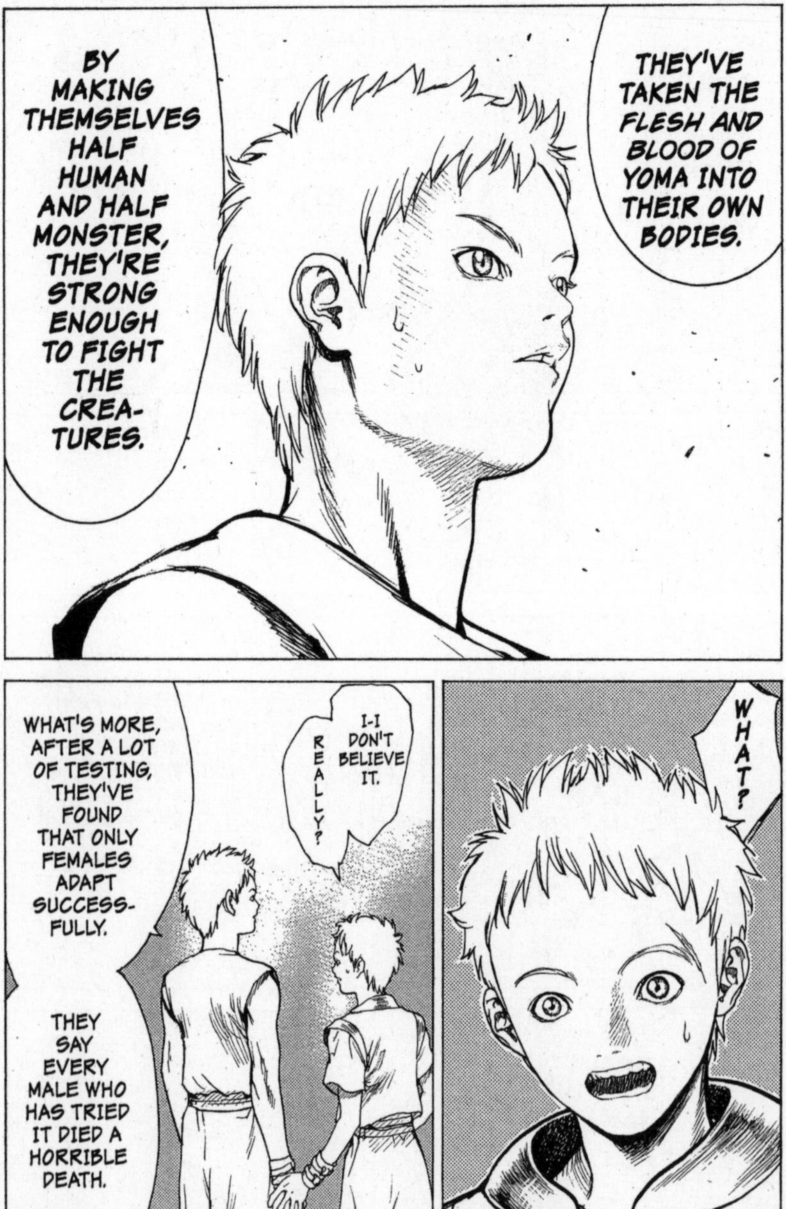
THEY'VE TAKEN THE FLESH AND BLOOD OF YOMA INTO THEIR OWN BODIES.
BY MAKING THEMSELVES HALF HUMAN AND HALF MONSTER, THEY'RE STRONG ENOUGH TO FIGHT THE CREA-TURES.
WHAT?
I-I DON'T BELIEVE IT.
REALLY?
WHAT'S MORE, AFTER A LOT OF TESTING, THEY'VE FOUND THAT ONLY FEMALES ADAPT SUCCESS-FULLY.
THEY SAY EVERY MALE WHO HAS TRIED IT DIED A HORRIBLE DEATH.

READ THIS WAY

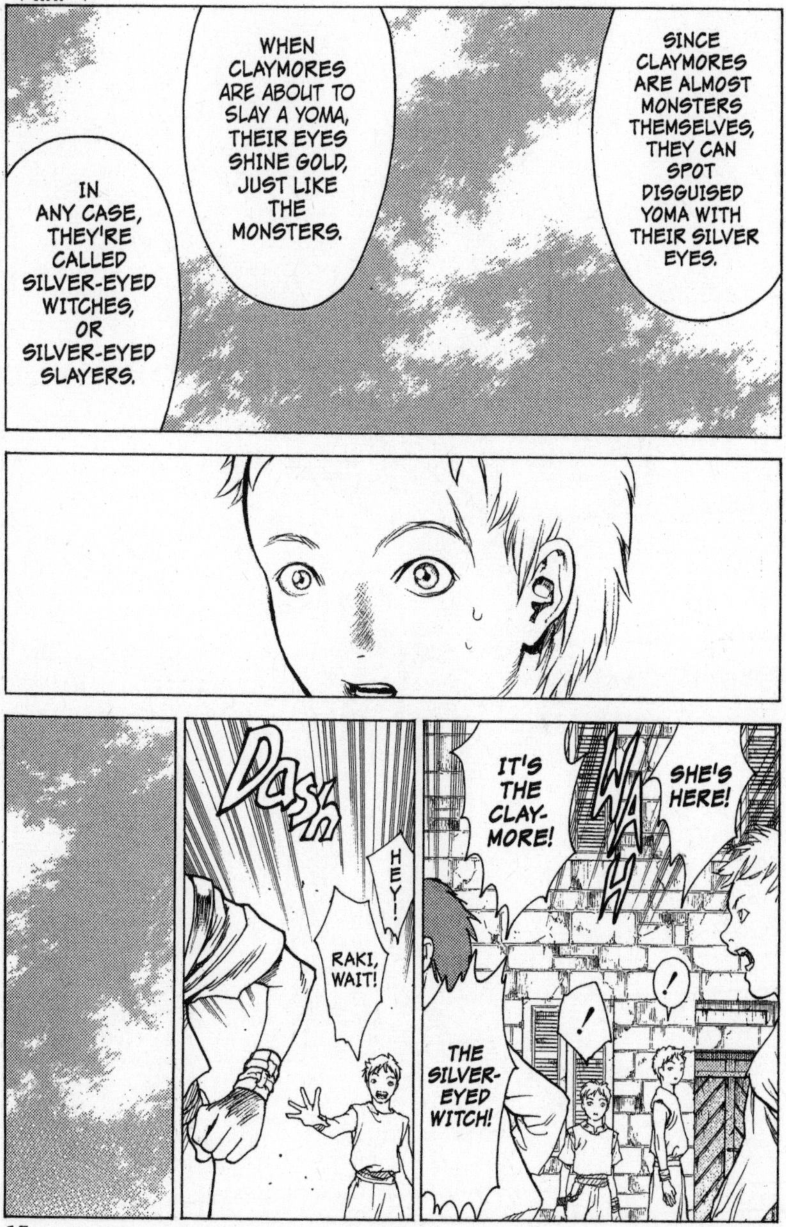
SINCE CLAYMORES ARE ALMOST MONSTERS THEMSELVES, THEY CAN SPOT DISGUISED YOMA WITH THEIR SILVER EYES.
WHEN CLAYMORES ARE ABOUT TO SLAY A YOMA, THEIR EYES SHINE GOLD, JUST LIKE THE MONSTERS.
IN ANY CASE, THEY'RE CALLED SILVER-EYED WITCHES, OR SILVER-EYED SLAYERS.
SHE'S HERE!
WAAH
IT'S THE CLAY-MORE!
!
!
THE SILVER-EYED WITCH!
Dash
HEY!
RAKI, WAIT!

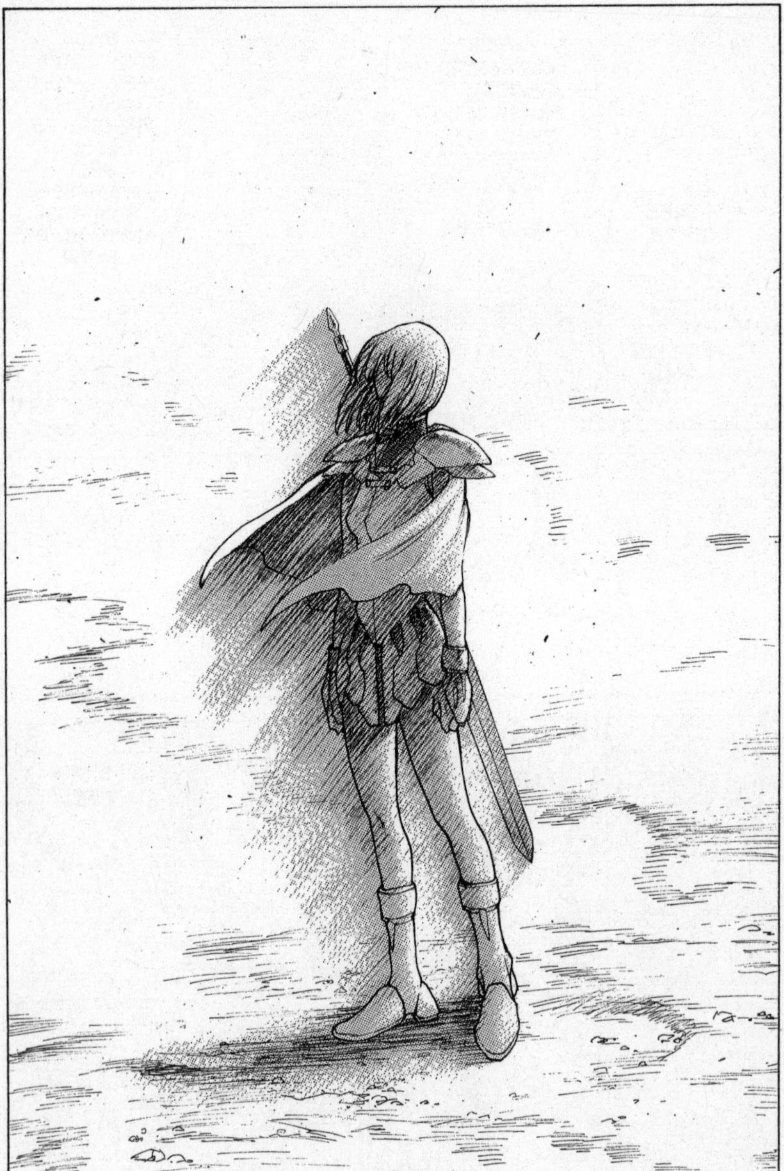

READ THIS WAY

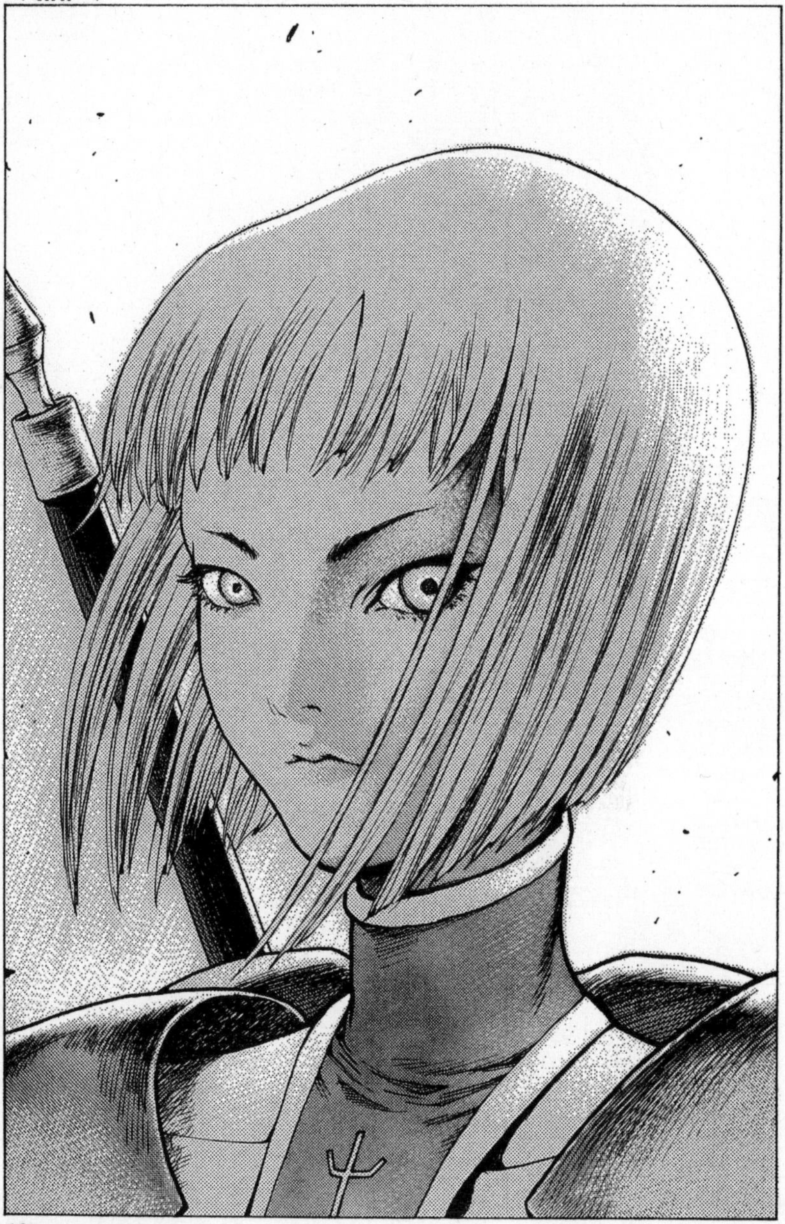

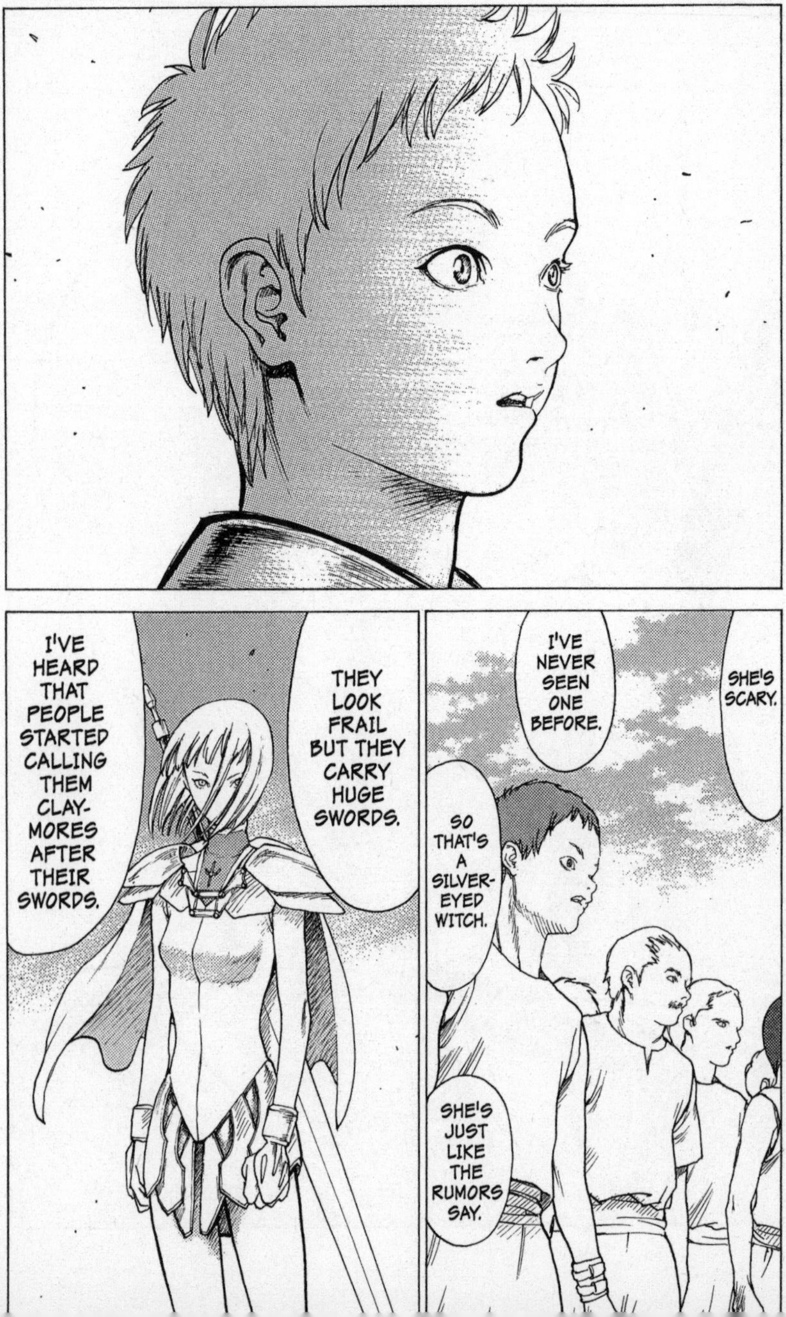
SHE'S SCARY.
I'VE NEVER SEEN ONE BEFORE.
SO THAT'S A SILVER-EYED WITCH.
SHE'S JUST LIKE THE RUMORS SAY.
THEY LOOK FRAIL BUT THEY CARRY HUGE SWORDS.
I'VE HEARD THAT PEOPLE STARTED CALLING THEM CLAYMORES AFTER THEIR SWORDS.

READ THIS WAY

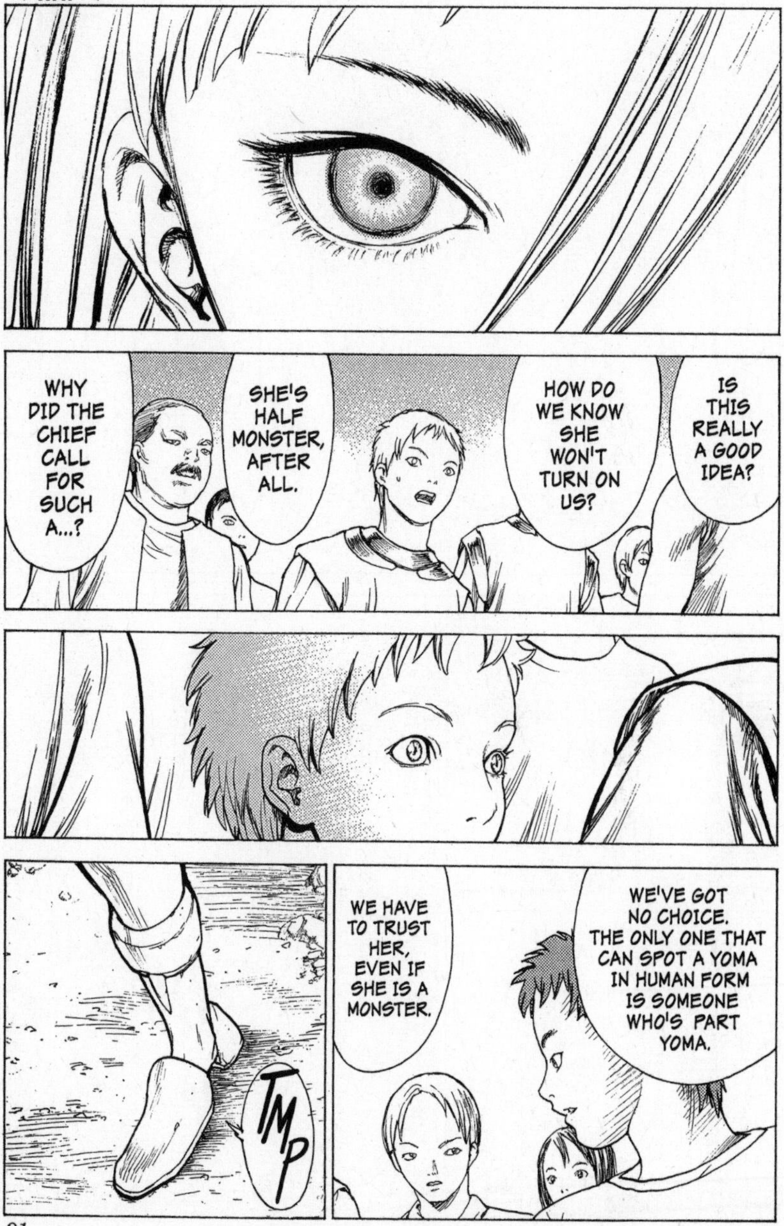
IS THIS REALLY A GOOD IDEA?
HOW DO WE KNOW SHE WON'T TURN ON US?
SHE'S HALF MONSTER, AFTER ALL.
WHY DID THE CHIEF CALL FOR SUCH A...?
WE'VE GOT NO CHOICE. THE ONLY ONE THAT CAN SPOT A YOMA IN HUMAN FORM IS SOMEONE WHO'S PART YOMA.
WE HAVE TO TRUST HER, EVEN IF SHE IS A MONSTER.
TMP

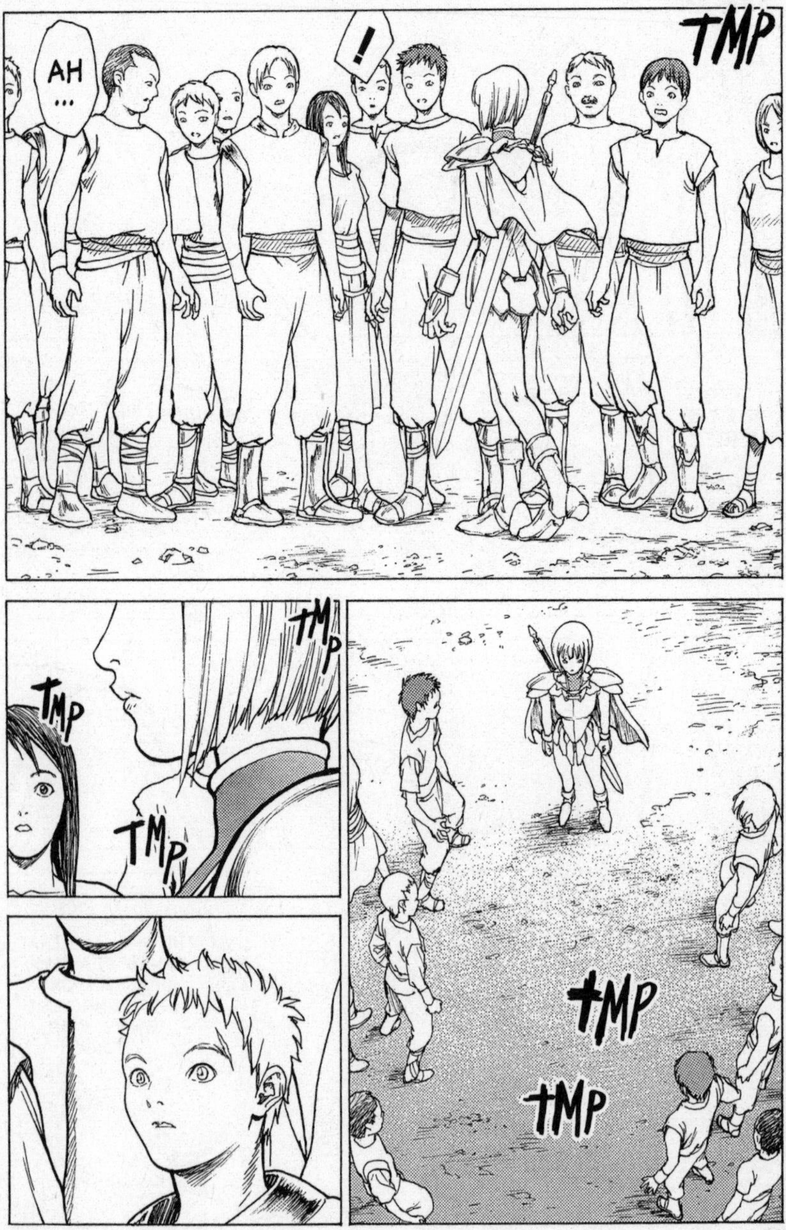
TMP
!
AH ...
TMP
TMP
TMP
TMP
TMP

READ THIS WAY

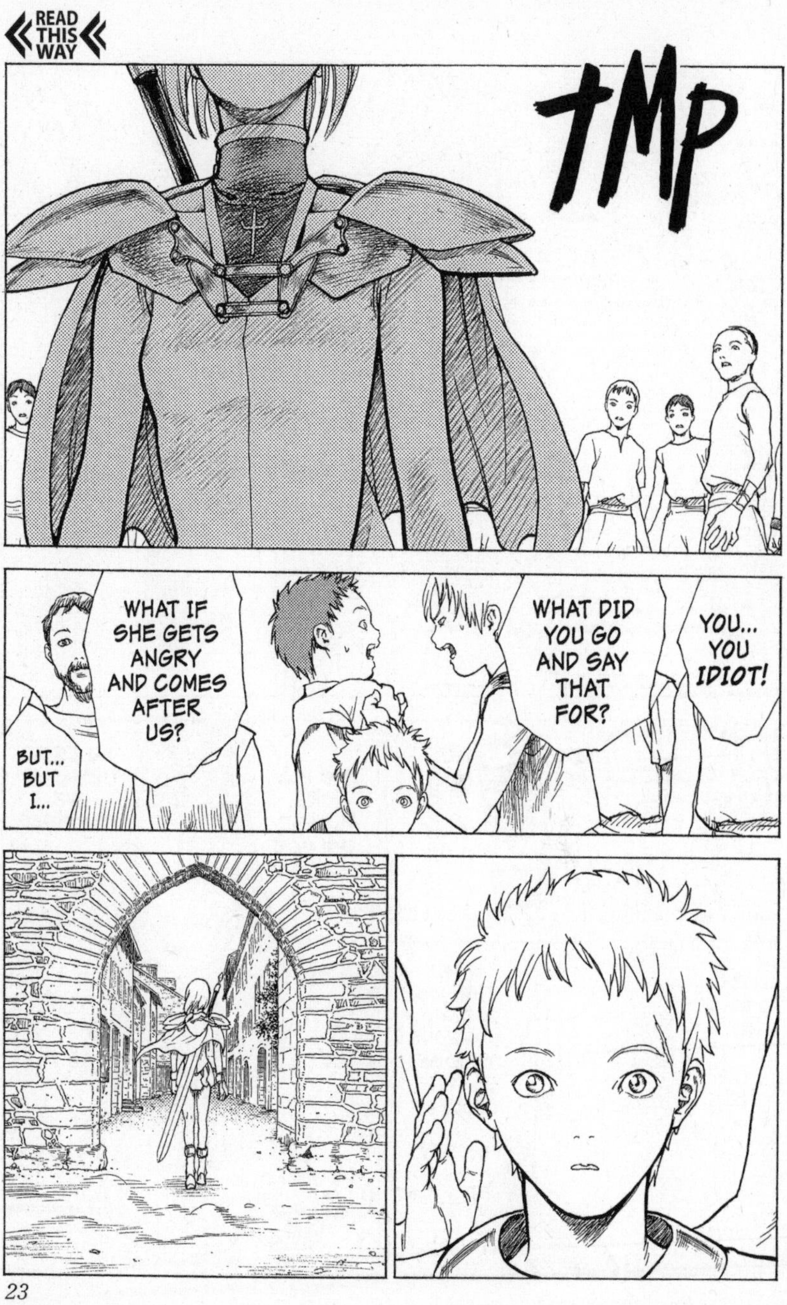
TMP
YOU... YOU IDIOT!
WHAT DID YOU GO AND SAY THAT FOR?
WHAT IF SHE GETS ANGRY AND COMES AFTER US?
BUT... BUT I...

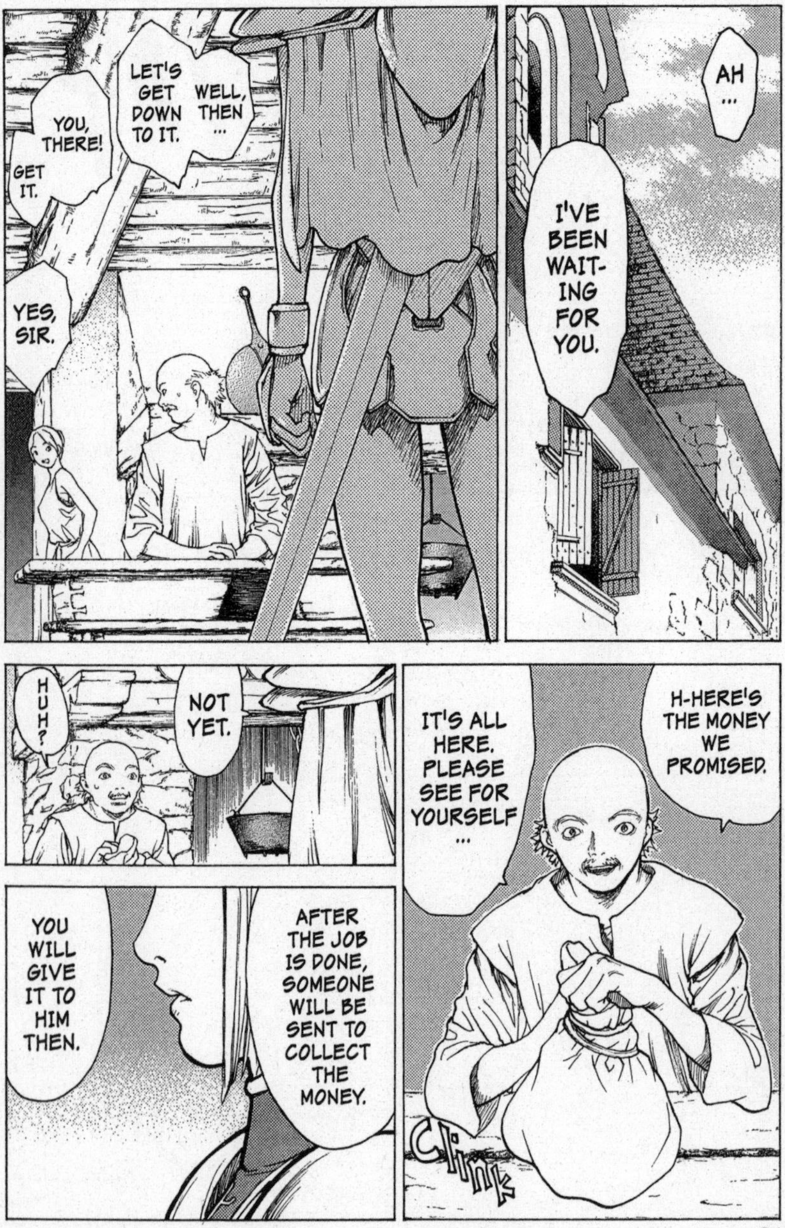
AH ...
I'VE BEEN WAITING FOR YOU.
WELL, THEN ...
LET'S GET DOWN TO IT.
YOU, THERE!
GET IT.
YES, SIR.
H-HERE'S THE MONEY WE PROMISED.
IT'S ALL HERE. PLEASE SEE FOR YOURSELF ...
Clink
NOT YET.
HUH?
AFTER THE JOB IS DONE, SOMEONE WILL BE SENT TO COLLECT THE MONEY.
YOU WILL GIVE IT TO HIM THEN.

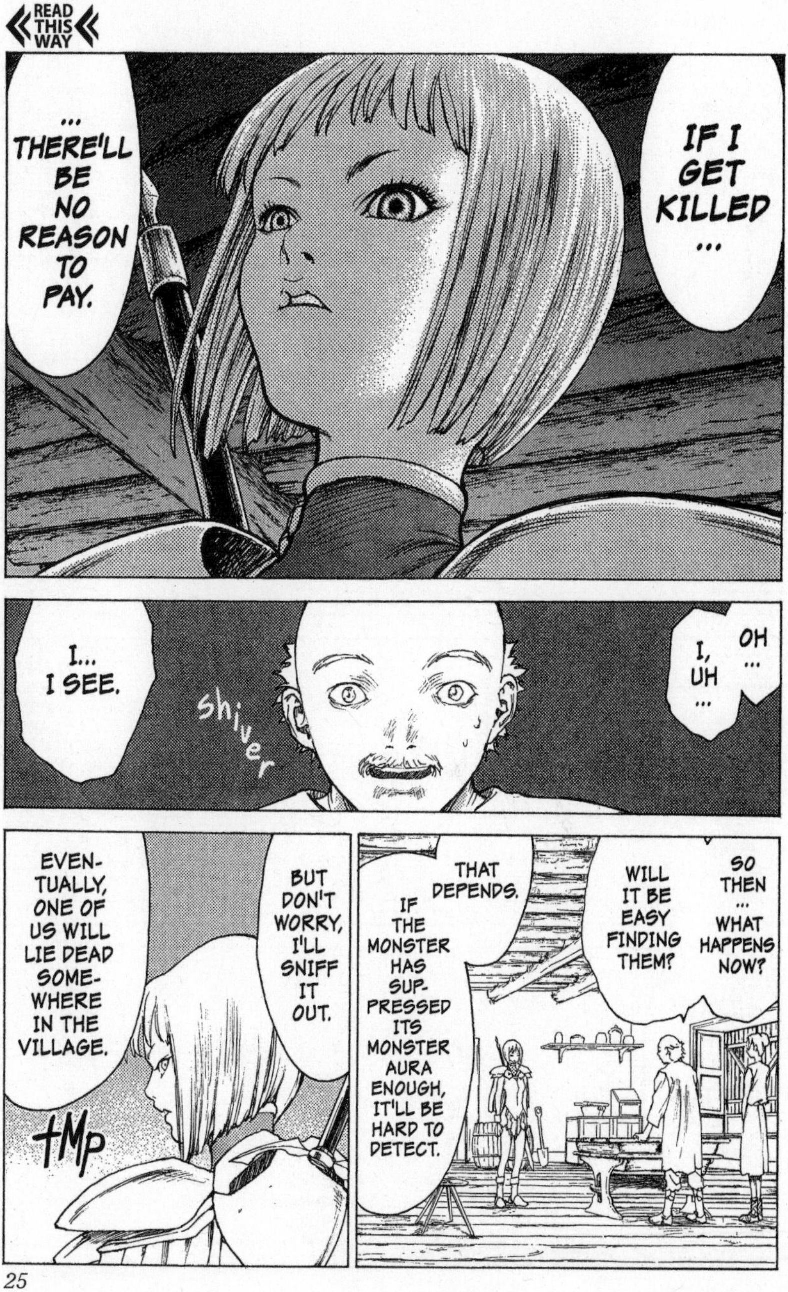
READ THIS WAY
IF I GET KILLED ...
... THERE'LL BE NO REASON TO PAY.
OH ...
I, UH ...
I... I SEE.
shiver
SO THEN ... WHAT HAPPENS NOW?
WILL IT BE EASY FINDING THEM?
THAT DEPENDS.
IF THE MONSTER HAS SUP-PRESSED ITS MONSTER AURA ENOUGH, IT'LL BE HARD TO DETECT.
BUT DON'T WORRY, I'LL SNIFF IT OUT.
EVEN-TUALLY, ONE OF US WILL LIE DEAD SOME-WHERE IN THE VILLAGE.
tMp

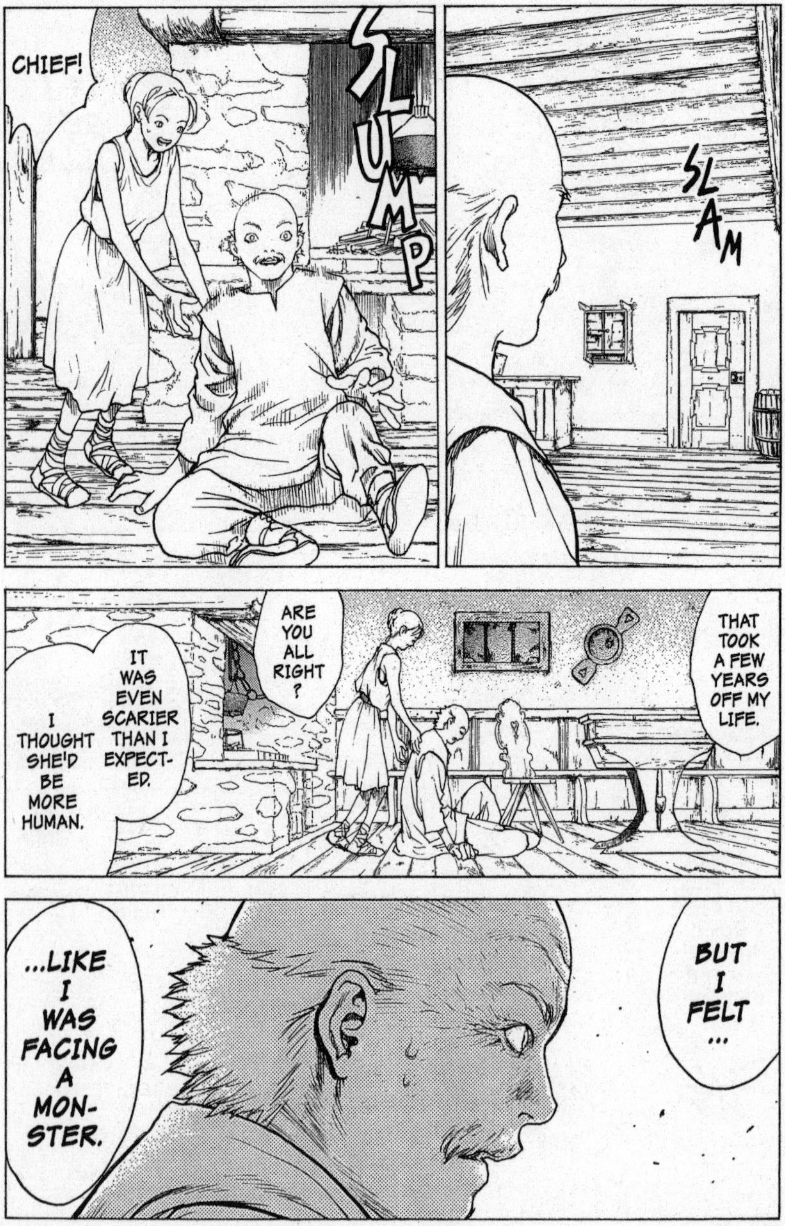
SLAM
SLUMP
CHIEF!
THAT TOOK A FEW YEARS OFF MY LIFE.
ARE YOU ALL RIGHT?
IT WAS EVEN SCARIER THAN I EXPECTED.
I THOUGHT SHE'D BE MORE HUMAN.
BUT I FELT...
...LIKE I WAS FACING A MONSTER.

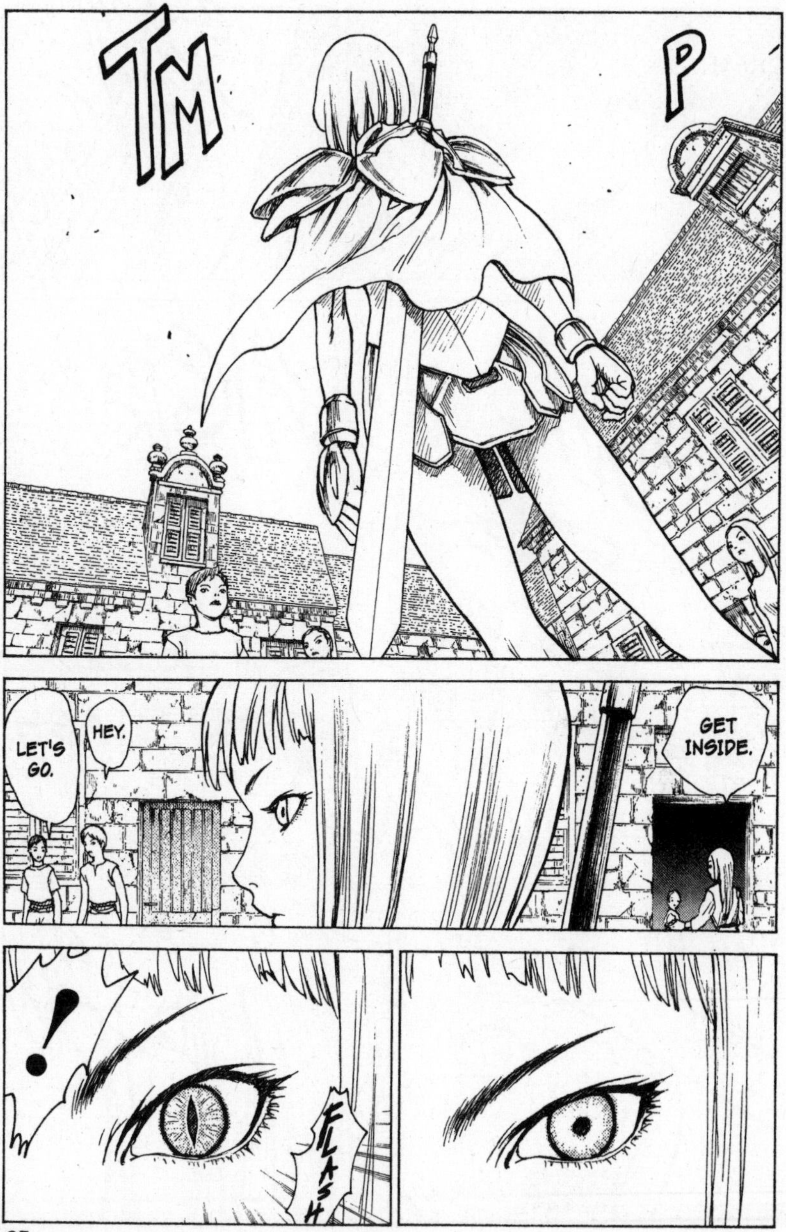
TMP
GET INSIDE.
HEY.
LET'S GO.
!
FLASH

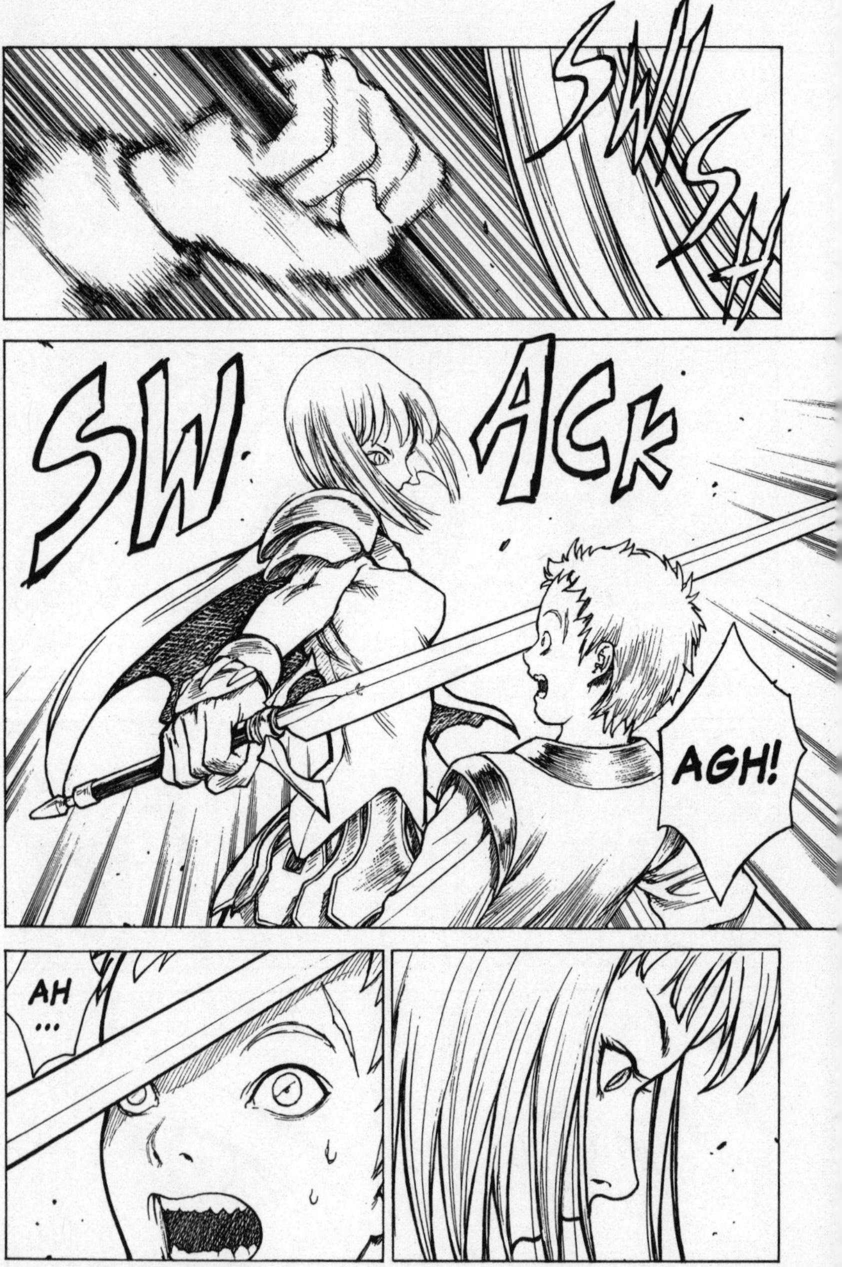
SWISH
SWACK
AGH!
AH ...

READ THIS WAY

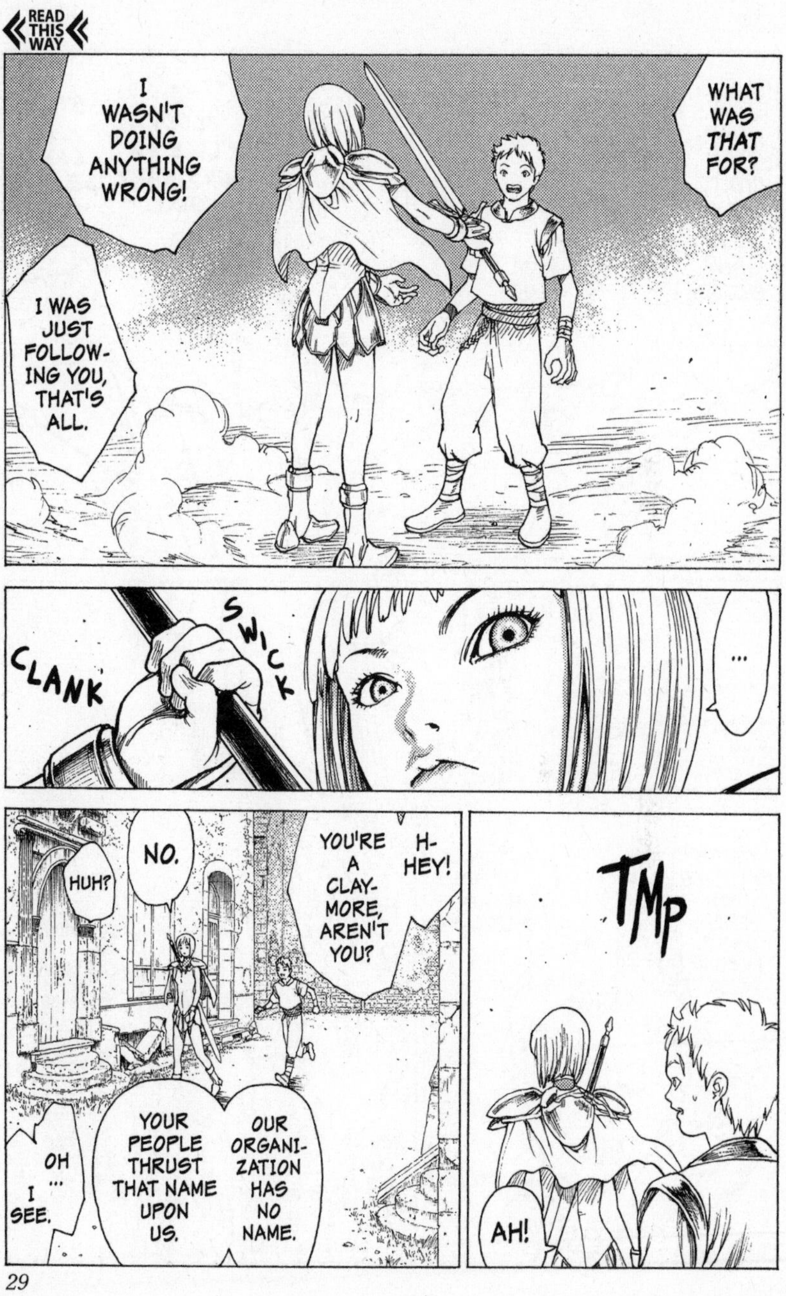

WHAT WAS THAT FOR?
I WASN'T DOING ANYTHING WRONG!
I WAS JUST FOLLOWING YOU, THAT'S ALL.
...
SWICK
CLANK
TMP
AH!
H-HEY!
YOU'RE A CLAYMORE, AREN'T YOU?
NO.
HUH?
OUR ORGANIZATION HAS NO NAME.
YOUR PEOPLE THRUST THAT NAME UPON US.
OH ... I SEE.

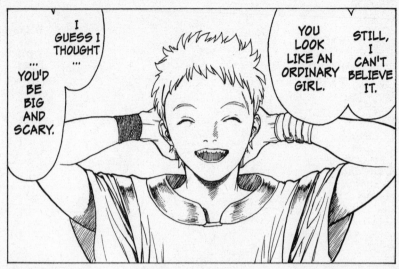

STILL, I CAN'T BELIEVE IT.
YOU LOOK LIKE AN ORDINARY GIRL.
I GUESS I THOUGHT ...
... YOU'D BE BIG AND SCARY.
YOU'RE NOT AFRAID OF ME?
HUH?
NO, NOT AT ALL.
YOU'RE JUST LIKE AN ORDINARY GIRL.
ACTUALLY, YOU'RE NOT SO ORDINARY.
Heh heh heh...
YOU'RE PRETTIER THAN THE GIRLS AROUND HERE.

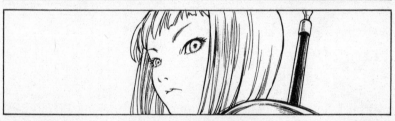

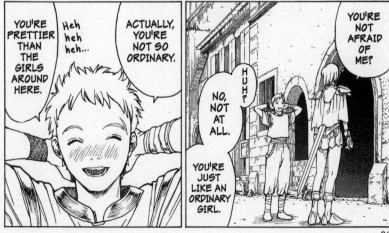

READ THIS WAY

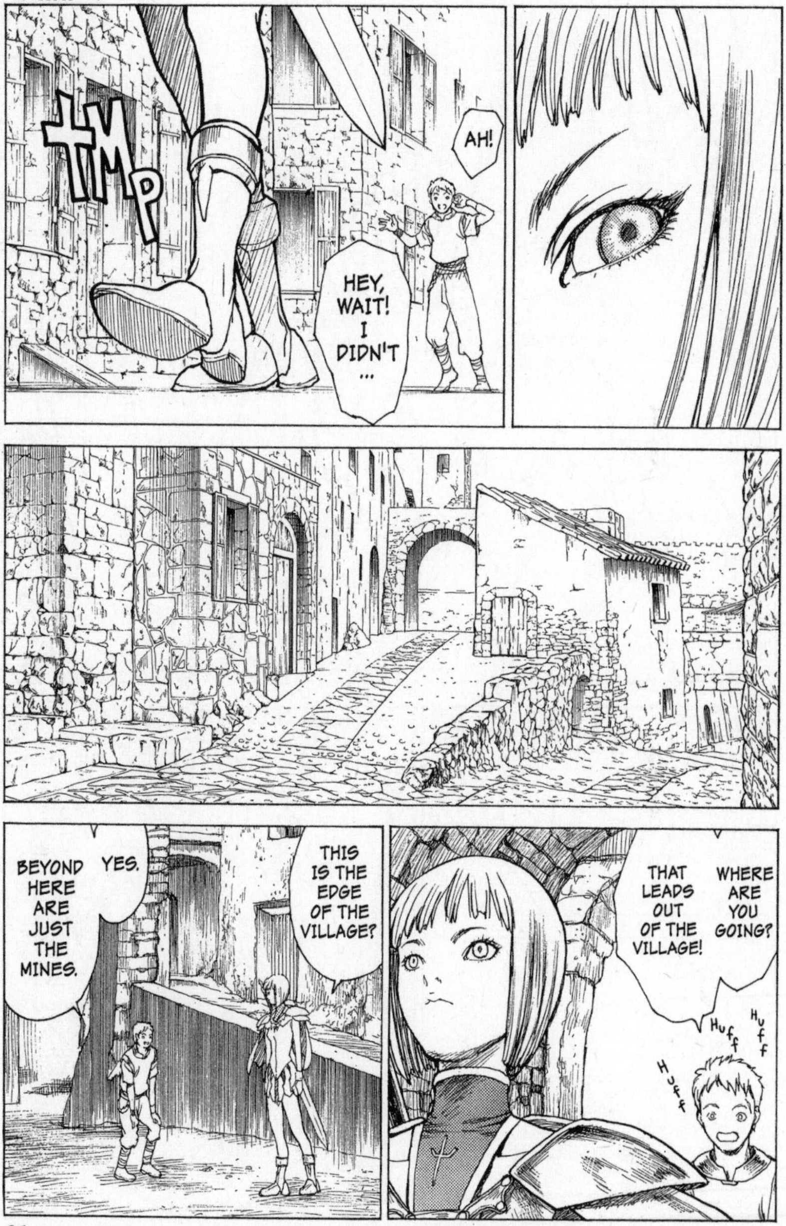

AH!
TMP
HEY, WAIT! I DIDN'T ...
WHERE ARE YOU GOING?
THAT LEADS OUT OF THE VILLAGE!
Huff
Huff
Huff
THIS IS THE EDGE OF THE VILLAGE?
YES.
BEYOND HERE ARE JUST THE MINES.

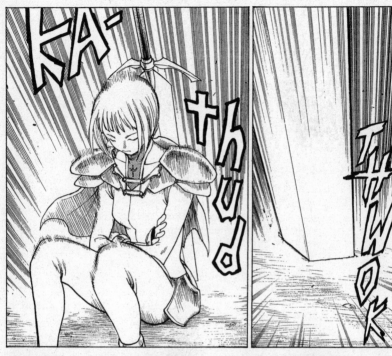

WHAT THE...?

REST TIME.

I'VE BEEN WALKING FOR THREE DAYS.

32

READ THIS WAY

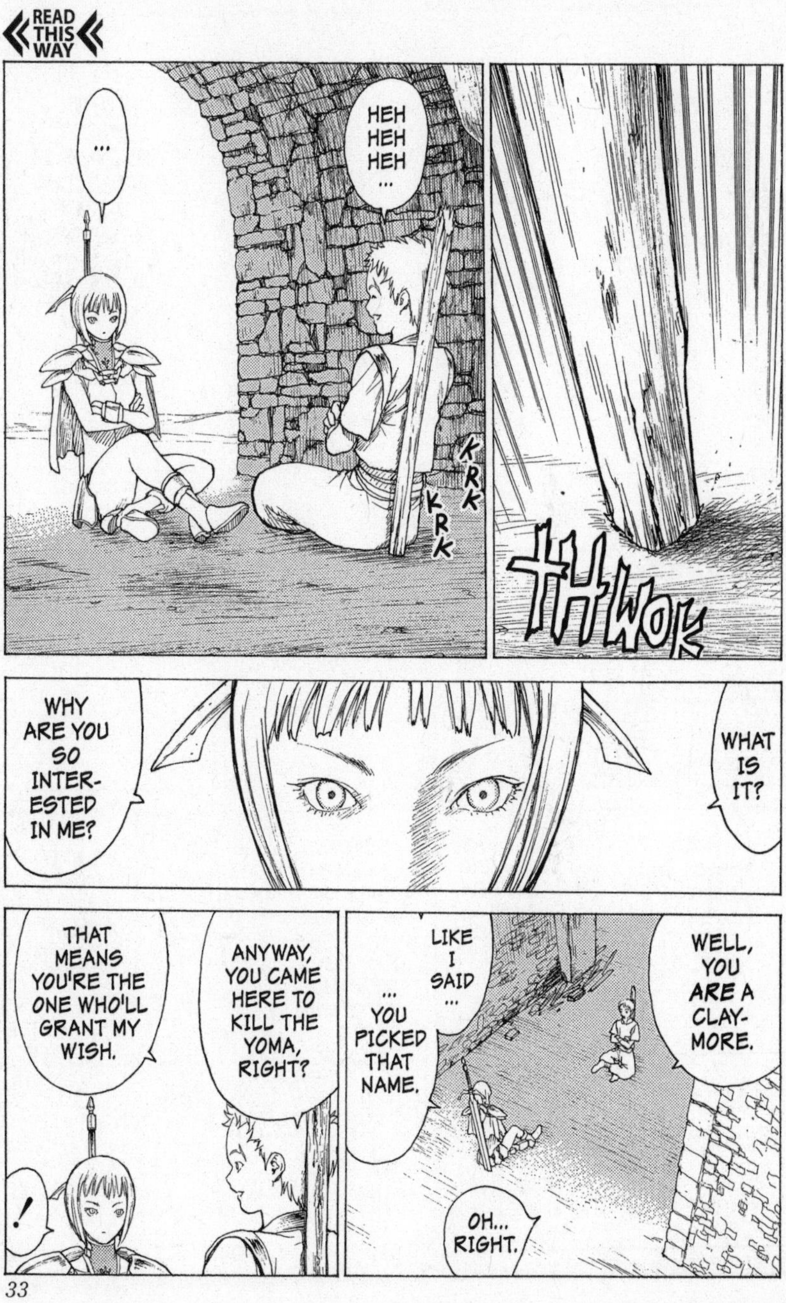
THWOK
HEH HEH HEH ...
...
KRK KRK
WHAT IS IT?
WHY ARE YOU SO INTER-ESTED IN ME?
WELL, YOU ARE A CLAY-MORE.
LIKE I SAID ...
... YOU PICKED THAT NAME.
OH... RIGHT.
ANYWAY, YOU CAME HERE TO KILL THE YOMA, RIGHT?
THAT MEANS YOU'RE THE ONE WHO'LL GRANT MY WISH.
!

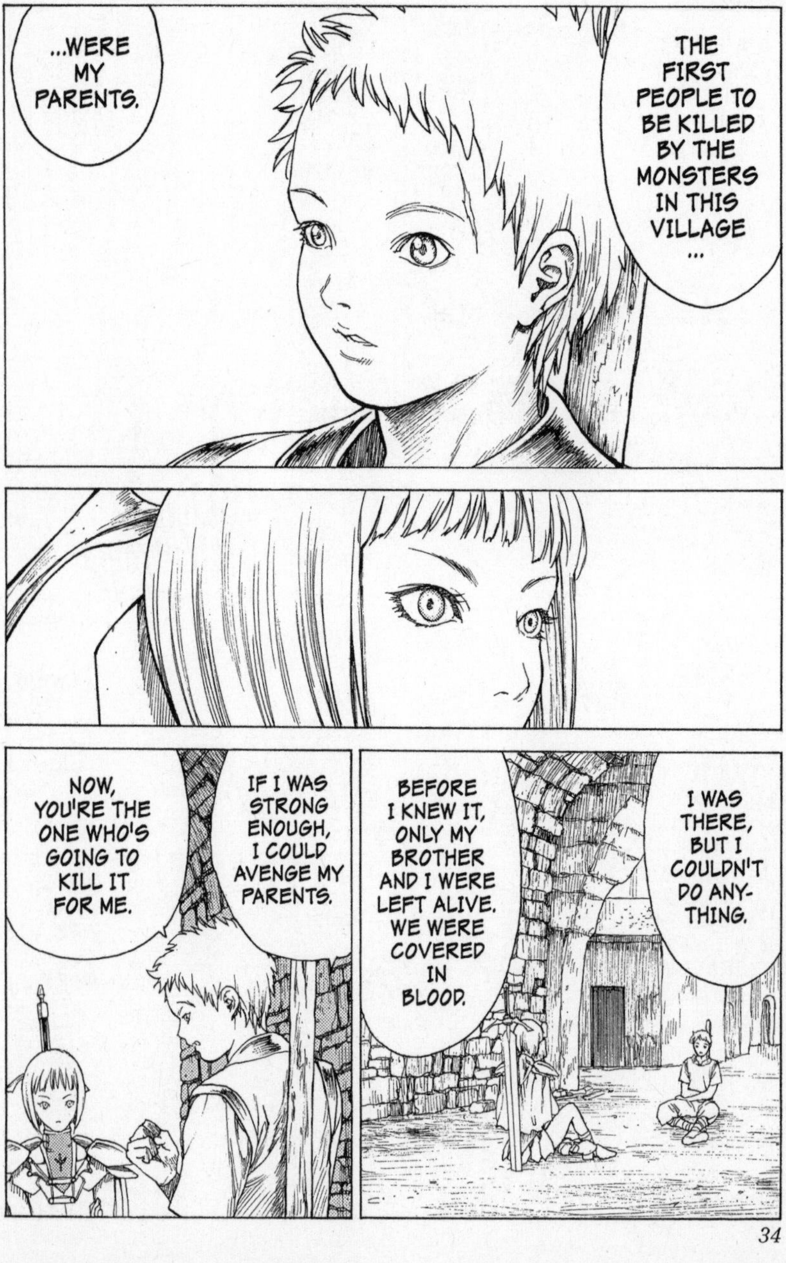
THE FIRST PEOPLE TO BE KILLED BY THE MONSTERS IN THIS VILLAGE ...
...WERE MY PARENTS.
I WAS THERE, BUT I COULDN'T DO ANY-THING.
BEFORE I KNEW IT, ONLY MY BROTHER AND I WERE LEFT ALIVE. WE WERE COVERED IN BLOOD.
IF I WAS STRONG ENOUGH, I COULD AVENGE MY PARENTS.
NOW, YOU'RE THE ONE WHO'S GOING TO KILL IT FOR ME.

READ THIS WAY

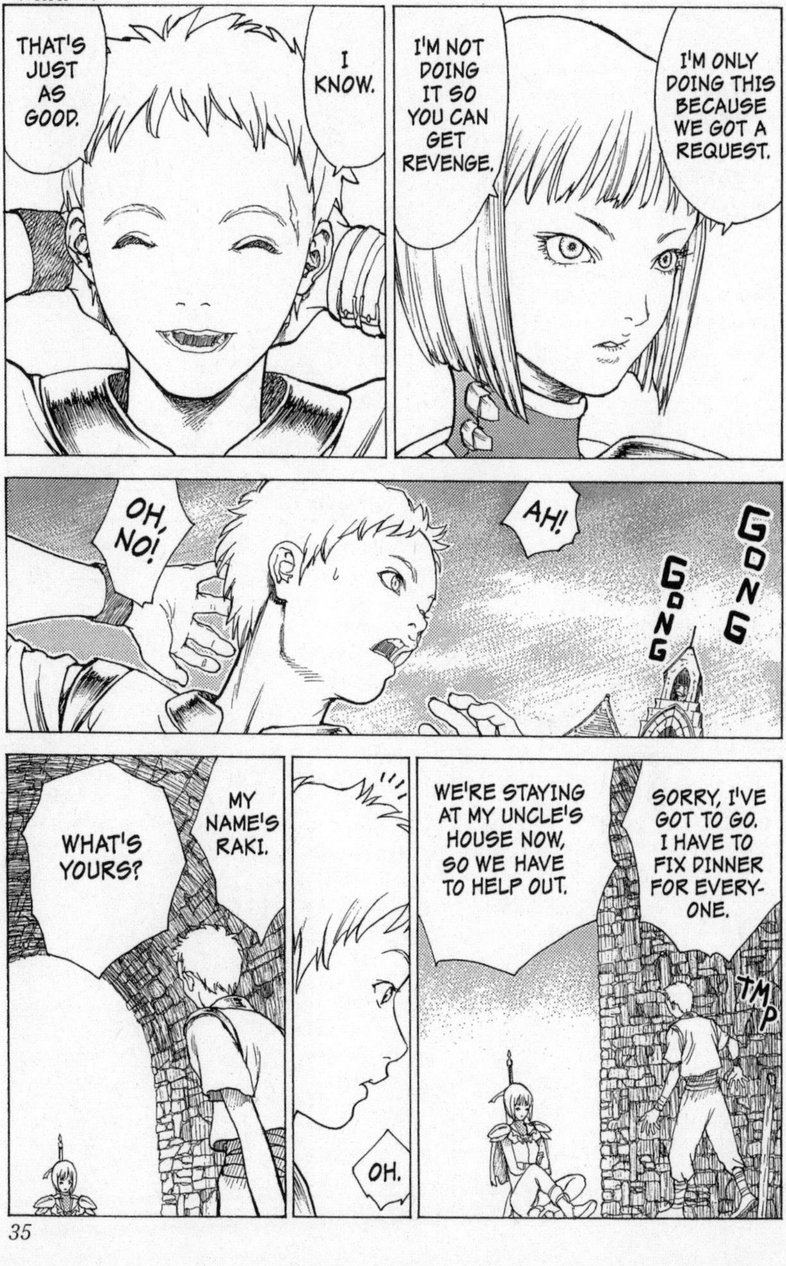
I'M ONLY DOING THIS BECAUSE WE GOT A REQUEST.
I'M NOT DOING IT SO YOU CAN GET REVENGE.
I KNOW.
THAT'S JUST AS GOOD.
GONG
GONG
AH!
OH, NO!
SORRY, I'VE GOT TO GO. I HAVE TO FIX DINNER FOR EVERY-ONE.
WE'RE STAYING AT MY UNCLE'S HOUSE NOW, SO WE HAVE TO HELP OUT.
TMP
OH.
MY NAME'S RAKI.
WHAT'S YOURS?

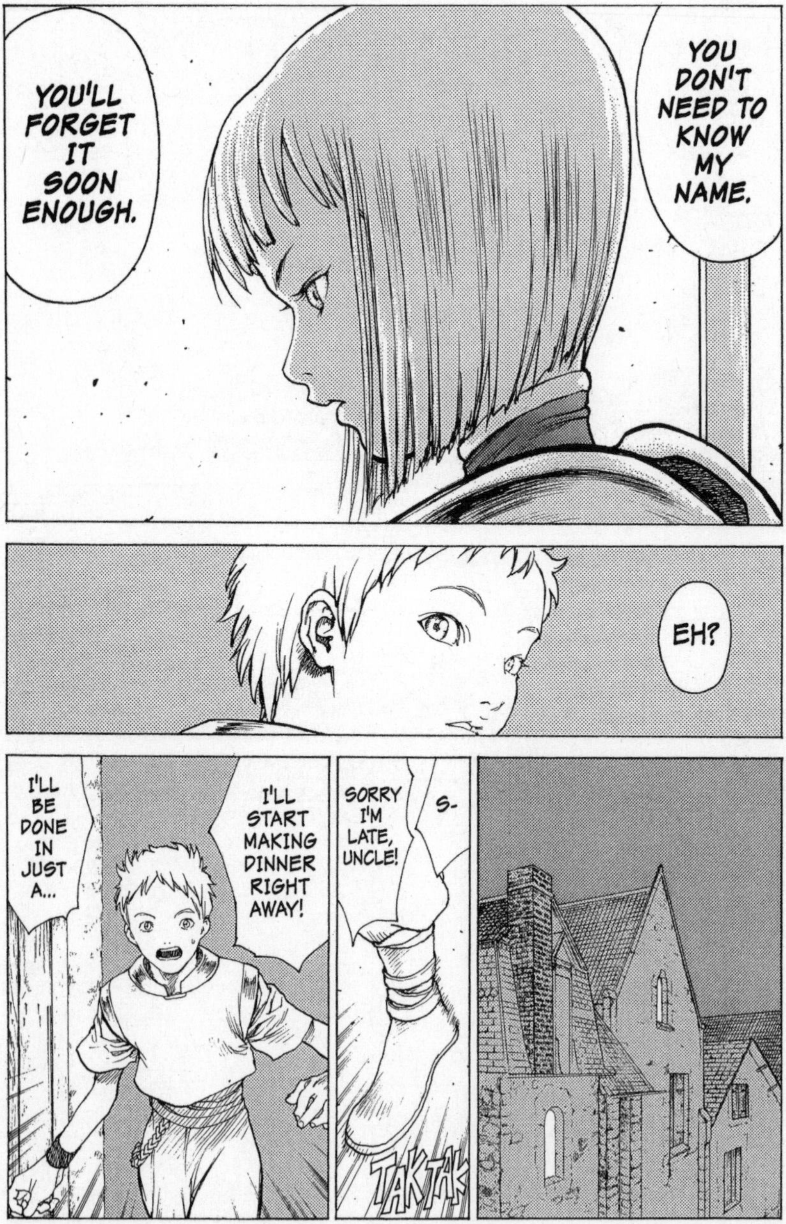
YOU DON'T NEED TO KNOW MY NAME.
YOU'LL FORGET IT SOON ENOUGH.
EH?
S-
SORRY I'M LATE, UNCLE!
TAK TAK
I'LL START MAKING DINNER RIGHT AWAY!
I'LL BE DONE IN JUST A...

READ THIS WAY

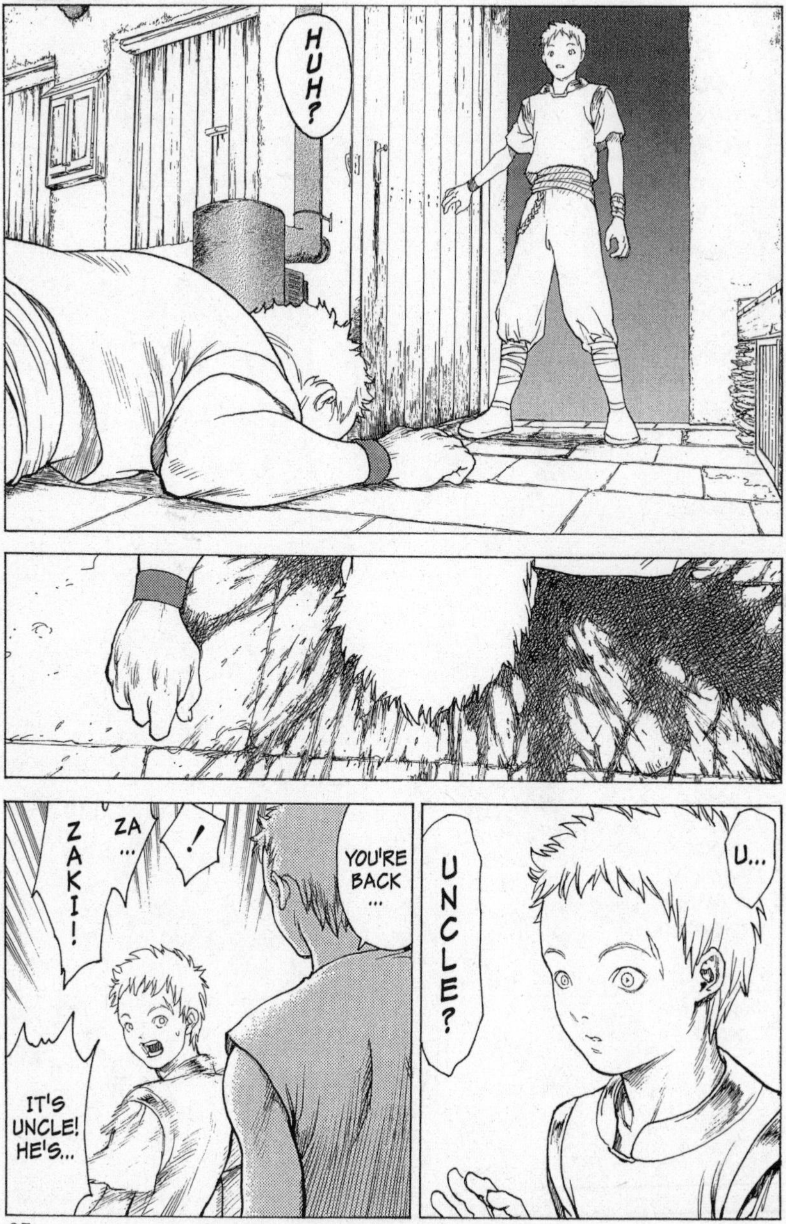
HUH?
U...
UNCLE?
YOU'RE BACK...
!
ZA... ZAKI!
IT'S UNCLE! HE'S...

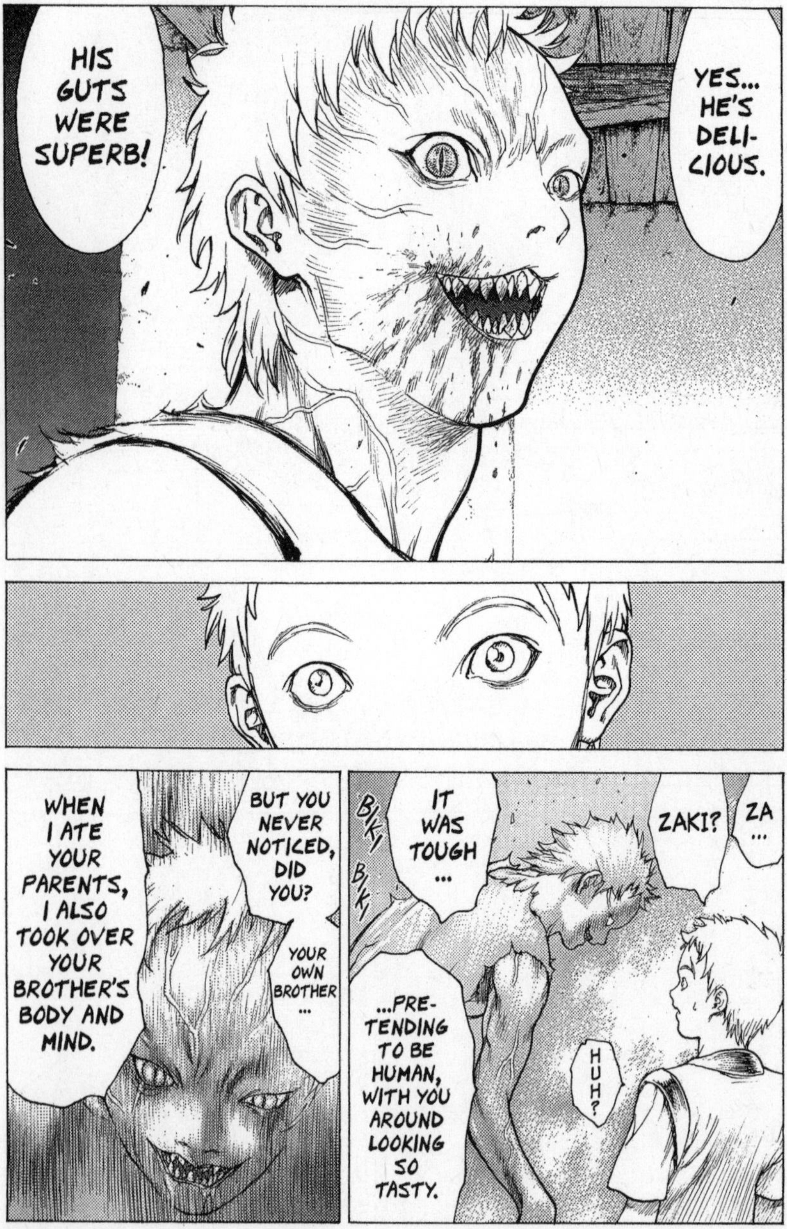
YES... HE'S DELI-CIOUS.
HIS GUTS WERE SUPERB!
ZA ...
ZAKI?
IT WAS TOUGH ...
BIKI BIKI
HUH?
...PRE-TENDING TO BE HUMAN, WITH YOU AROUND LOOKING SO TASTY.
WHEN I ATE YOUR PARENTS, I ALSO TOOK OVER YOUR BROTHER'S BODY AND MIND.
BUT YOU NEVER NOTICED, DID YOU?
YOUR OWN BROTHER ...

READ THIS WAY

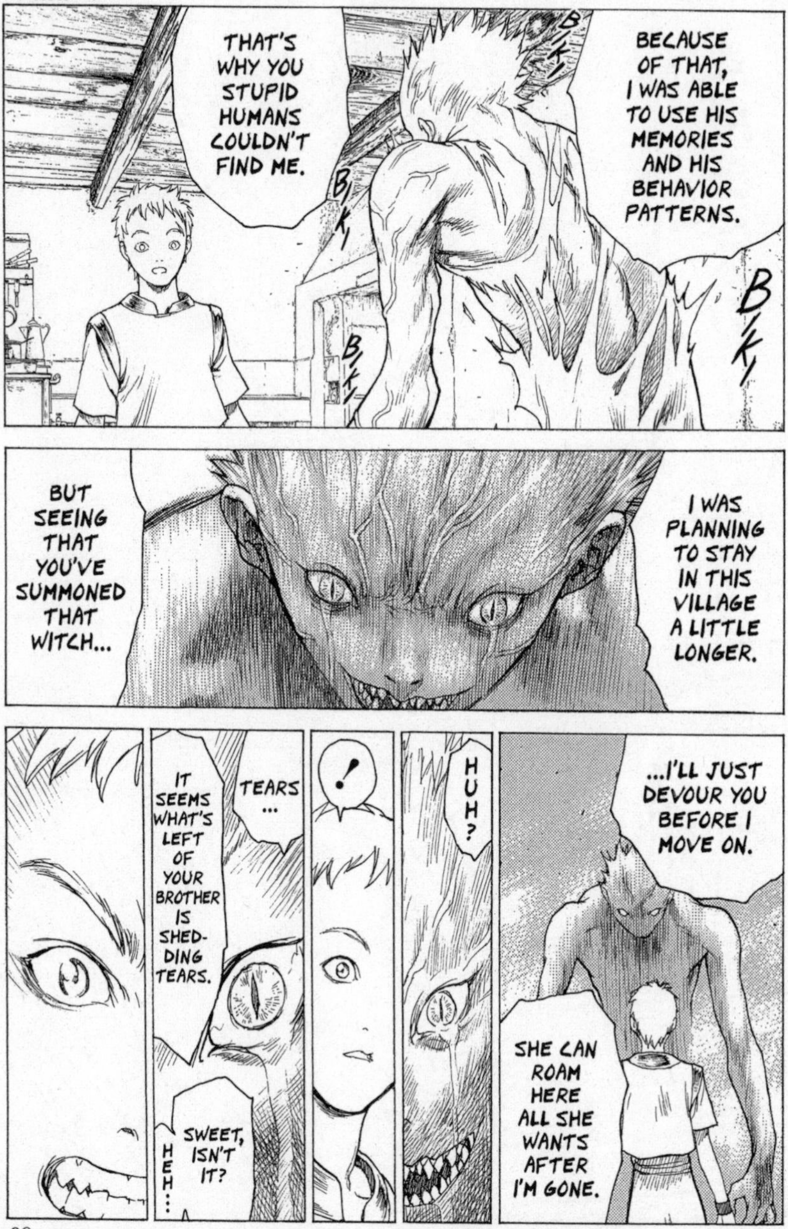
BECAUSE OF THAT, I WAS ABLE TO USE HIS MEMORIES AND HIS BEHAVIOR PATTERNS.
BIKI
BIKI
THAT'S WHY YOU STUPID HUMANS COULDN'T FIND ME.
BIKI
BIKI
I WAS PLANNING TO STAY IN THIS VILLAGE A LITTLE LONGER.
BUT SEEING THAT YOU'VE SUMMONED THAT WITCH...
...I'LL JUST DEVOUR YOU BEFORE I MOVE ON.
SHE CAN ROAM HERE ALL SHE WANTS AFTER I'M GONE.
HUH?
!
TEARS...
IT SEEMS WHAT'S LEFT OF YOUR BROTHER IS SHEDDING TEARS.
SWEET, ISN'T IT?
HEH...

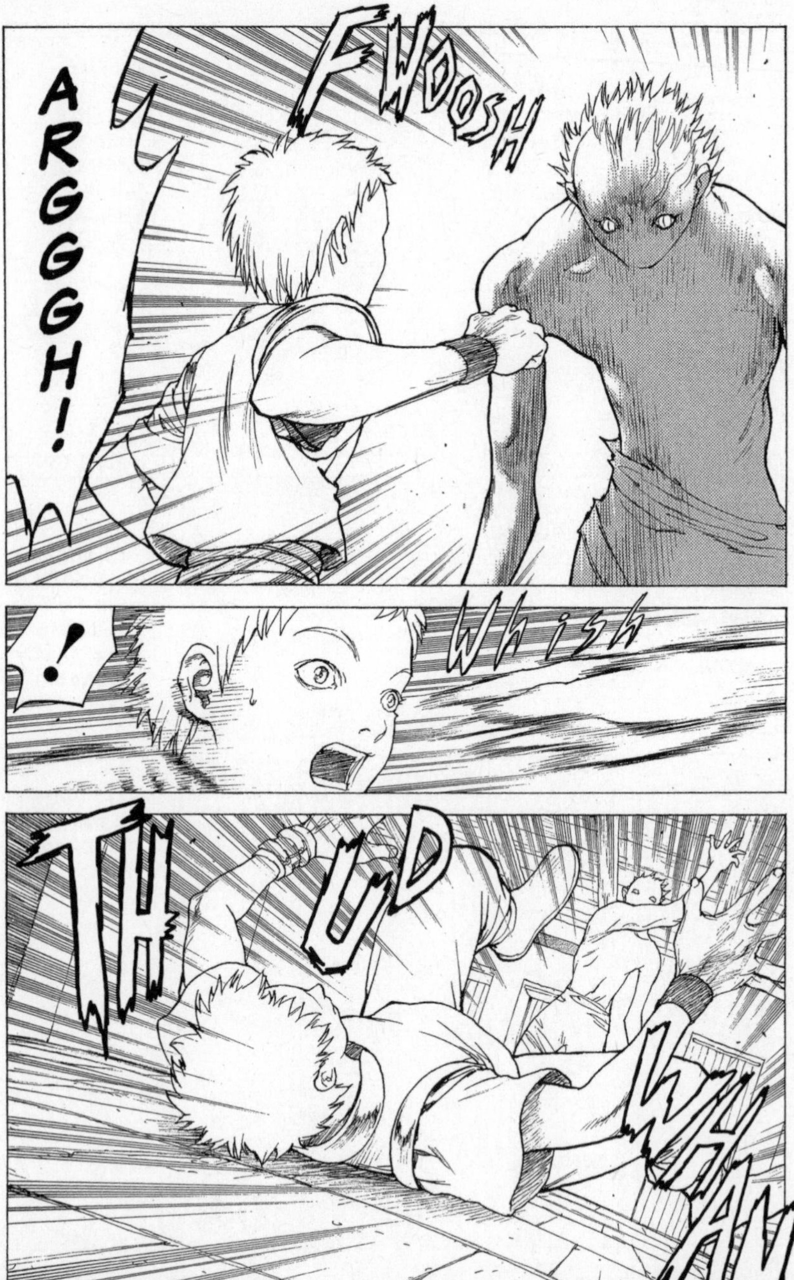
FWOOSH
ARGGGGH!
Whish
!
THUD
WHAM

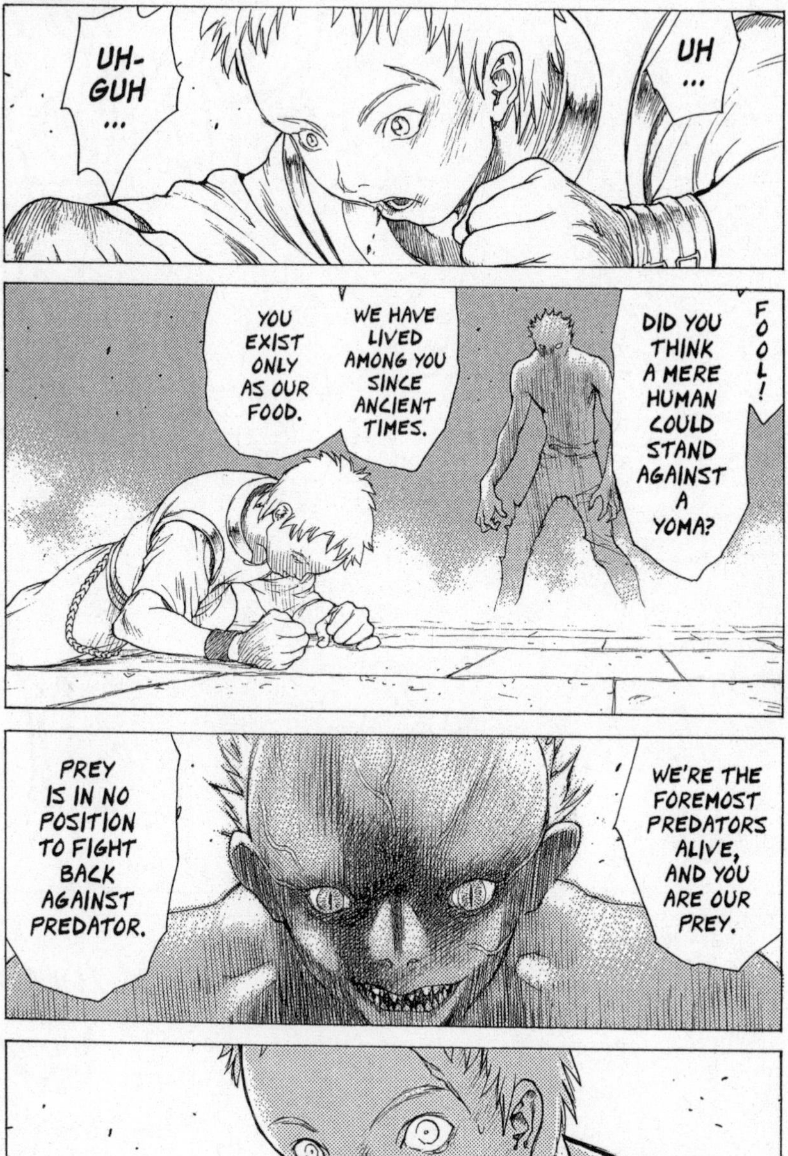
UH ...
UH-GUH ...
FOOL!
DID YOU THINK A MERE HUMAN COULD STAND AGAINST A YOMA?
WE HAVE LIVED AMONG YOU SINCE ANCIENT TIMES.
YOU EXIST ONLY AS OUR FOOD.
WE'RE THE FOREMOST PREDATORS ALIVE, AND YOU ARE OUR PREY.
PREY IS IN NO POSITION TO FIGHT BACK AGAINST PREDATOR.

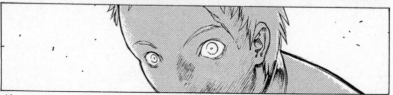

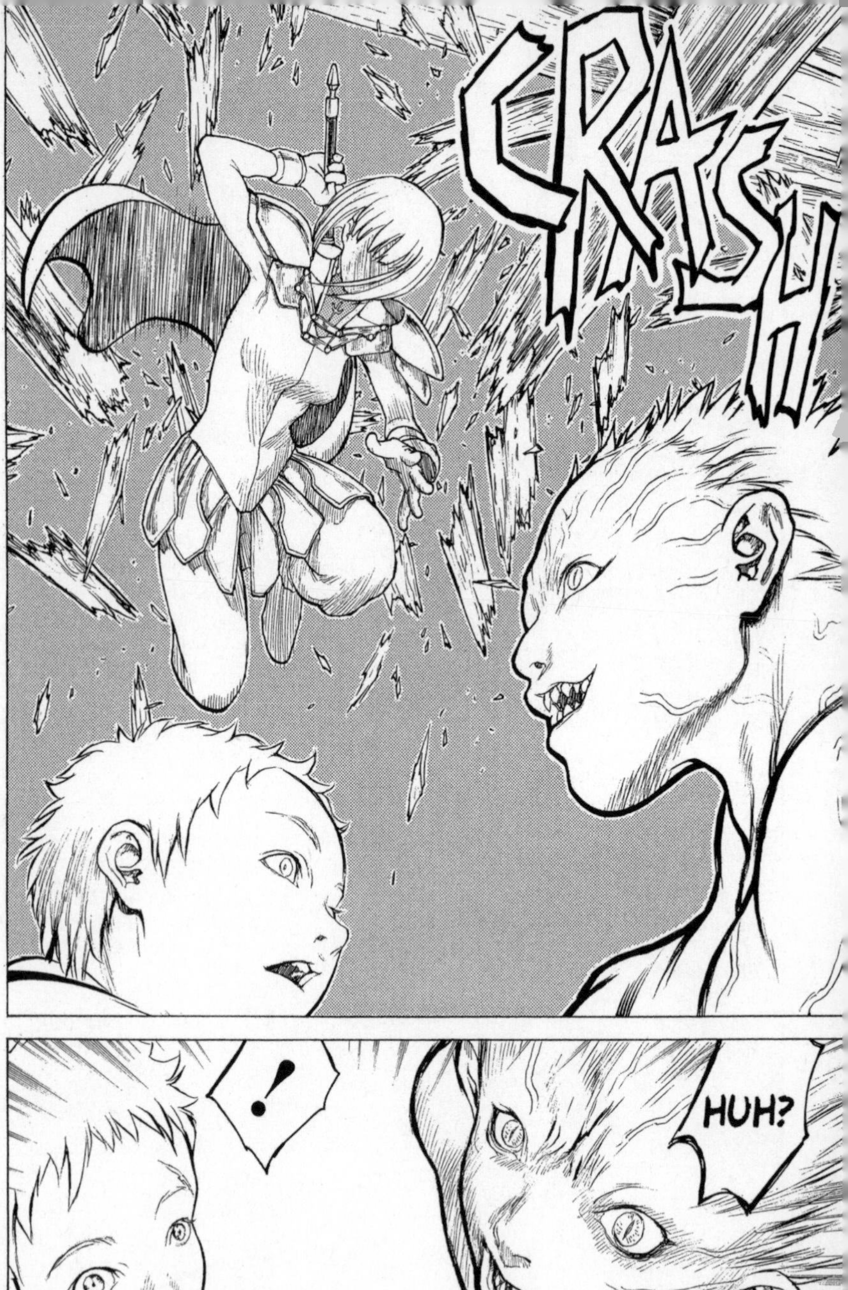
CRASH
HUH?
!

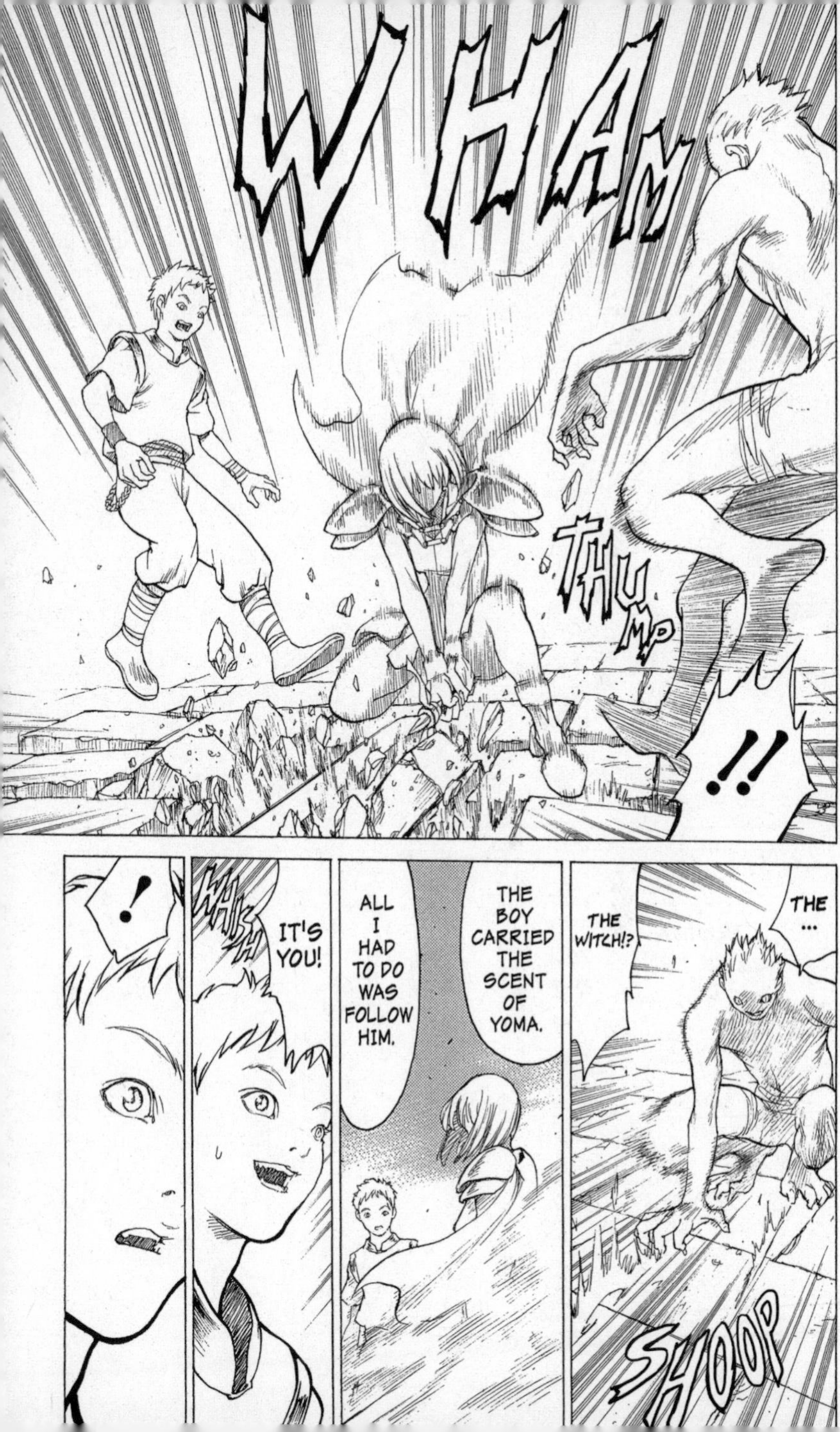
WHAM
THUMP
!!
THE ...
THE WITCH!?
SHOOP
THE BOY CARRIED THE SCENT OF YOMA.
ALL I HAD TO DO WAS FOLLOW HIM.
IT'S YOU!
WHISH
!

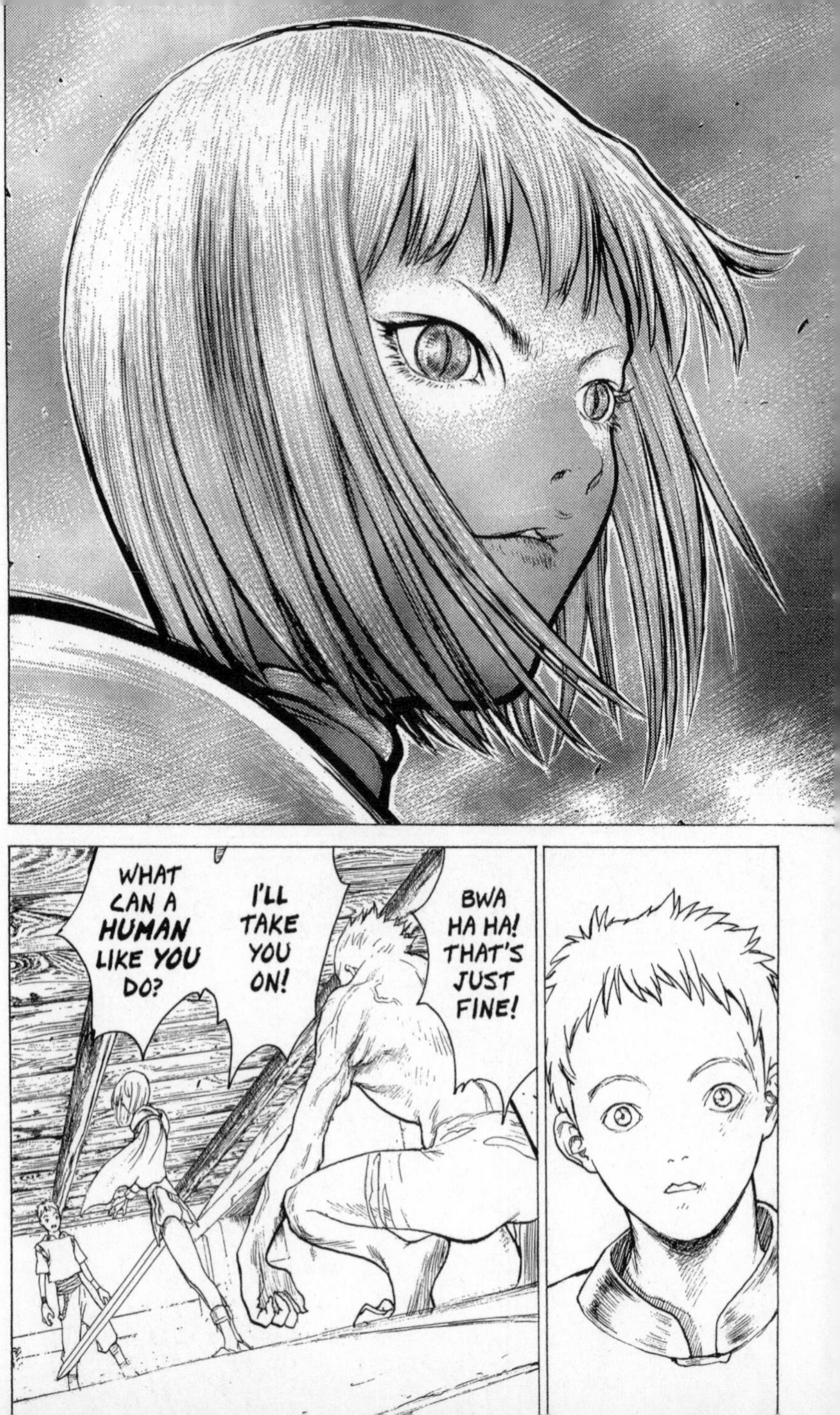
BWA HA HA! THAT'S JUST FINE!
I'LL TAKE YOU ON!
WHAT CAN A HUMAN LIKE YOU DO?

READ THIS WAY

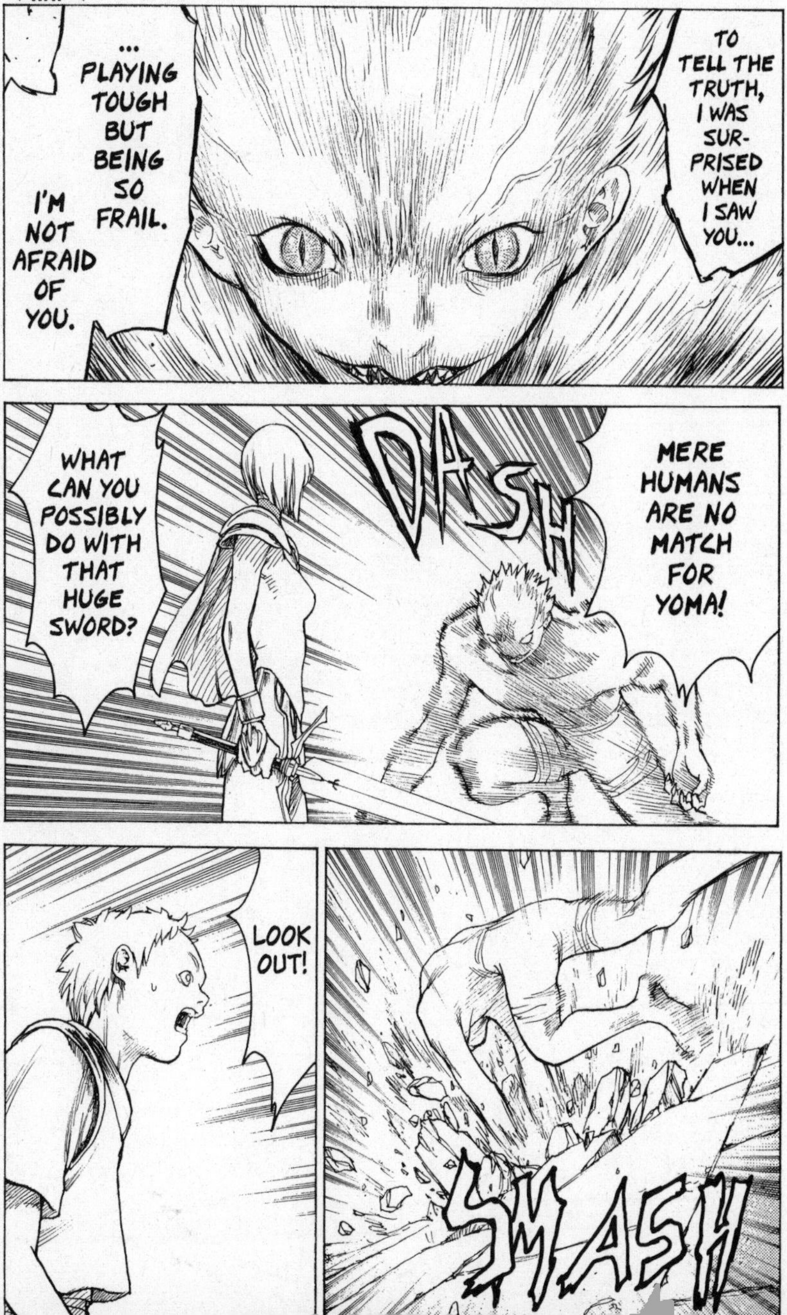
TO TELL THE TRUTH, I WAS SUR-PRISED WHEN I SAW YOU...
...PLAYING TOUGH BUT BEING SO FRAIL.
I'M NOT AFRAID OF YOU.
MERE HUMANS ARE NO MATCH FOR YOMA!
DASH
WHAT CAN YOU POSSIBLY DO WITH THAT HUGE SWORD?
SMASH
LOOK OUT!

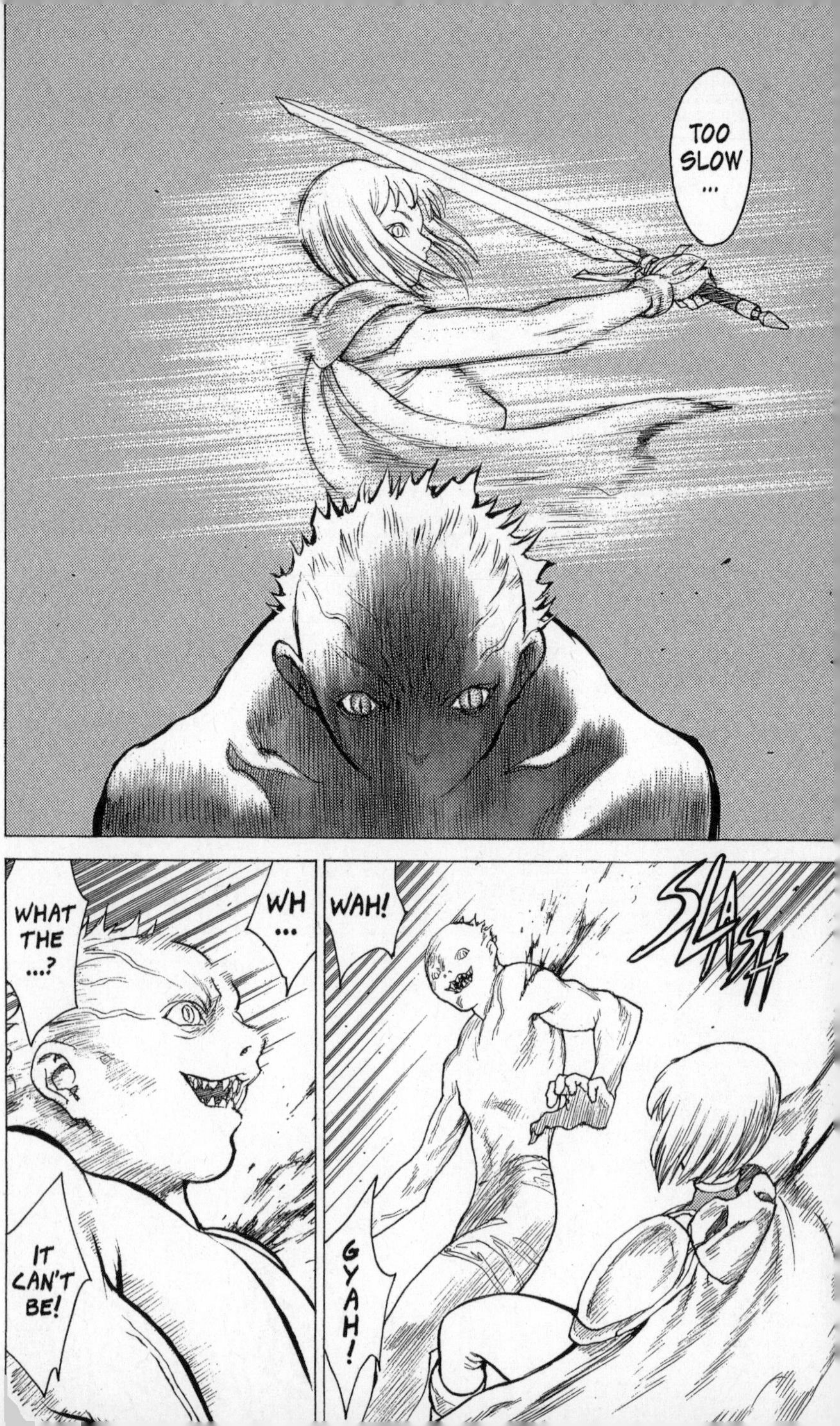
TOO SLOW ...
SLASH
WAH!
GYAH!
WH ...
WHAT THE ...?
IT CAN'T BE!

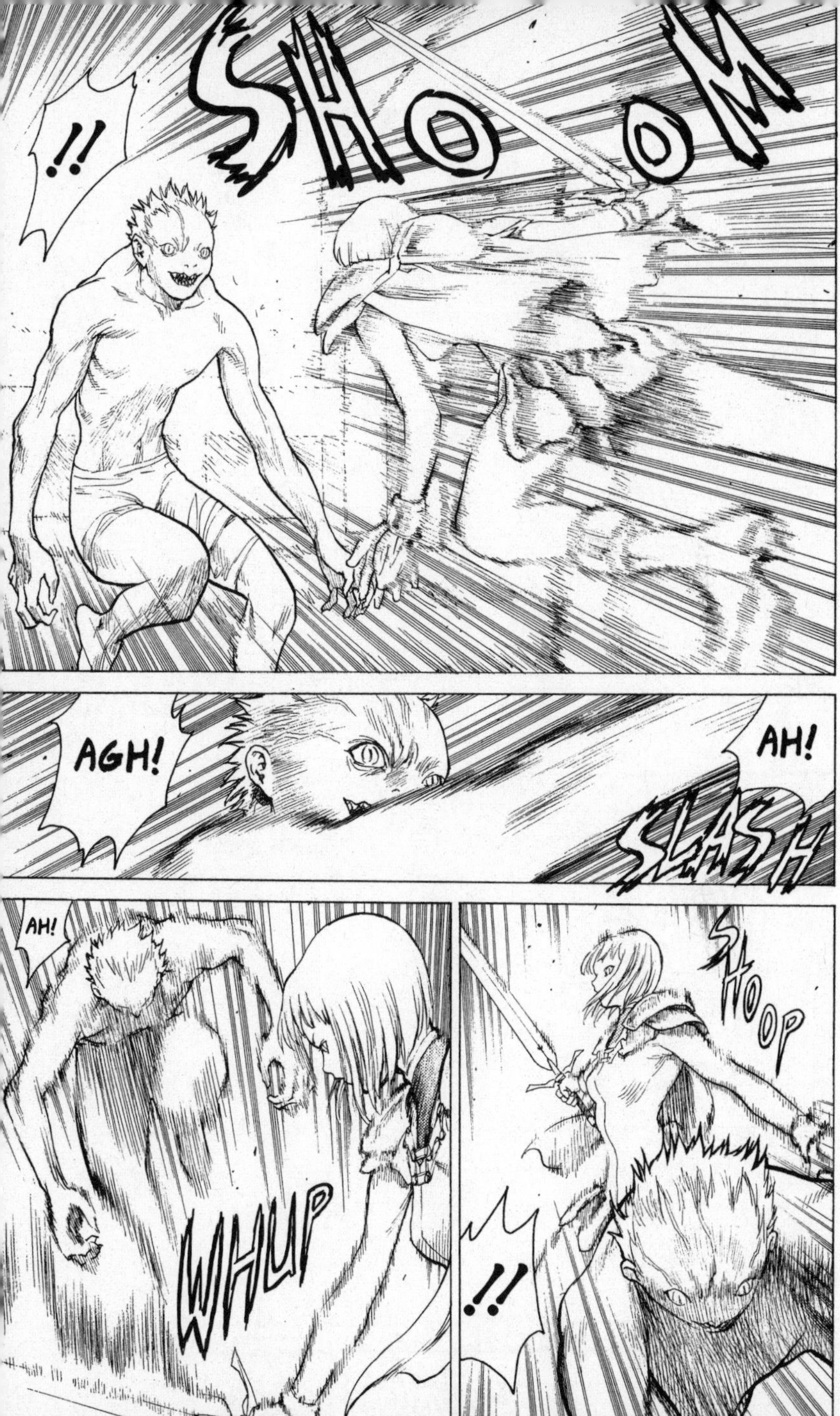
SHOOM
!!
AH!
SLASH
AGH!
SHOOP
!!
AH!
WHUP

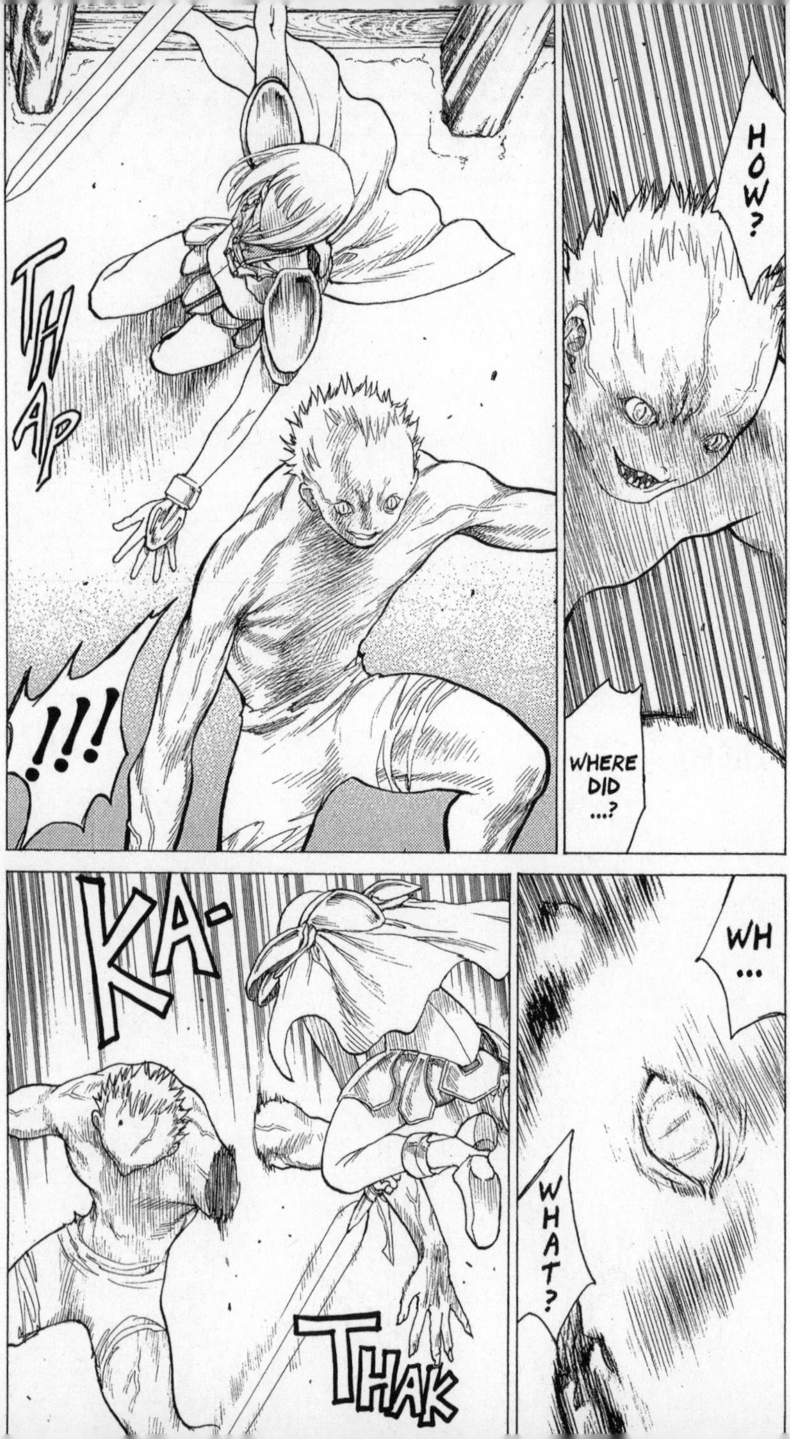
HOW?
WHERE DID ...?
THAP
!!!
WH ...
WHAT?
KA-
THAK

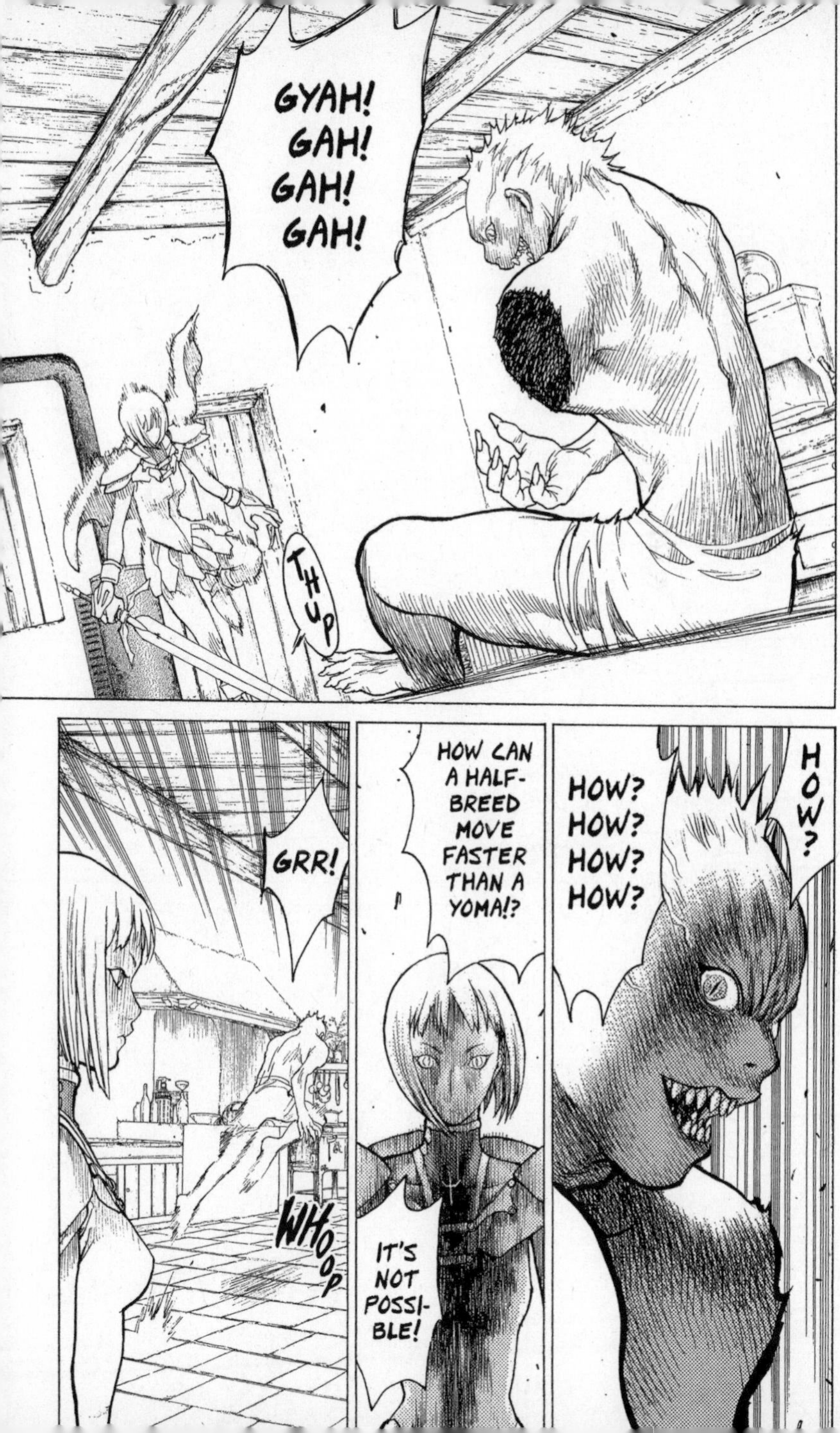
GYAH! GAH! GAH! GAH!
THUP
HOW?
HOW? HOW? HOW? HOW?
HOW CAN A HALF-BREED MOVE FASTER THAN A YOMA!?
IT'S NOT POSSI-BLE!
GRR!
WHOOP

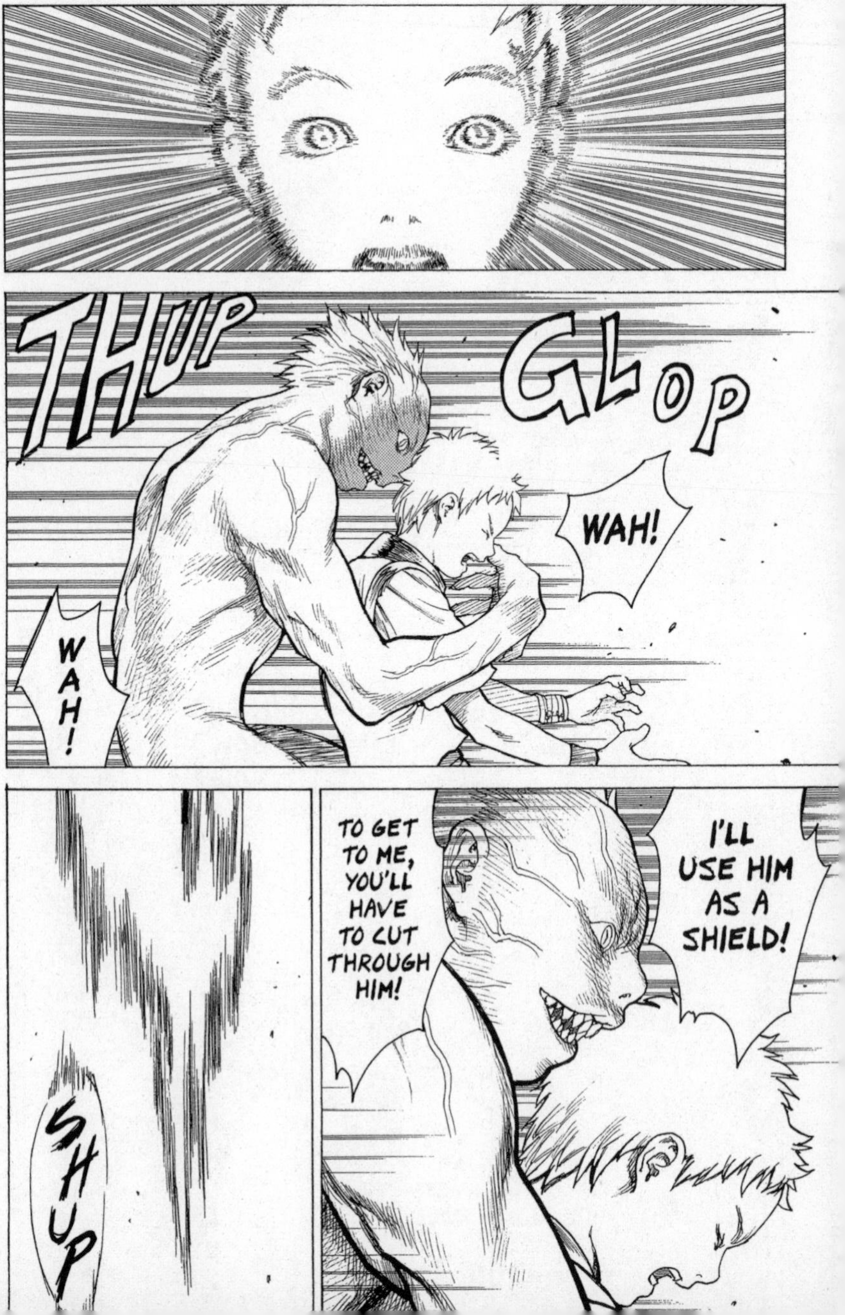
GLOP
WAH!
THUP
WAH!
I'LL USE HIM AS A SHIELD!
TO GET TO ME, YOU'LL HAVE TO CUT THROUGH HIM!
SHUP

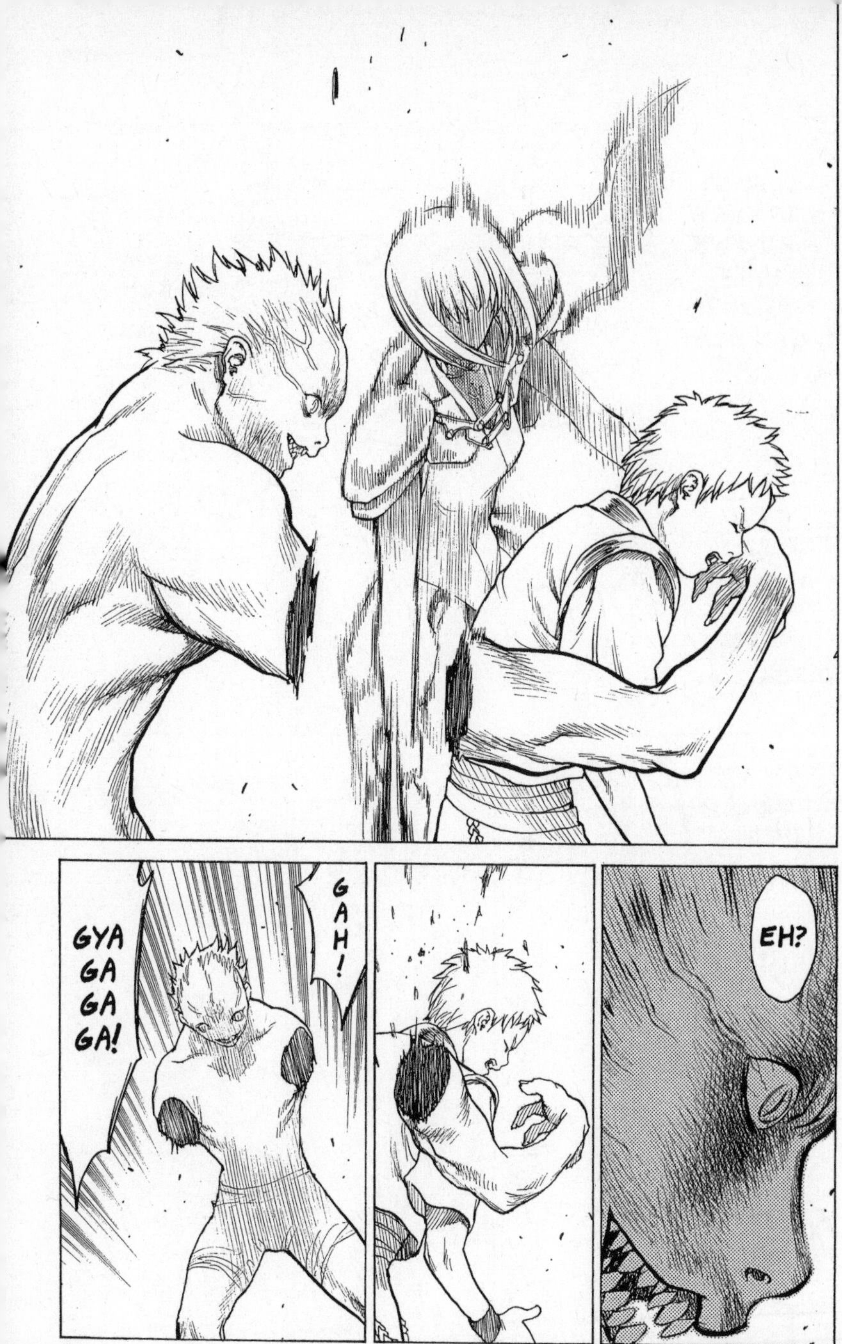
EH?
GAH!
GYA GA GA GA!

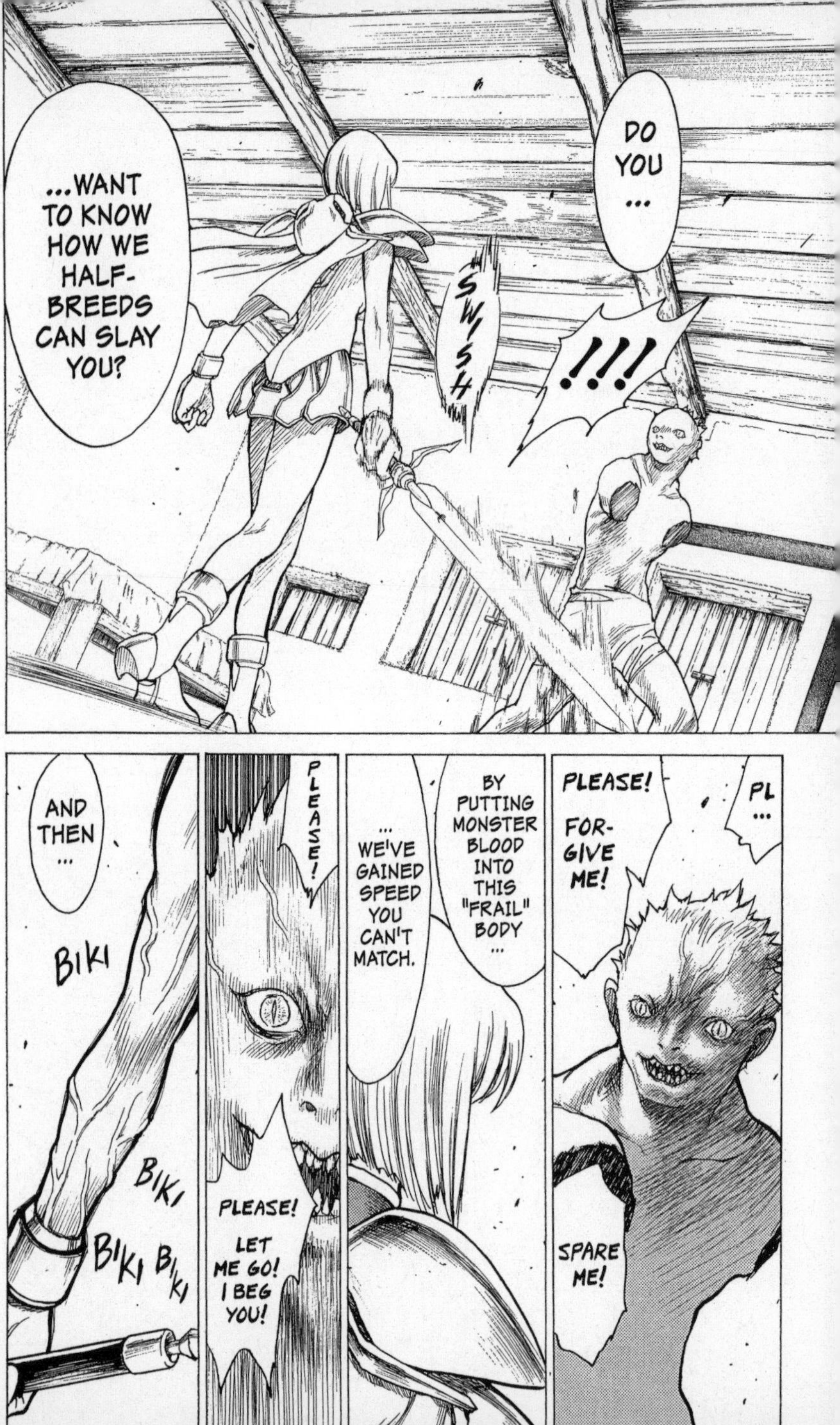
DO YOU ...
...WANT TO KNOW HOW WE HALF-BREEDS CAN SLAY YOU?
SWISH
!!!
PL ...
PLEASE!
FOR-GIVE ME!
SPARE ME!
BY PUTTING MONSTER BLOOD INTO THIS "FRAIL" BODY ...
... WE'VE GAINED SPEED YOU CAN'T MATCH.
PLEASE!
PLEASE!
LET ME GO! I BEG YOU!
AND THEN ...
BIKI
BIKI
BIKI
BIKI

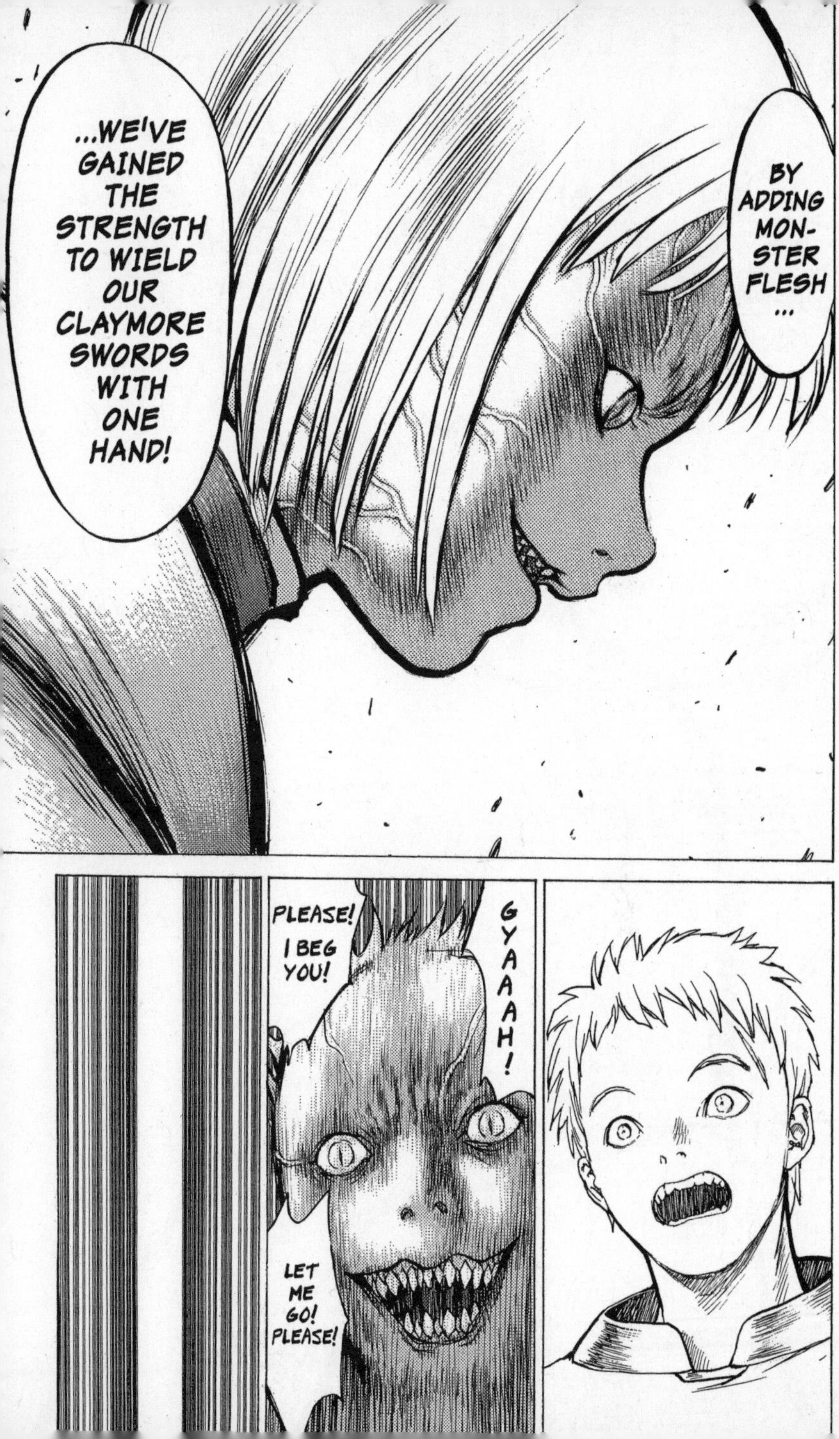
BY ADDING MON-STER FLESH...
...WE'VE GAINED THE STRENGTH TO WIELD OUR CLAYMORE SWORDS WITH ONE HAND!
GYAAAAH!
PLEASE! I BEG YOU!
LET ME GO! PLEASE!

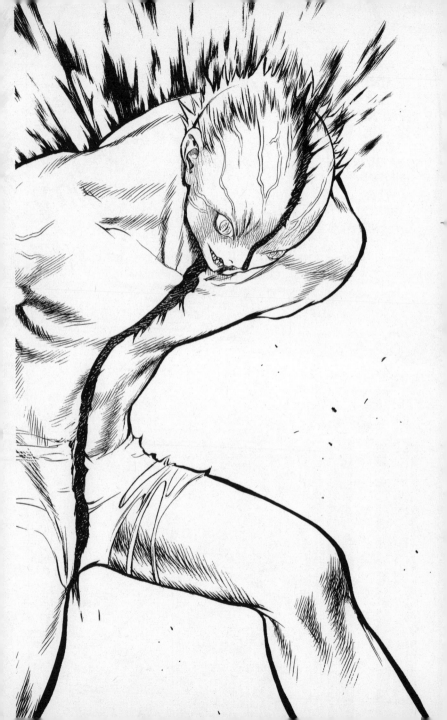

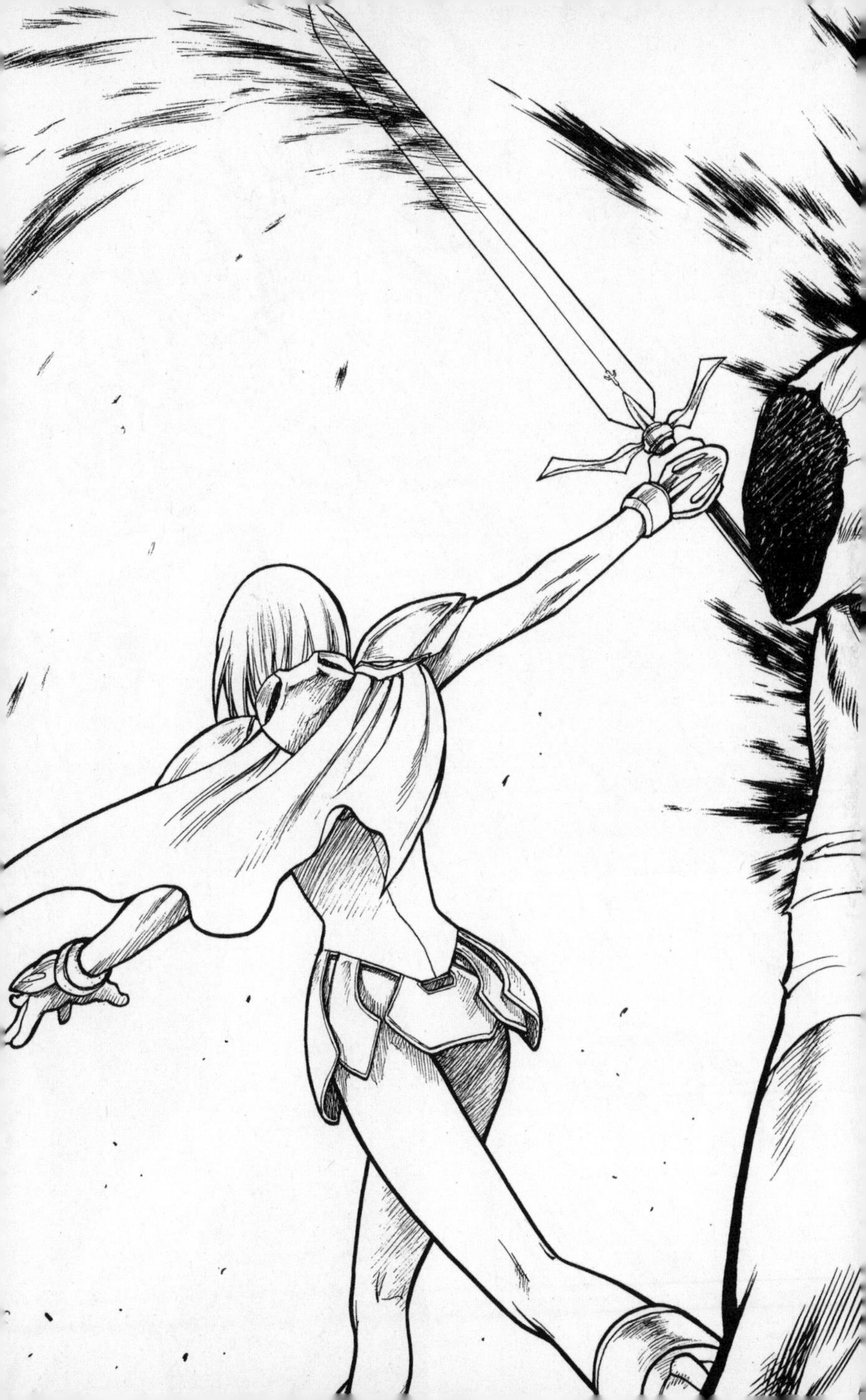

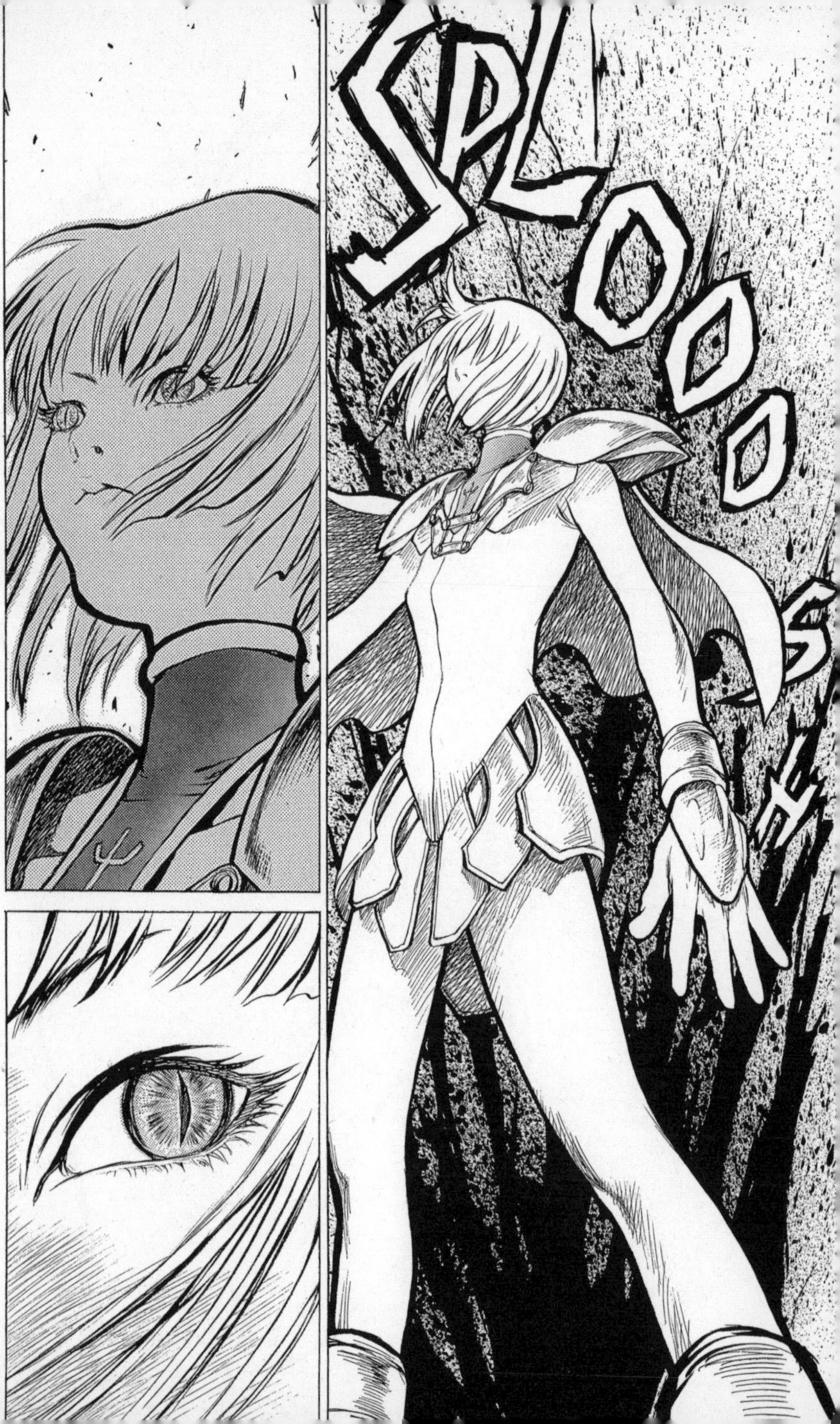
SPLOOOOSH

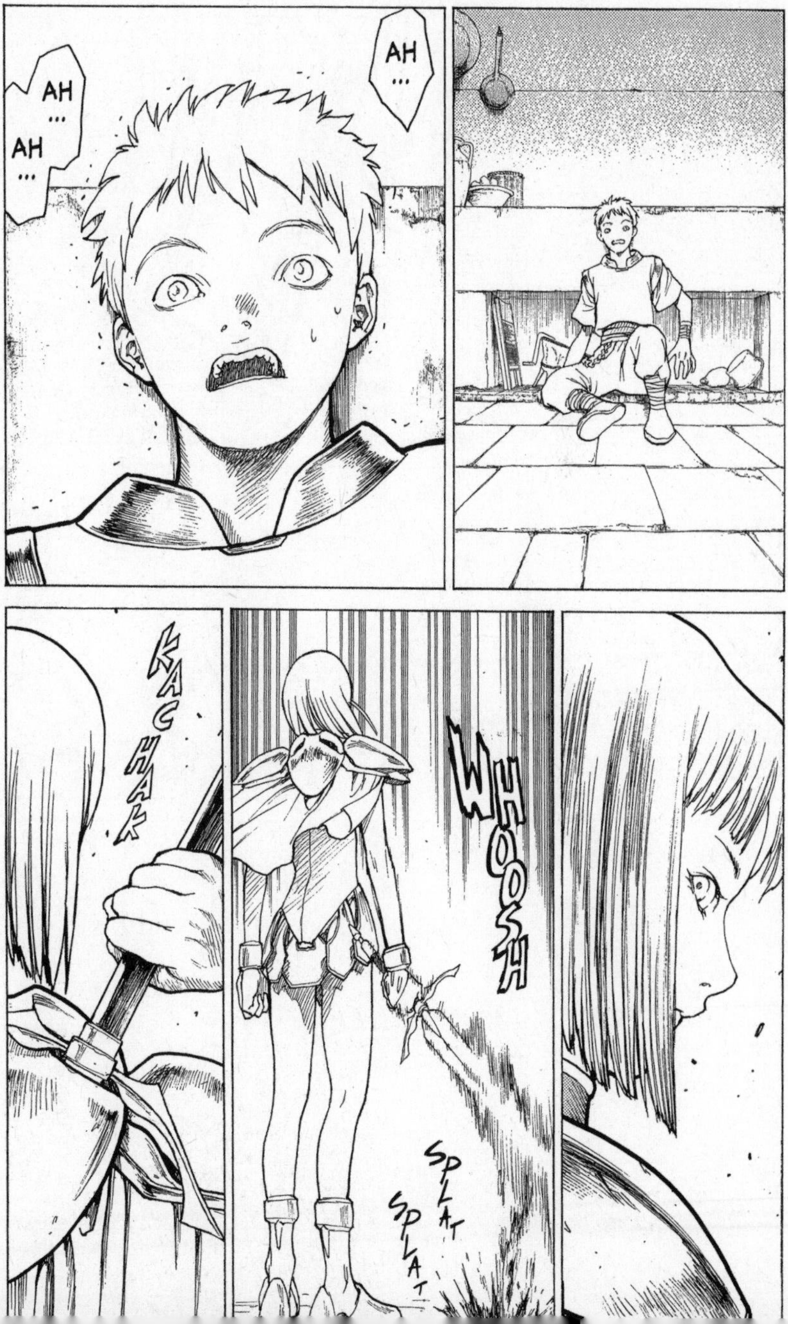
AH ...
AH ... AH ...
WHOOSH
SPLAT SPLAT
KACHAK

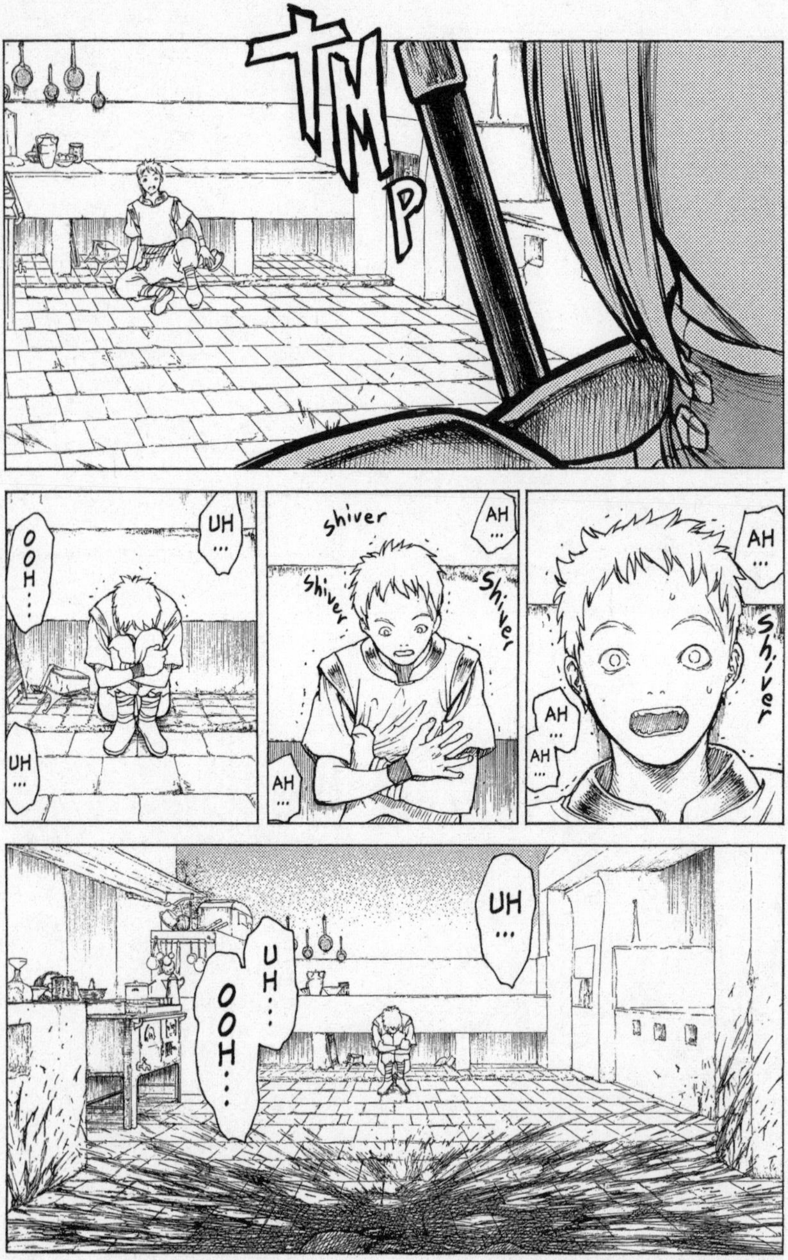
TMP
AH ...
Shiver
AH ...
AH ...
AH ...
shiver
Shiver
Shiver
AH ...
UH ...
OOH...
UH ...
UH ...
UH...
OOH...

READ THIS WAY

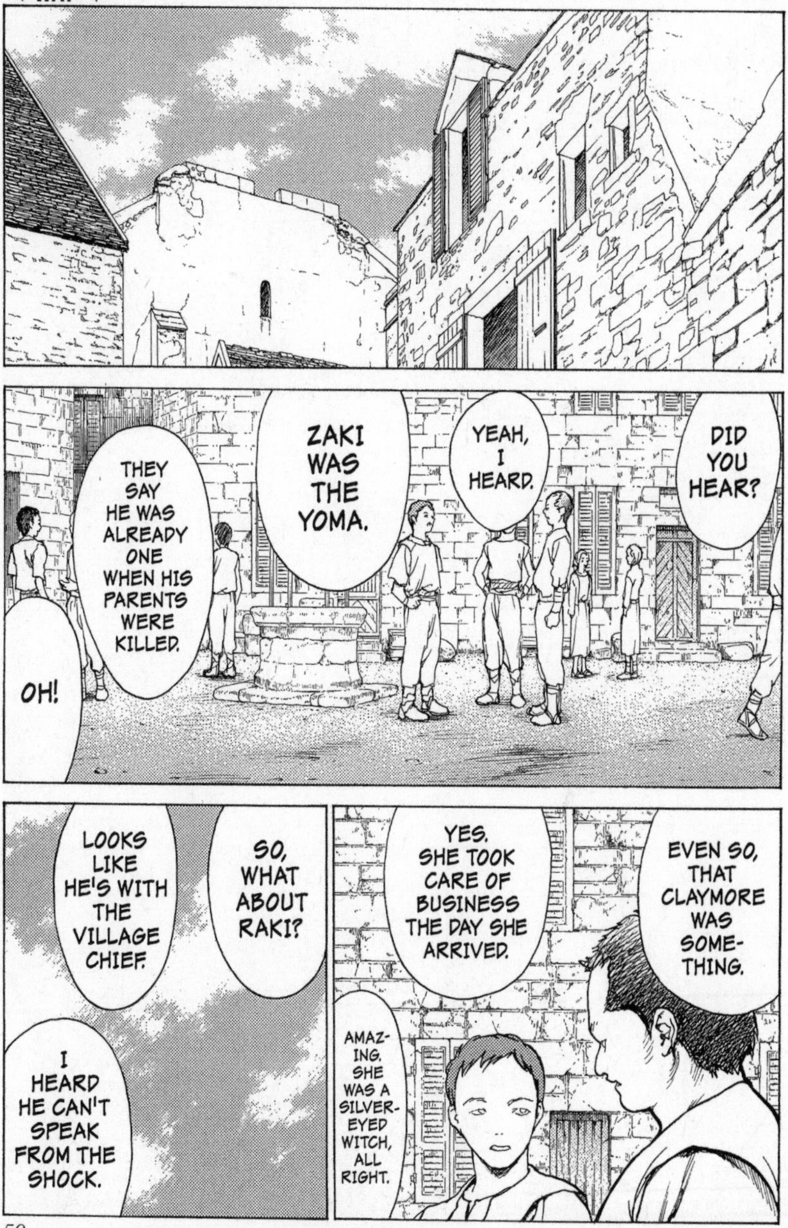
DID YOU HEAR?
YEAH, I HEARD.
ZAKI WAS THE YOMA.
THEY SAY HE WAS ALREADY ONE WHEN HIS PARENTS WERE KILLED.
OH!
EVEN SO, THAT CLAYMORE WAS SOME-THING.
YES. SHE TOOK CARE OF BUSINESS THE DAY SHE ARRIVED.
AMAZ-ING. SHE WAS A SILVER-EYED WITCH, ALL RIGHT.
SO, WHAT ABOUT RAKI?
LOOKS LIKE HE'S WITH THE VILLAGE CHIEF.
I HEARD HE CAN'T SPEAK FROM THE SHOCK.

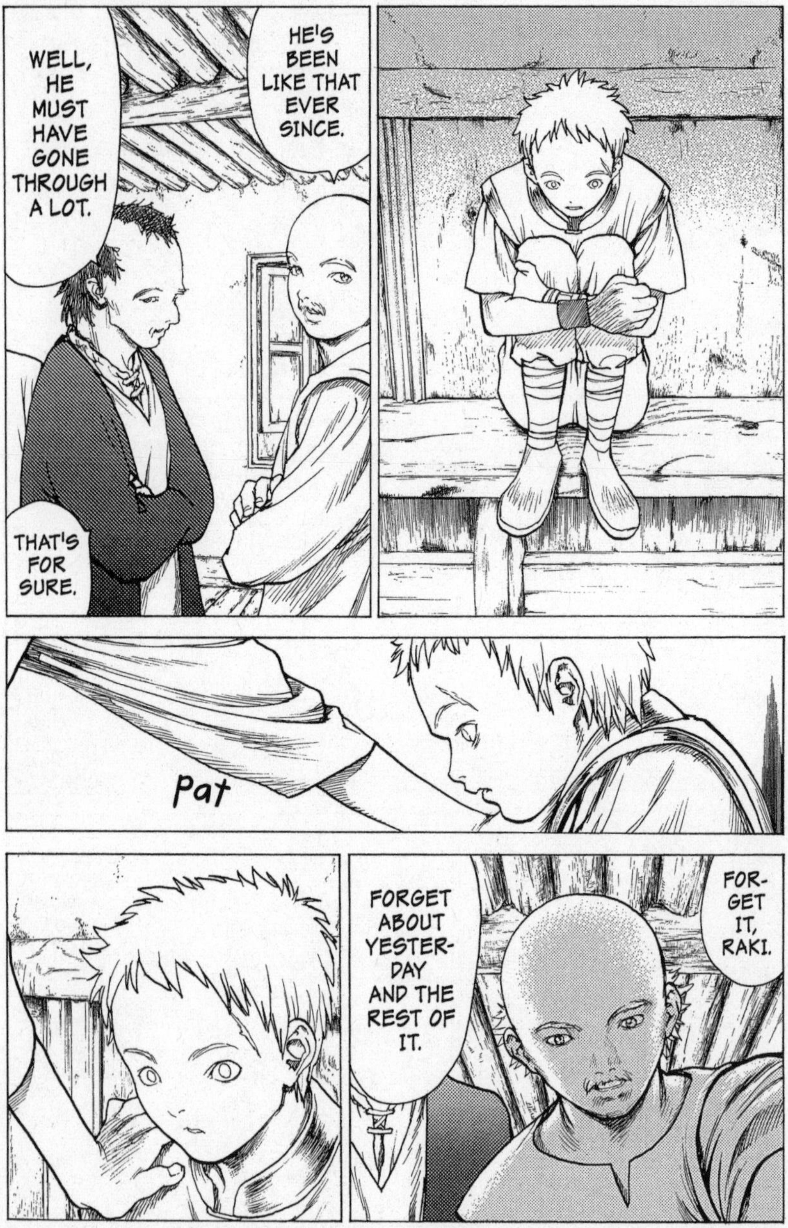
HE'S BEEN LIKE THAT EVER SINCE.
WELL, HE MUST HAVE GONE THROUGH A LOT.
THAT'S FOR SURE.
Pat
FOR-GET IT, RAKI.
FORGET ABOUT YESTER-DAY AND THE REST OF IT.

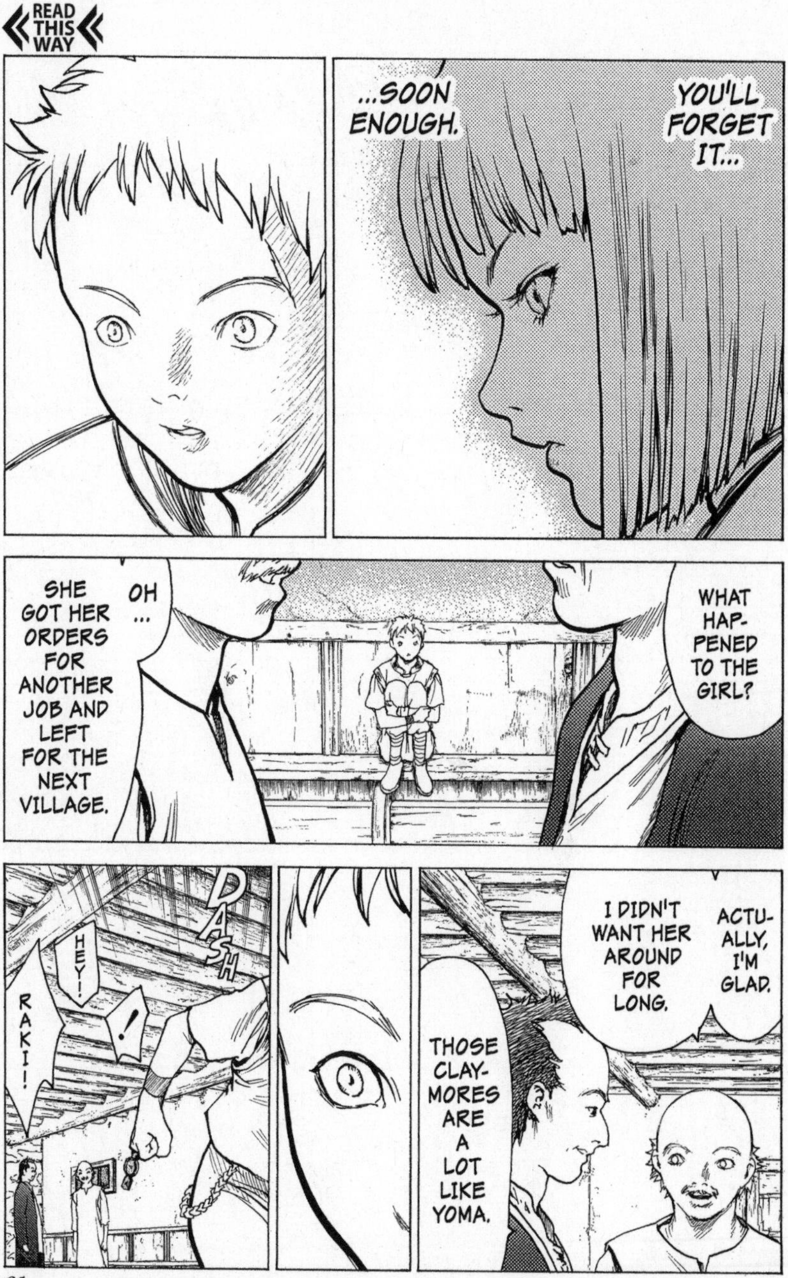
READ THIS WAY
YOU'LL FORGET IT...
...SOON ENOUGH.
WHAT HAPPENED TO THE GIRL?
OH ...
SHE GOT HER ORDERS FOR ANOTHER JOB AND LEFT FOR THE NEXT VILLAGE.
ACTUALLY, I'M GLAD.
I DIDN'T WANT HER AROUND FOR LONG.
THOSE CLAYMORES ARE A LOT LIKE YOMA.
DASH
HEY!
!
RAKI!

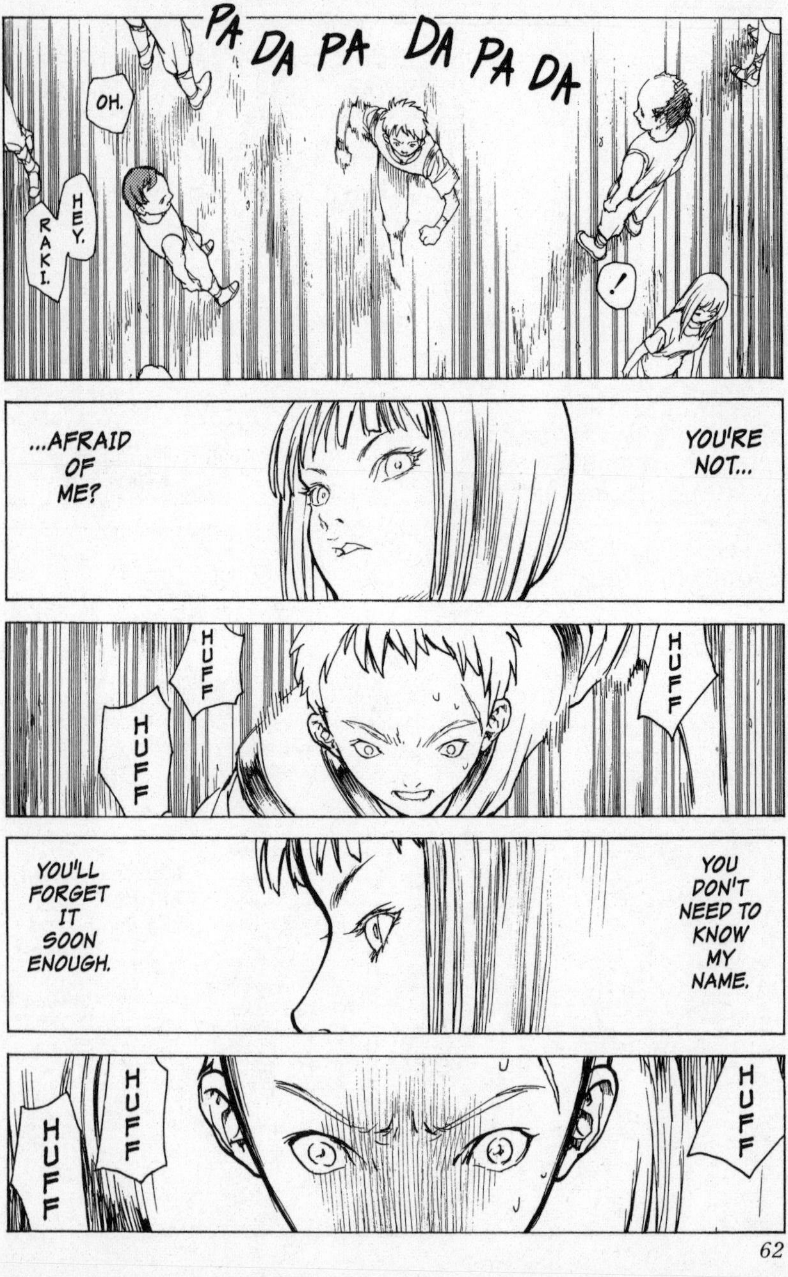

PA DA PA DA PA DA
!
OH.
HEY. RAKI.
YOU'RE NOT...
...AFRAID OF ME?
HUFF
HUFF
HUFF
YOU DON'T NEED TO KNOW MY NAME.
YOU'LL FORGET IT SOON ENOUGH.
HUFF
HUFF
HUFF

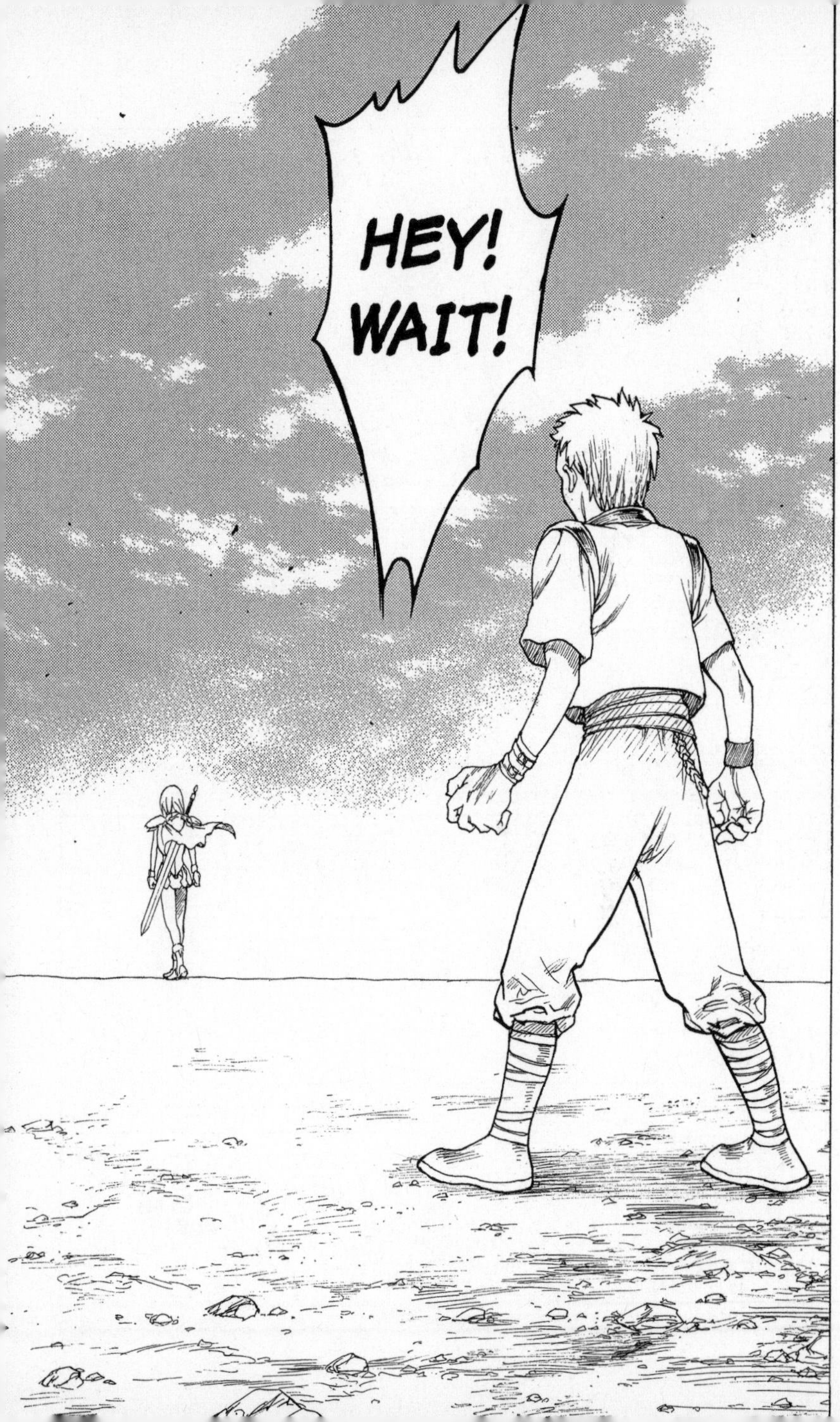
HEY! WAIT!

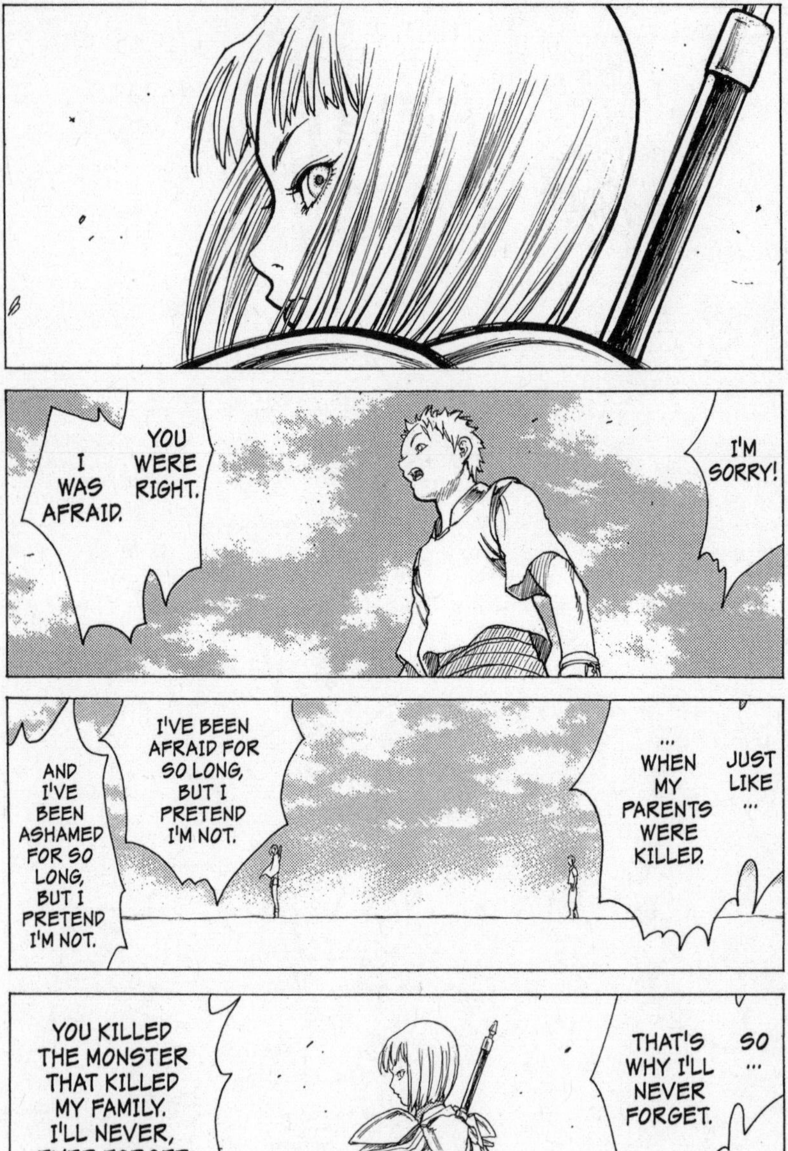
I'M SORRY!
YOU WERE RIGHT.
I WAS AFRAID.
JUST LIKE ...
... WHEN MY PARENTS WERE KILLED.
I'VE BEEN AFRAID FOR SO LONG, BUT I PRETEND I'M NOT.
AND I'VE BEEN ASHAMED FOR SO LONG, BUT I PRETEND I'M NOT.
SO ...
THAT'S WHY I'LL NEVER FORGET.
YOU KILLED THE MONSTER THAT KILLED MY FAMILY. I'LL NEVER, EVER FORGET YOU.

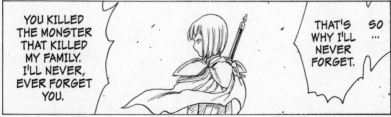

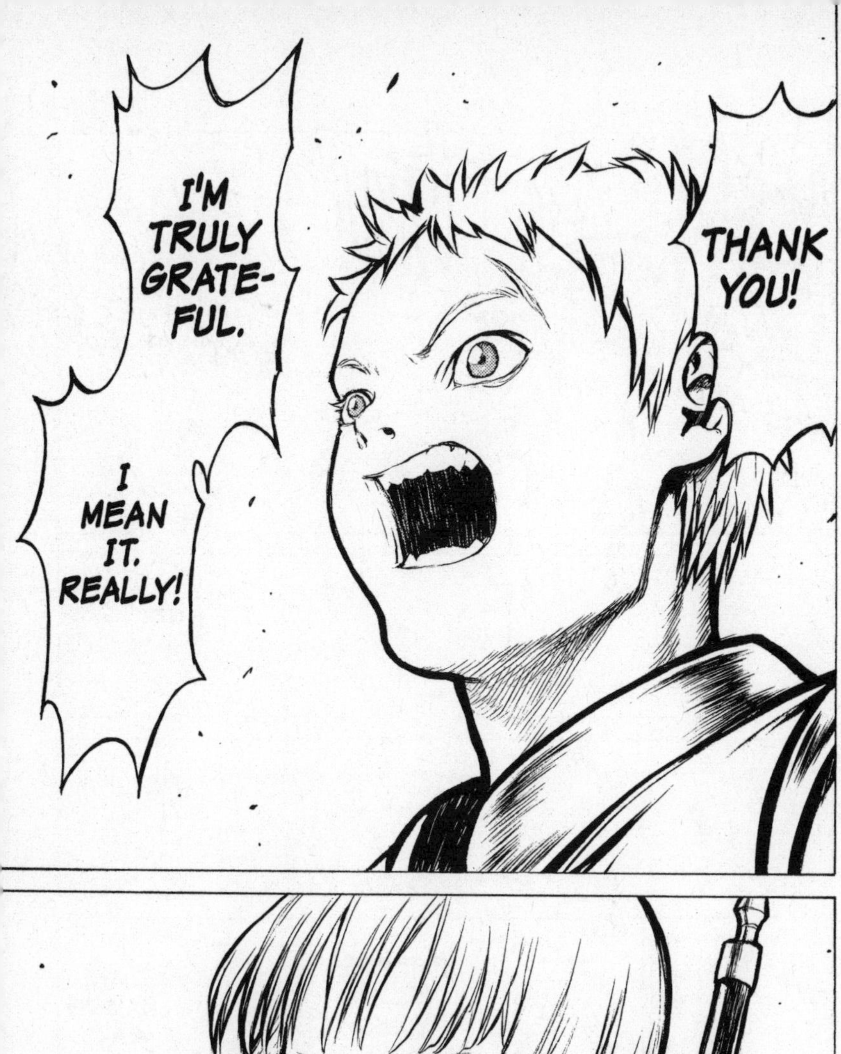
THANK YOU!
I'M TRULY GRATE-FUL.
I MEAN IT. REALLY!
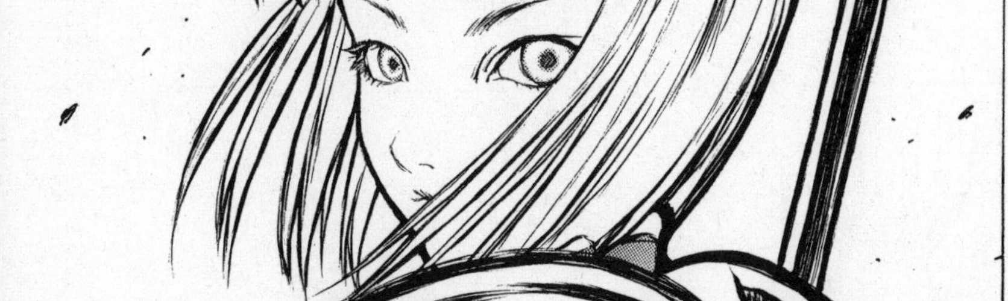

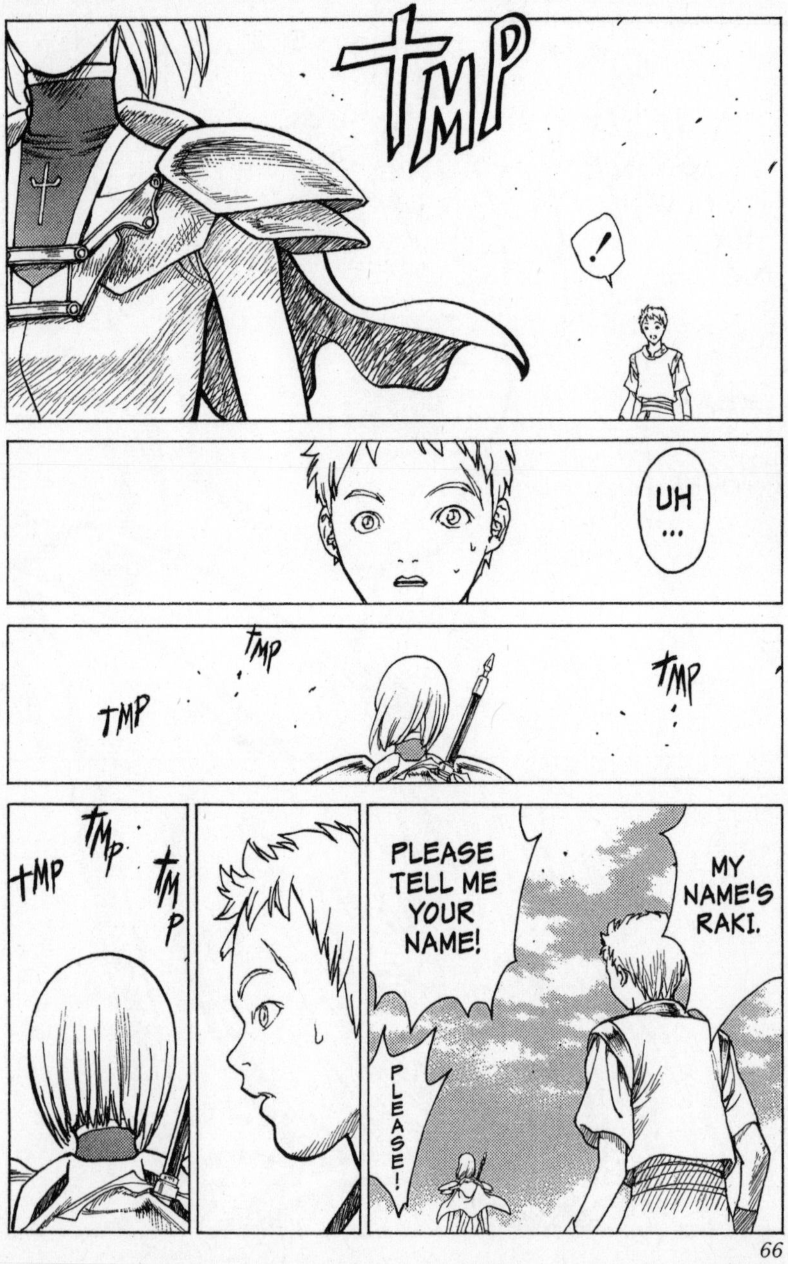
TMP
!
UH ...
TMP
TMP
TMP
MY NAME'S RAKI.
PLEASE TELL ME YOUR NAME!
PLEASE!
TMP
TMP
TMP

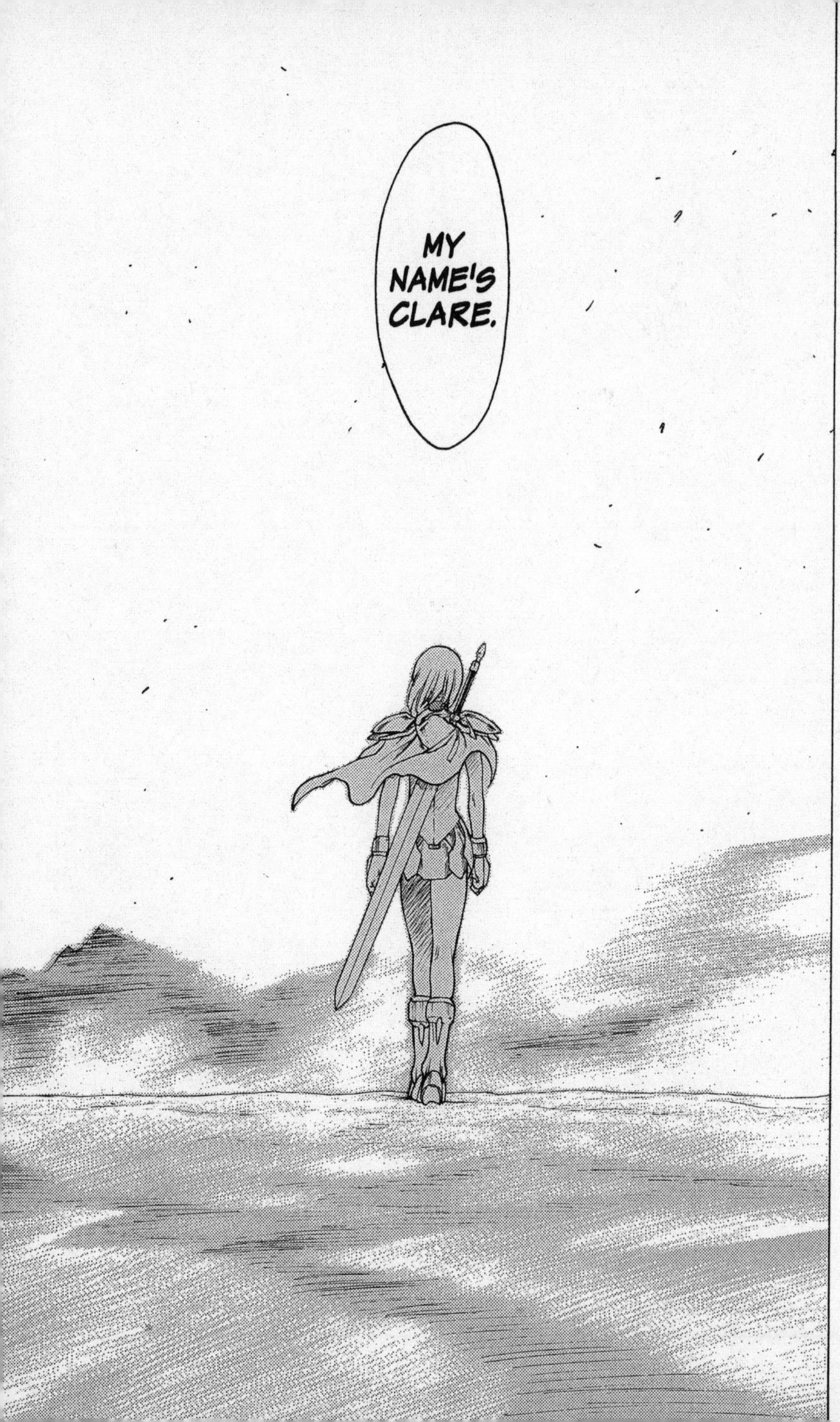
MY NAME'S CLARE.

クレイモア
Claymore

Scene 2: Claws in the Sky

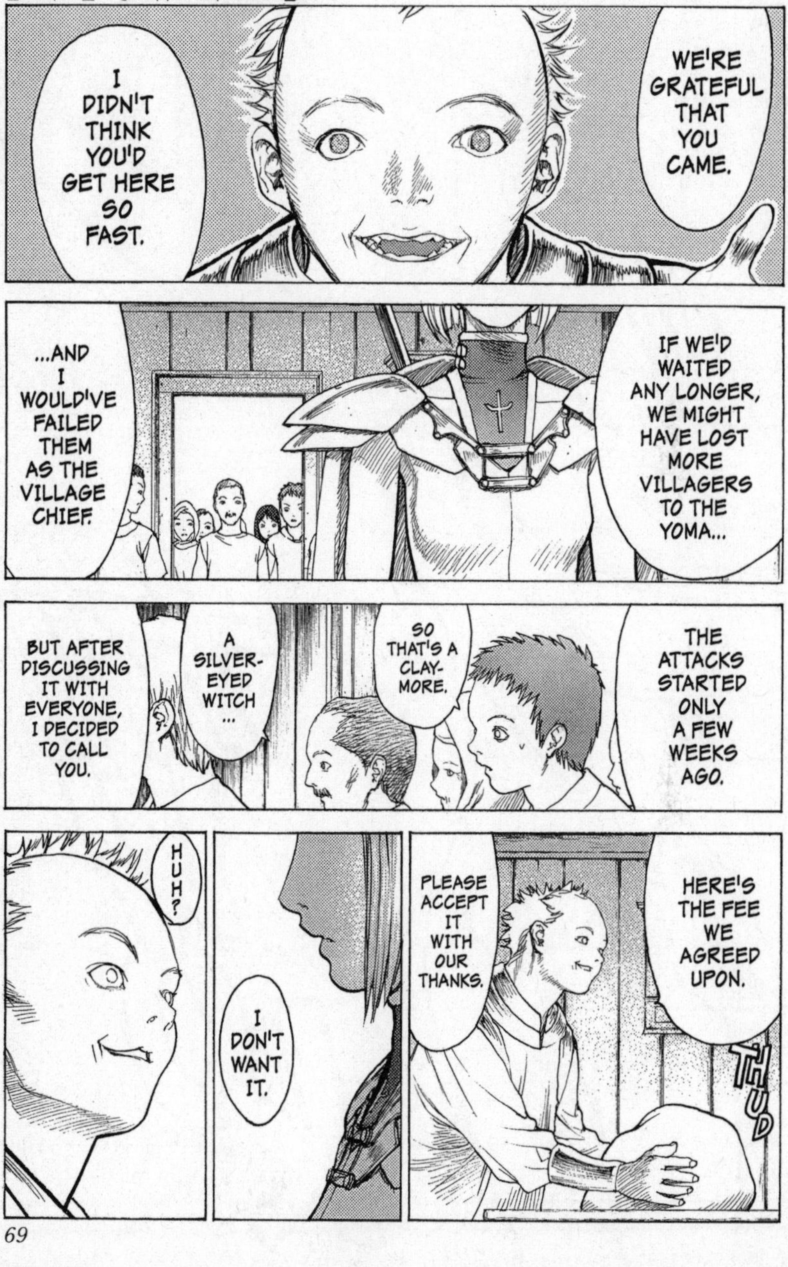

WE'RE GRATEFUL THAT YOU CAME.
I DIDN'T THINK YOU'D GET HERE SO FAST.
IF WE'D WAITED ANY LONGER, WE MIGHT HAVE LOST MORE VILLAGERS TO THE YOMA...
...AND I WOULD'VE FAILED THEM AS THE VILLAGE CHIEF.
THE ATTACKS STARTED ONLY A FEW WEEKS AGO.
SO THAT'S A CLAY-MORE.
A SILVER-EYED WITCH...
BUT AFTER DISCUSSING IT WITH EVERYONE, I DECIDED TO CALL YOU.
HERE'S THE FEE WE AGREED UPON.
THUD
PLEASE ACCEPT IT WITH OUR THANKS.
I DON'T WANT IT.
HUH?

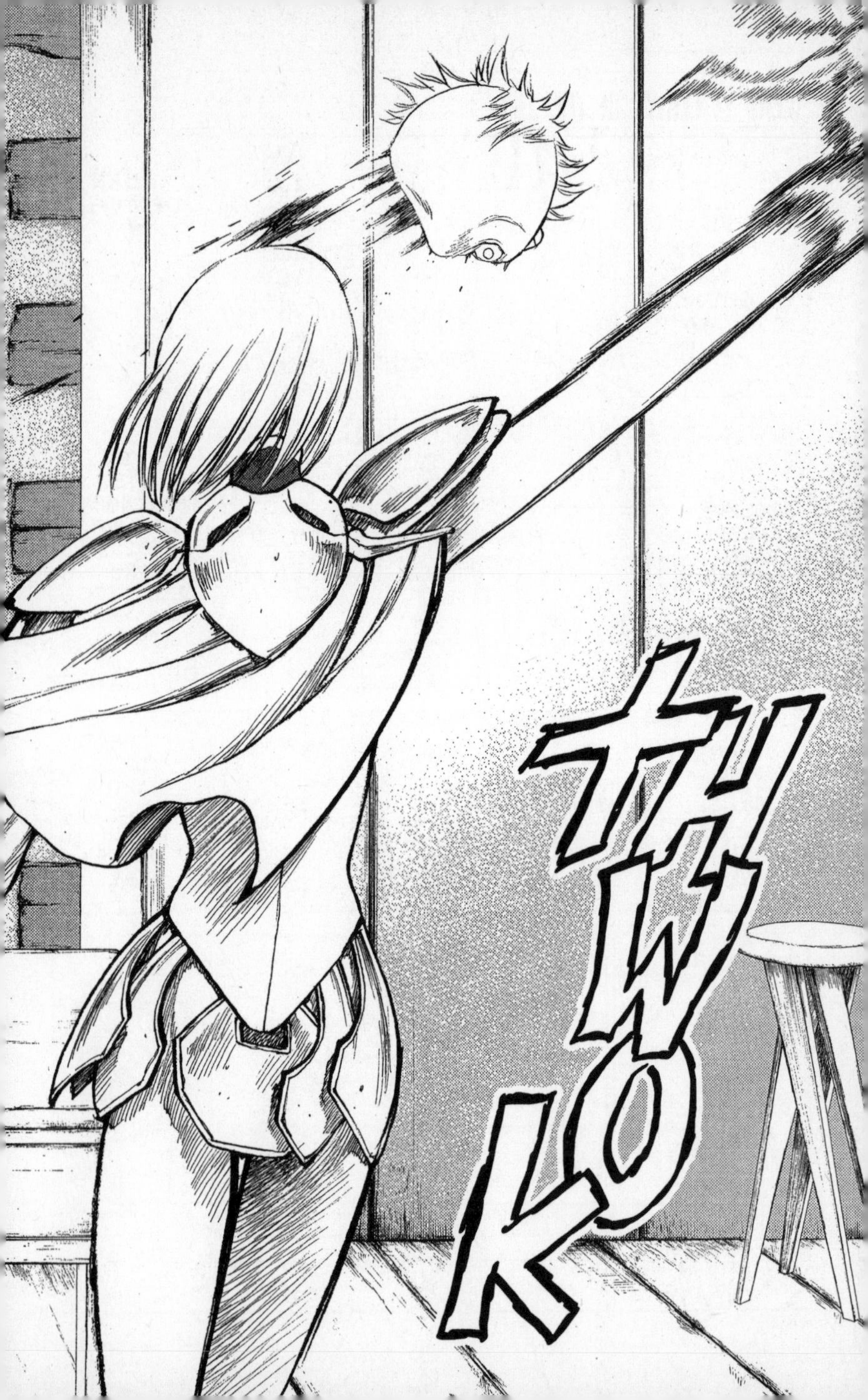
THWOK

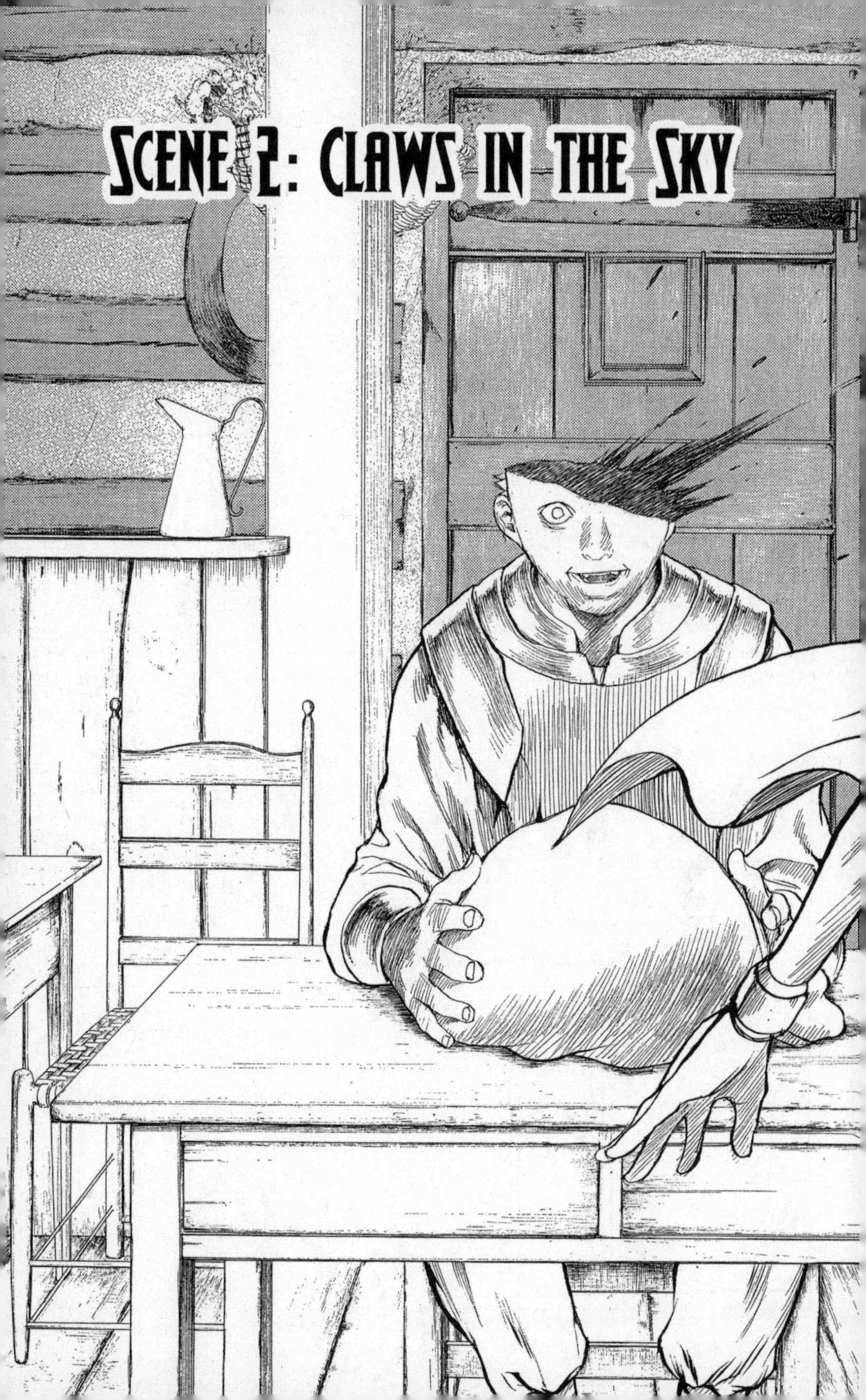
SCENE 2: CLAWS IN THE SKY

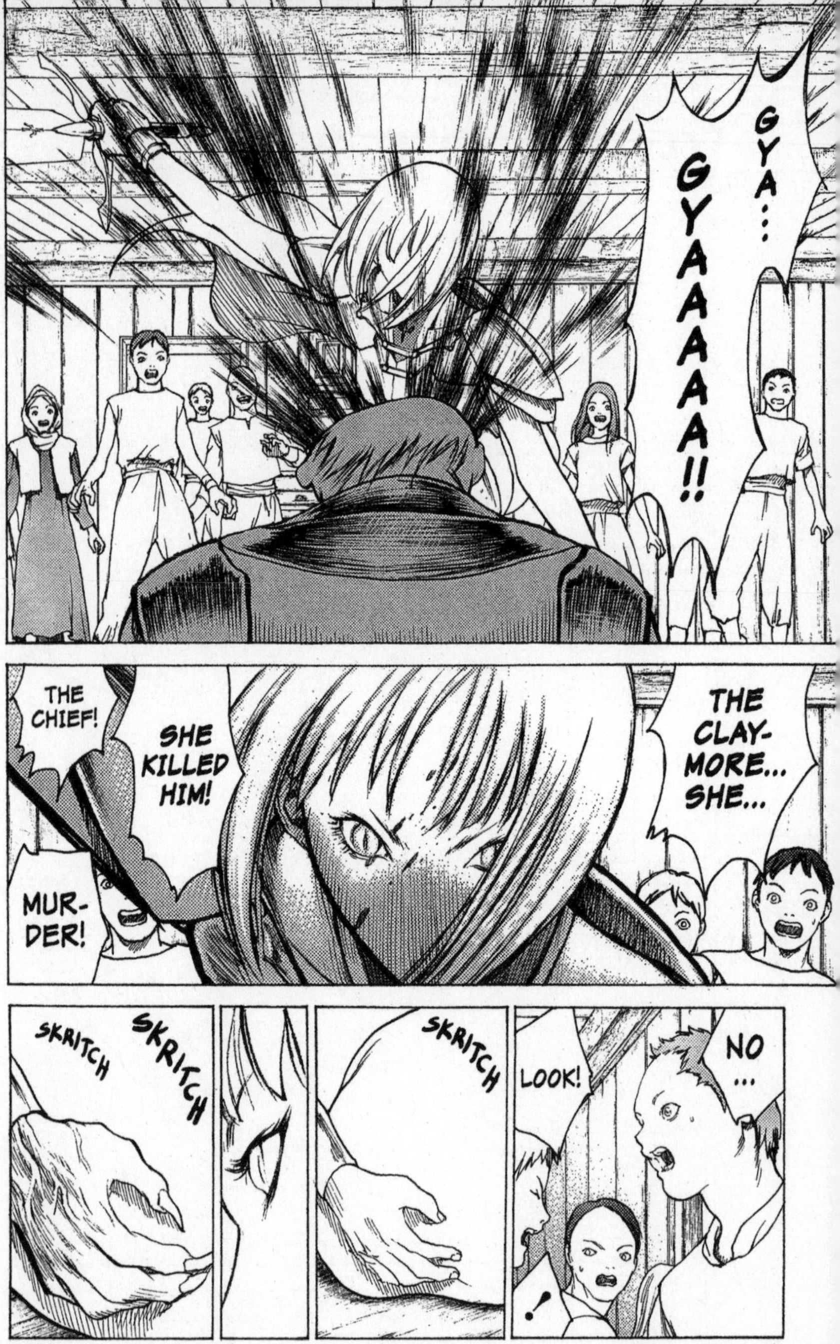
GYA...
GYAAAAAA!!
THE CLAY-MORE... SHE...
SHE KILLED HIM!
THE CHIEF!
MUR-DER!
NO ...
LOOK!
!
SKRITCH
SKRITCH
SKRITCH

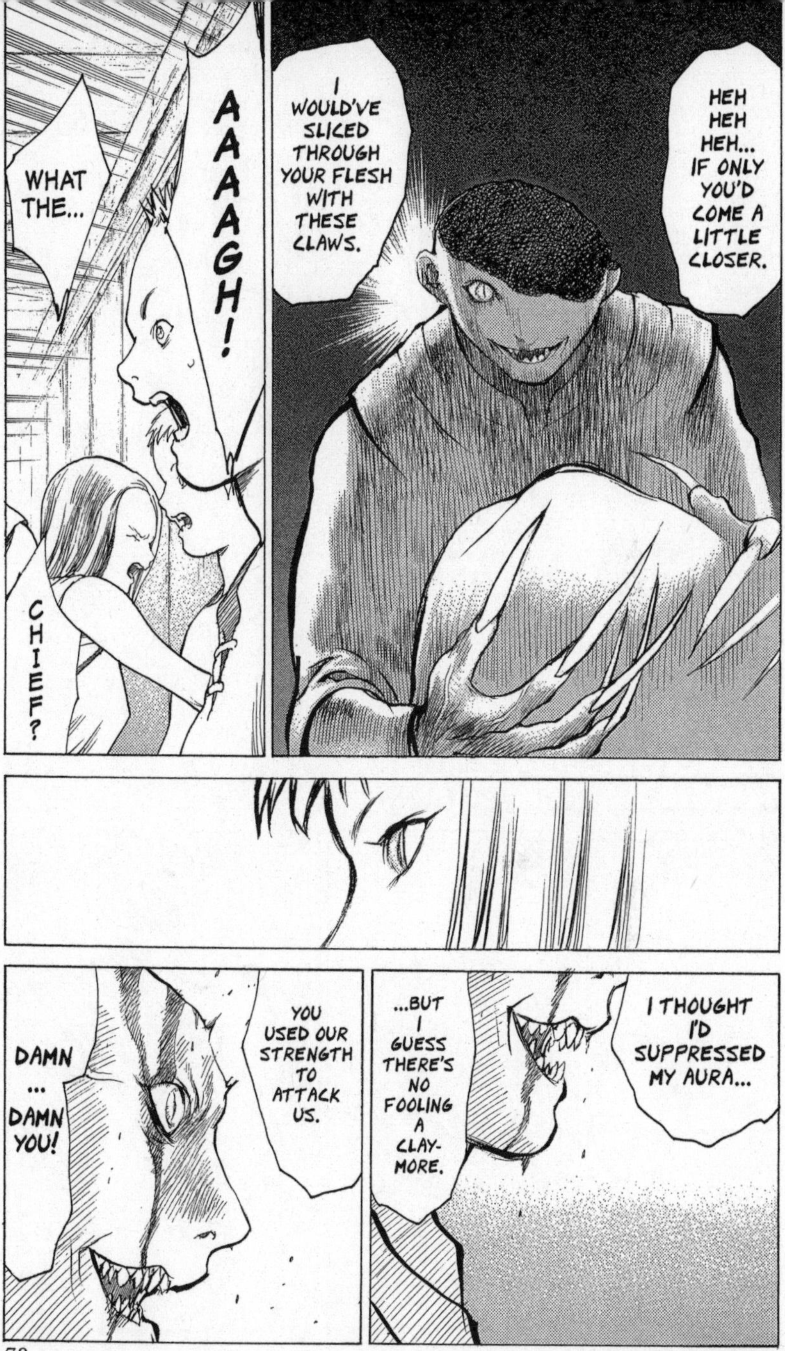
HEH HEH HEH... IF ONLY YOU'D COME A LITTLE CLOSER.
I WOULD'VE SLICED THROUGH YOUR FLESH WITH THESE CLAWS.
AAAAAGH!
WHAT THE...
CHIEF?
I THOUGHT I'D SUPPRESSED MY AURA...
...BUT I GUESS THERE'S NO FOOLING A CLAY-MORE.
YOU USED OUR STRENGTH TO ATTACK US.
DAMN ... DAMN YOU!

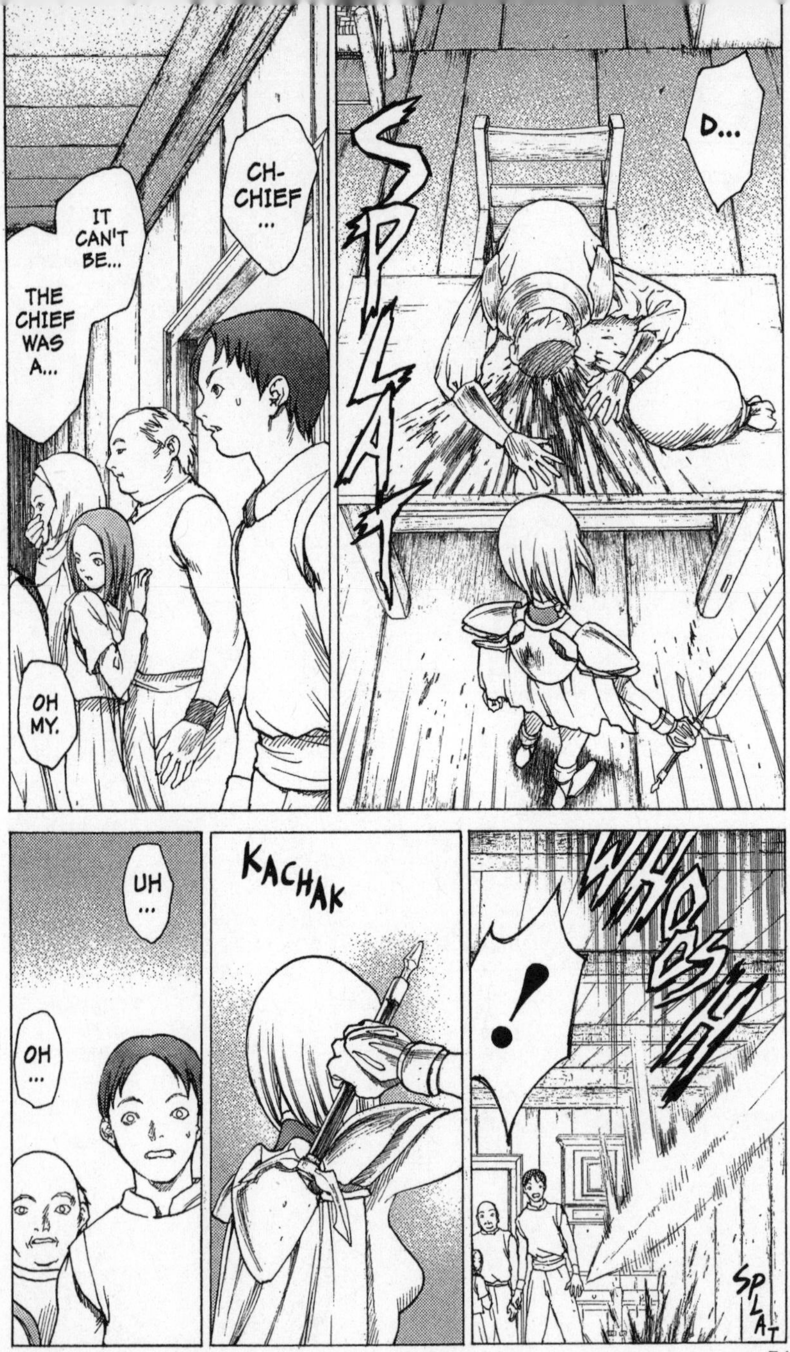
D...
SPLAT
CH-CHIEF...
IT CAN'T BE...
THE CHIEF WAS A...
OH MY.
WHOOSH
!
SPLAT
KACHAK
UH...
OH...

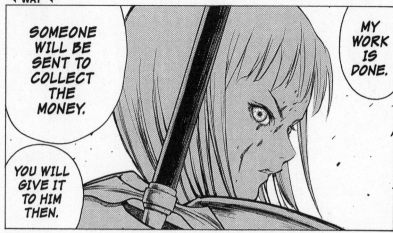

READ THIS WAY

MY WORK IS DONE.
SOMEONE WILL BE SENT TO COLLECT THE MONEY.
YOU WILL GIVE IT TO HIM THEN.
BSSH

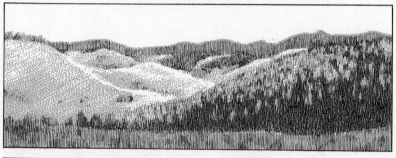

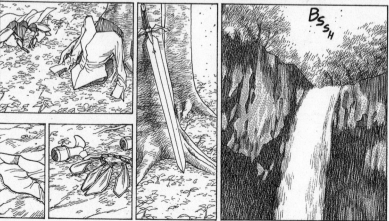

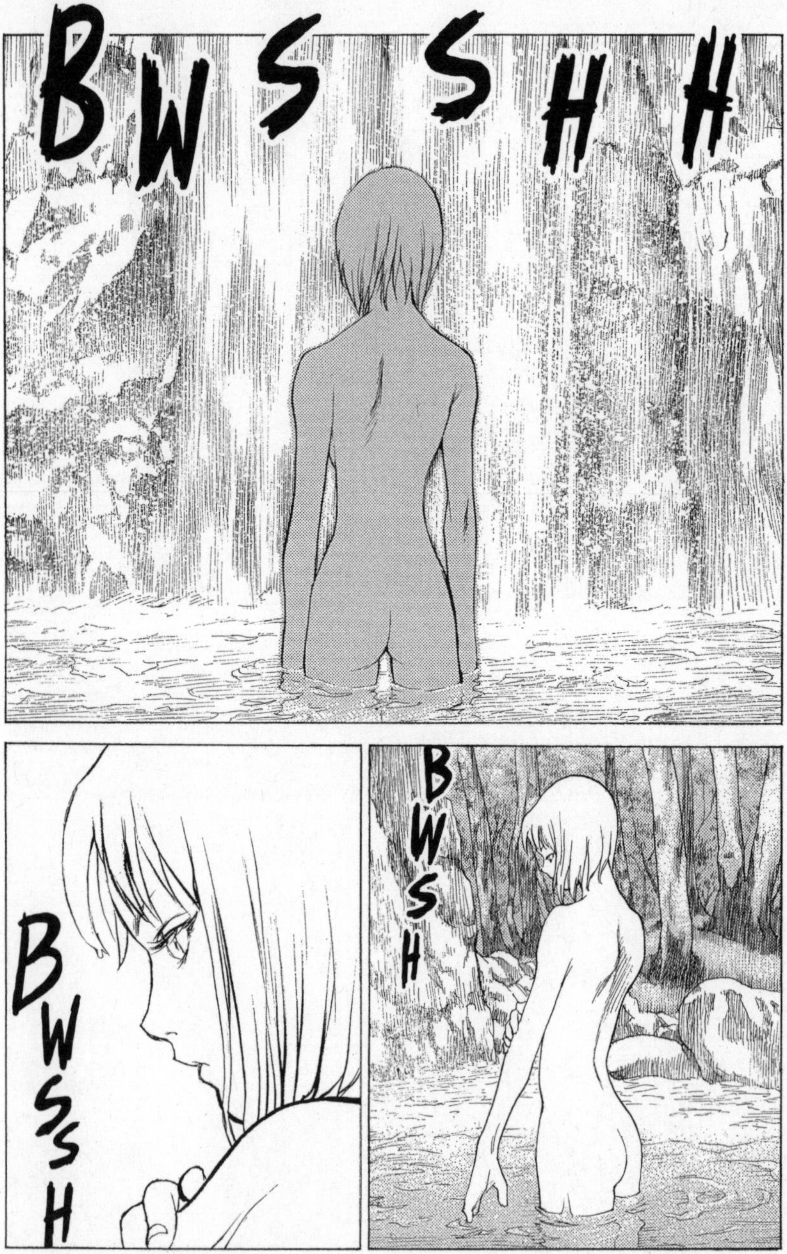
BWSSHH
BWSSH
BWSSH

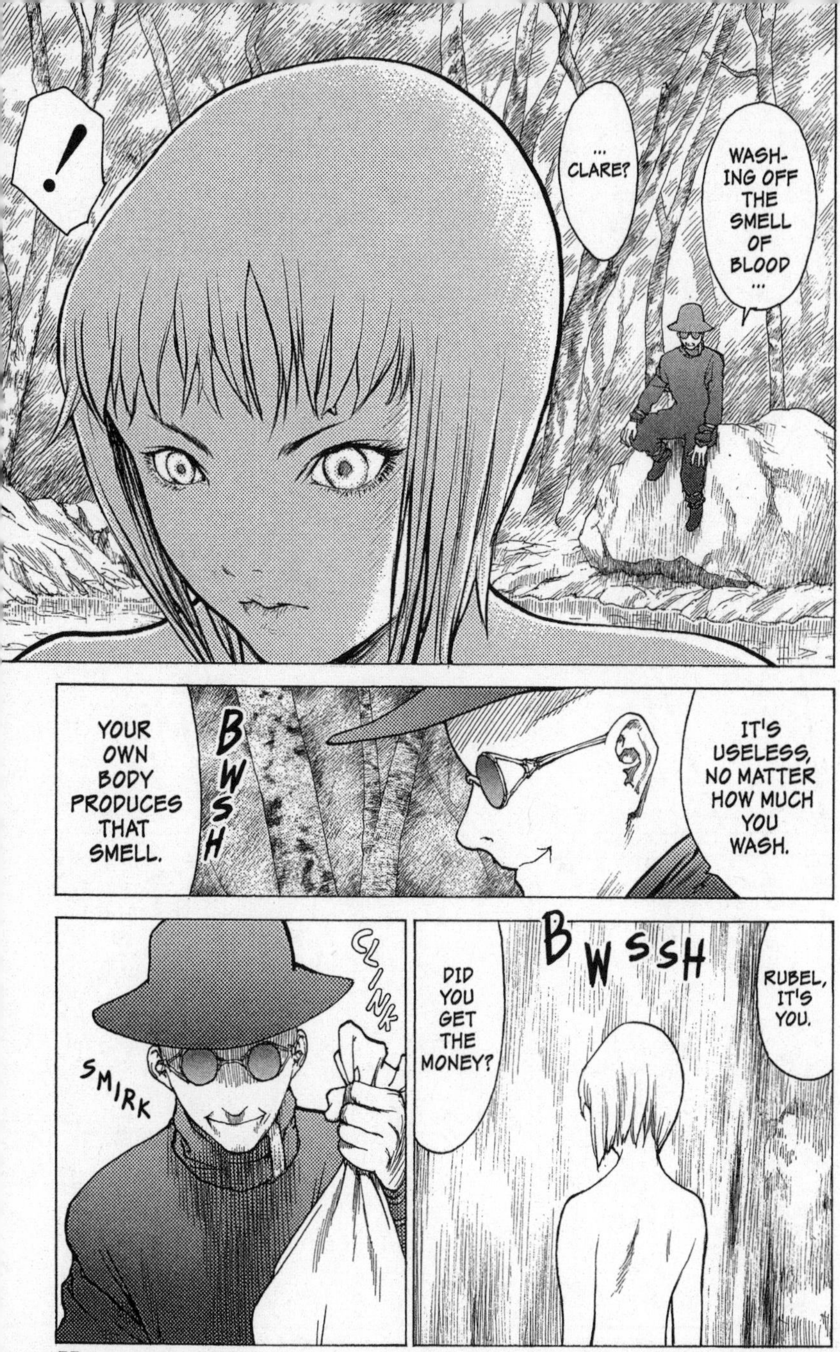
WASHING OFF THE SMELL OF BLOOD ...
... CLARE?
!
IT'S USELESS, NO MATTER HOW MUCH YOU WASH.
BWSH
YOUR OWN BODY PRODUCES THAT SMELL.
RUBEL, IT'S YOU.
BWSSH
DID YOU GET THE MONEY?
CLINK
SMIRK

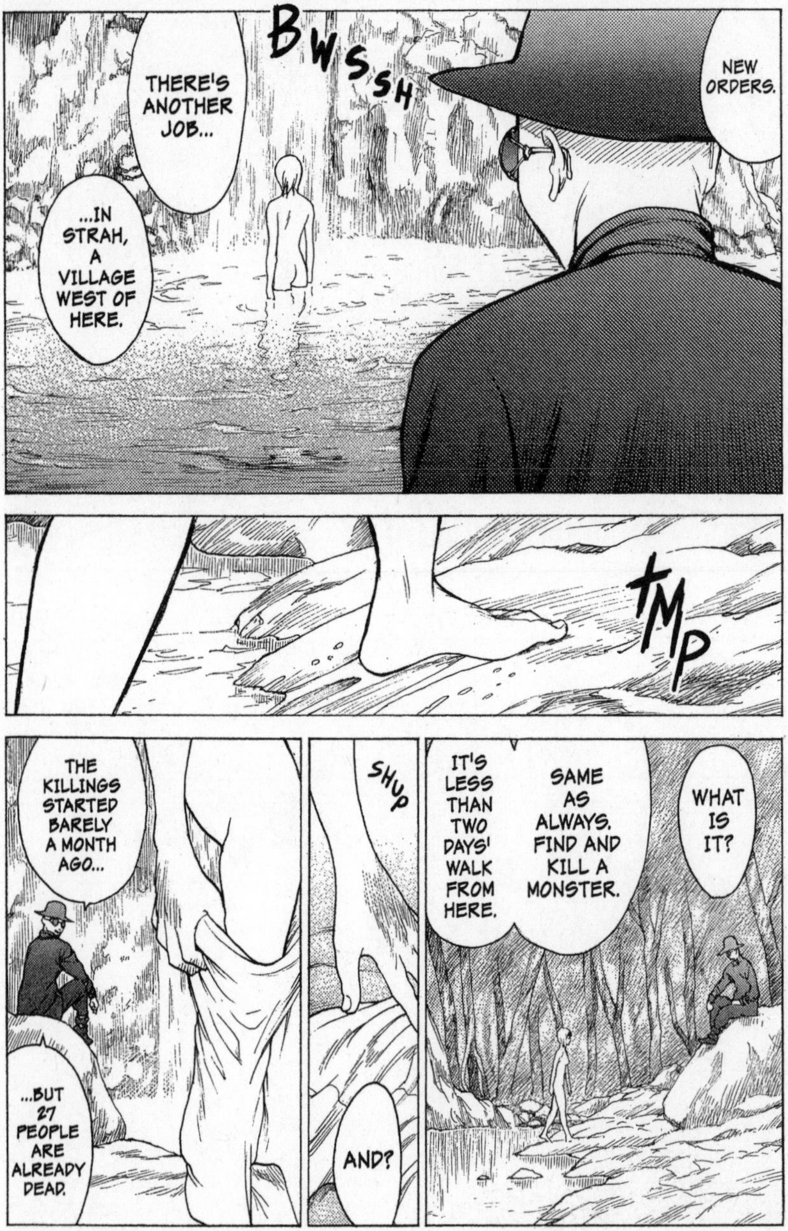
NEW ORDERS.
BWSSH
THERE'S ANOTHER JOB...
...IN STRAH, A VILLAGE WEST OF HERE.
TMP
WHAT IS IT?
SAME AS ALWAYS. FIND AND KILL A MONSTER.
IT'S LESS THAN TWO DAYS' WALK FROM HERE.
SHUP
AND?
THE KILLINGS STARTED BARELY A MONTH AGO...
...BUT 27 PEOPLE ARE ALREADY DEAD.

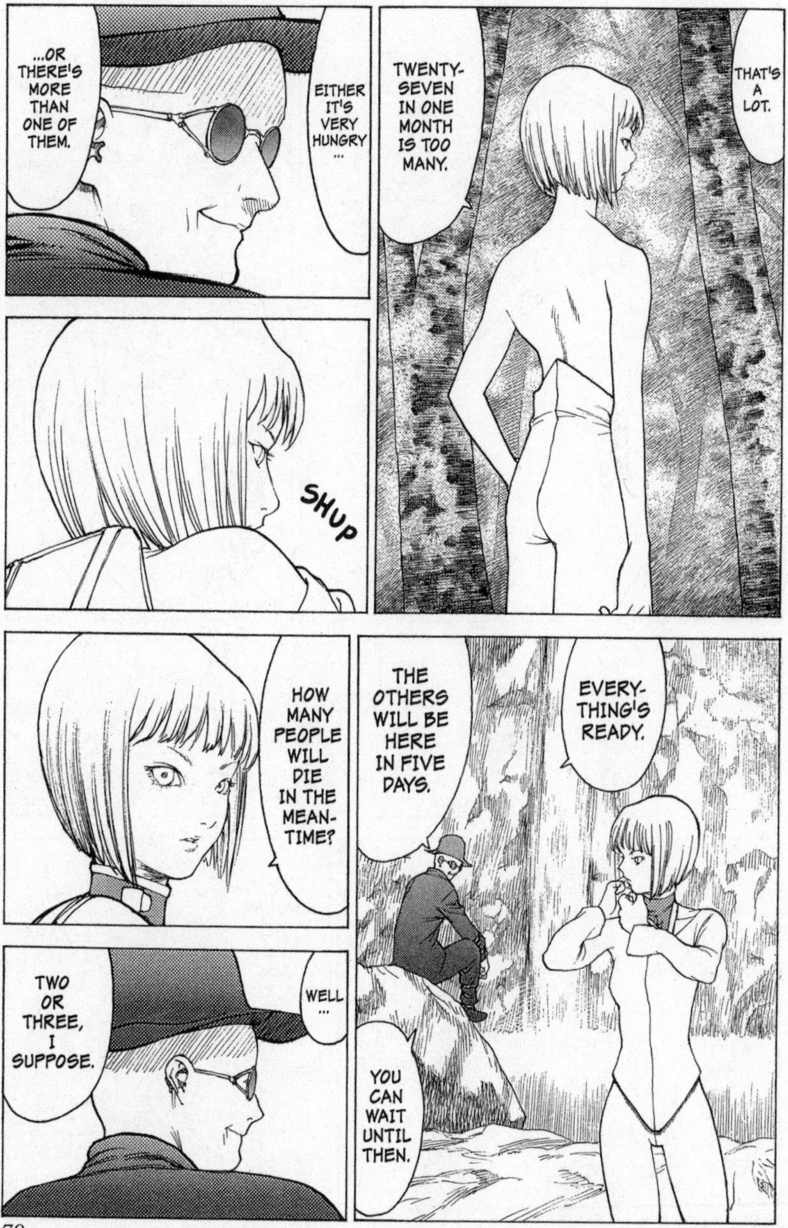
THAT'S A LOT.
TWENTY-SEVEN IN ONE MONTH IS TOO MANY.
EITHER IT'S VERY HUNGRY...
...OR THERE'S MORE THAN ONE OF THEM.
SHUP
EVERYTHING'S READY.
THE OTHERS WILL BE HERE IN FIVE DAYS.
YOU CAN WAIT UNTIL THEN.
HOW MANY PEOPLE WILL DIE IN THE MEANTIME?
WELL...
TWO OR THREE, I SUPPOSE.

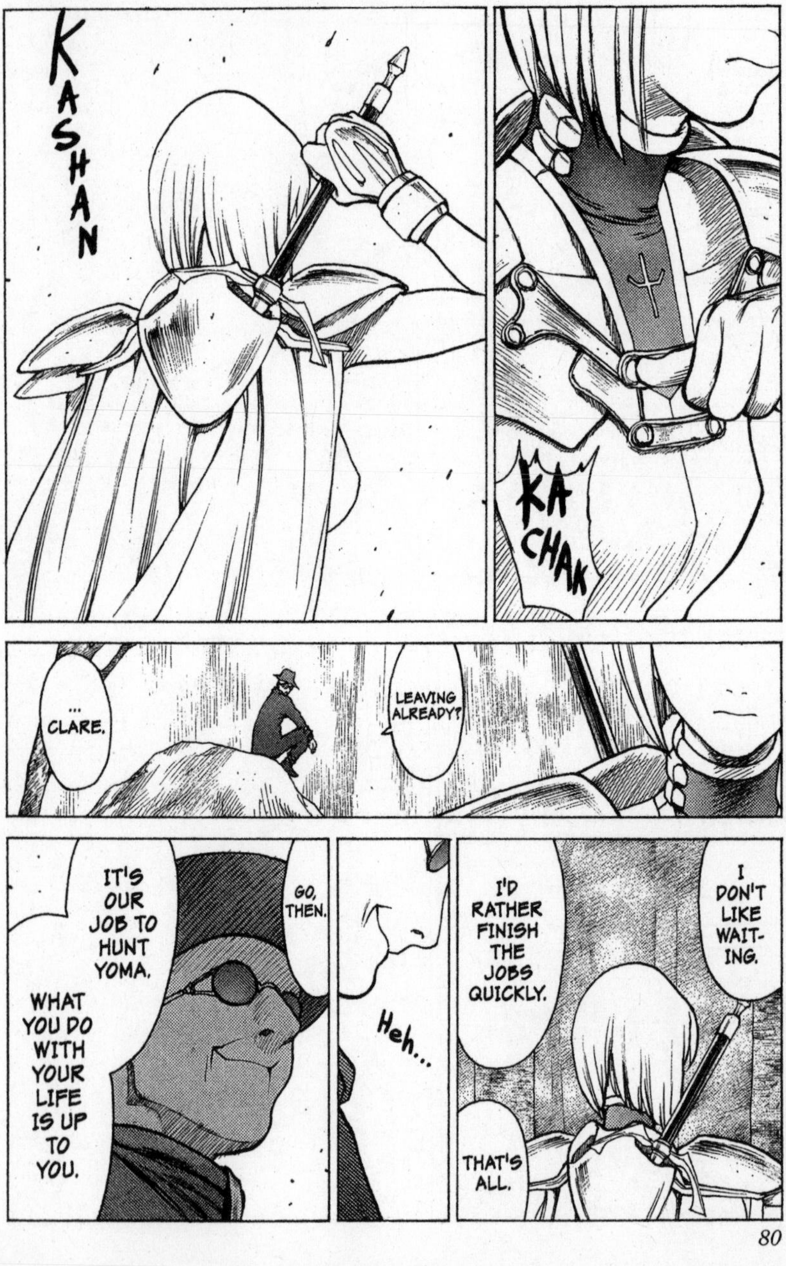
KA CHAK
KASHAN
LEAVING ALREADY?
... CLARE.
I DON'T LIKE WAIT-ING.
I'D RATHER FINISH THE JOBS QUICKLY.
THAT'S ALL.
GO, THEN.
Heh...
IT'S OUR JOB TO HUNT YOMA.
WHAT YOU DO WITH YOUR LIFE IS UP TO YOU.

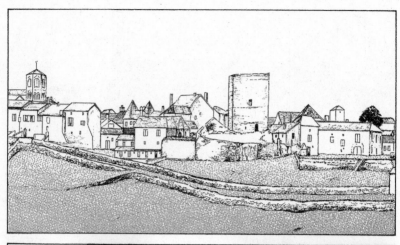

WHOOSH

TM

P

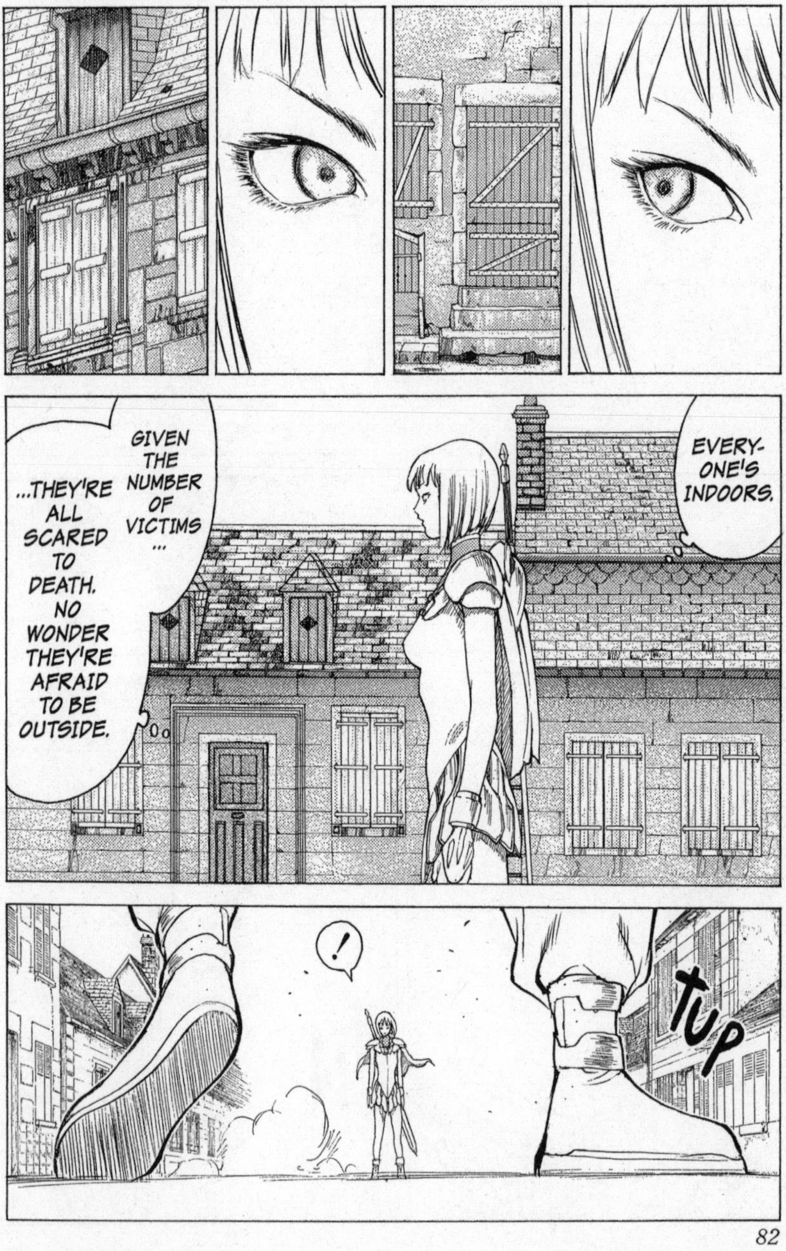
EVERY-ONE'S INDOORS.
GIVEN THE NUMBER OF VICTIMS ...
...THEY'RE ALL SCARED TO DEATH. NO WONDER THEY'RE AFRAID TO BE OUTSIDE.
TUP
!

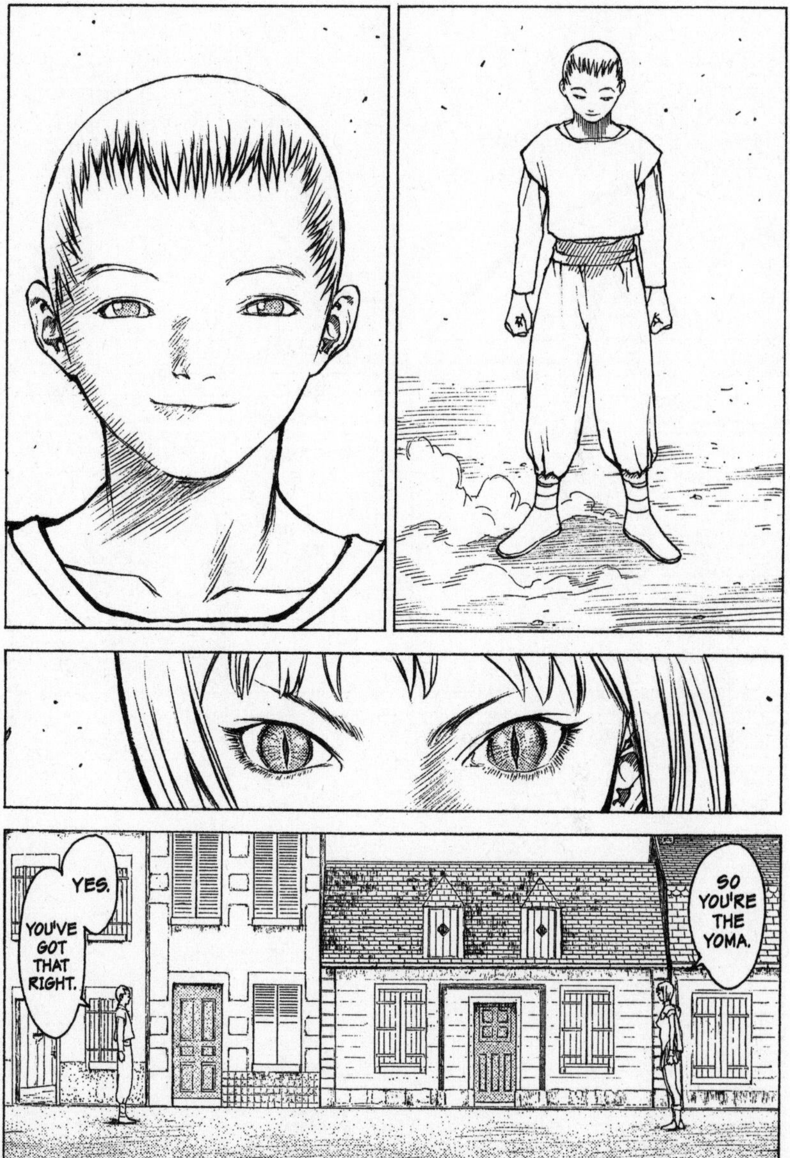
SO YOU'RE THE YOMA.
YES.
YOU'VE GOT THAT RIGHT.

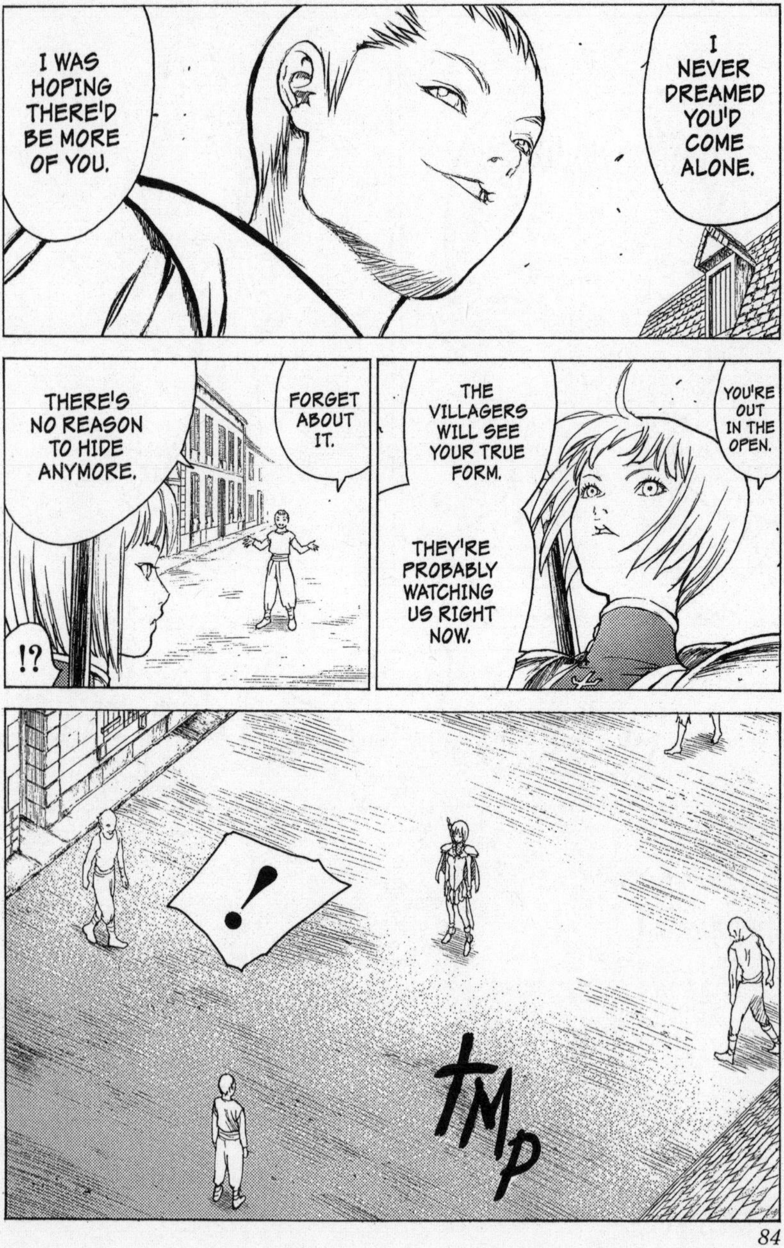
I NEVER DREAMED YOU'D COME ALONE.
I WAS HOPING THERE'D BE MORE OF YOU.
YOU'RE OUT IN THE OPEN.
THE VILLAGERS WILL SEE YOUR TRUE FORM.
THEY'RE PROBABLY WATCHING US RIGHT NOW.
FORGET ABOUT IT.
THERE'S NO REASON TO HIDE ANYMORE.
!?
!
TMP

READ THIS WAY

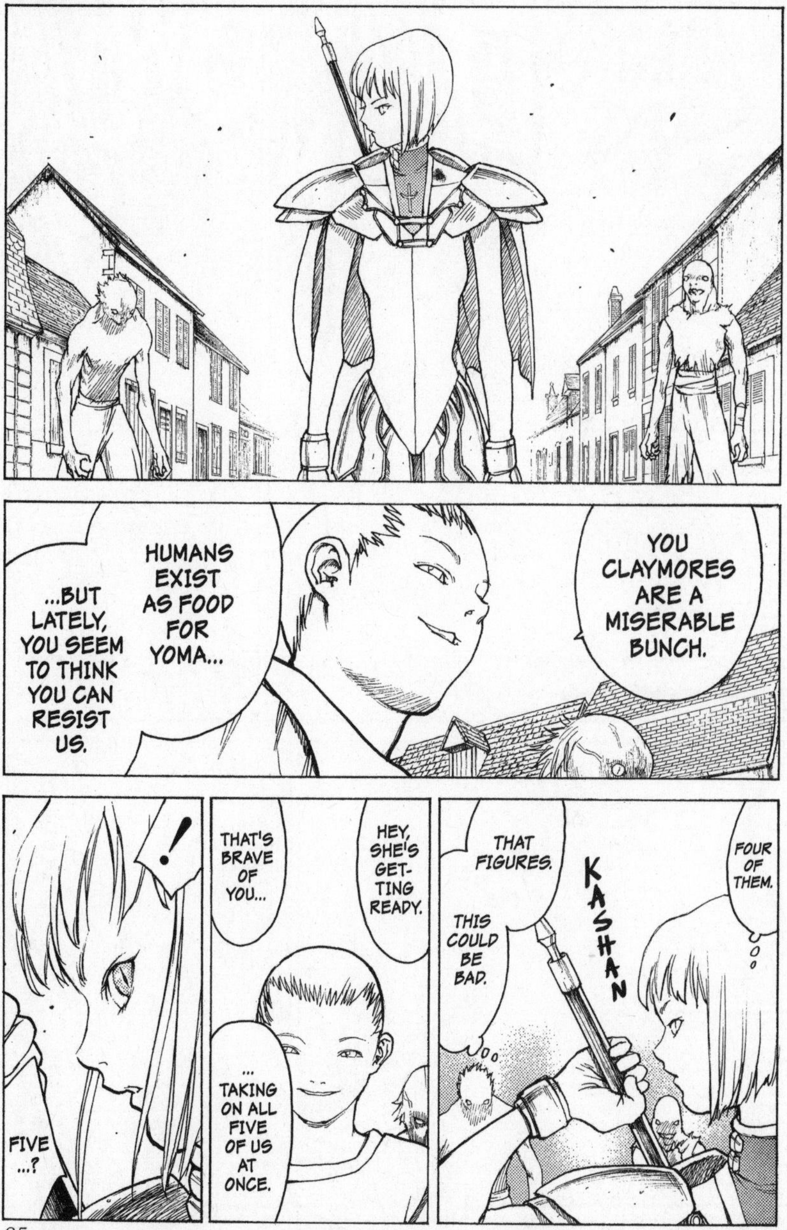
YOU CLAYMORES ARE A MISERABLE BUNCH.
HUMANS EXIST AS FOOD FOR YOMA...
...BUT LATELY, YOU SEEM TO THINK YOU CAN RESIST US.
FOUR OF THEM.
THAT FIGURES.
KASHAN
THIS COULD BE BAD.
HEY, SHE'S GET-TING READY.
THAT'S BRAVE OF YOU...
...TAKING ON ALL FIVE OF US AT ONCE.
!
FIVE ...?

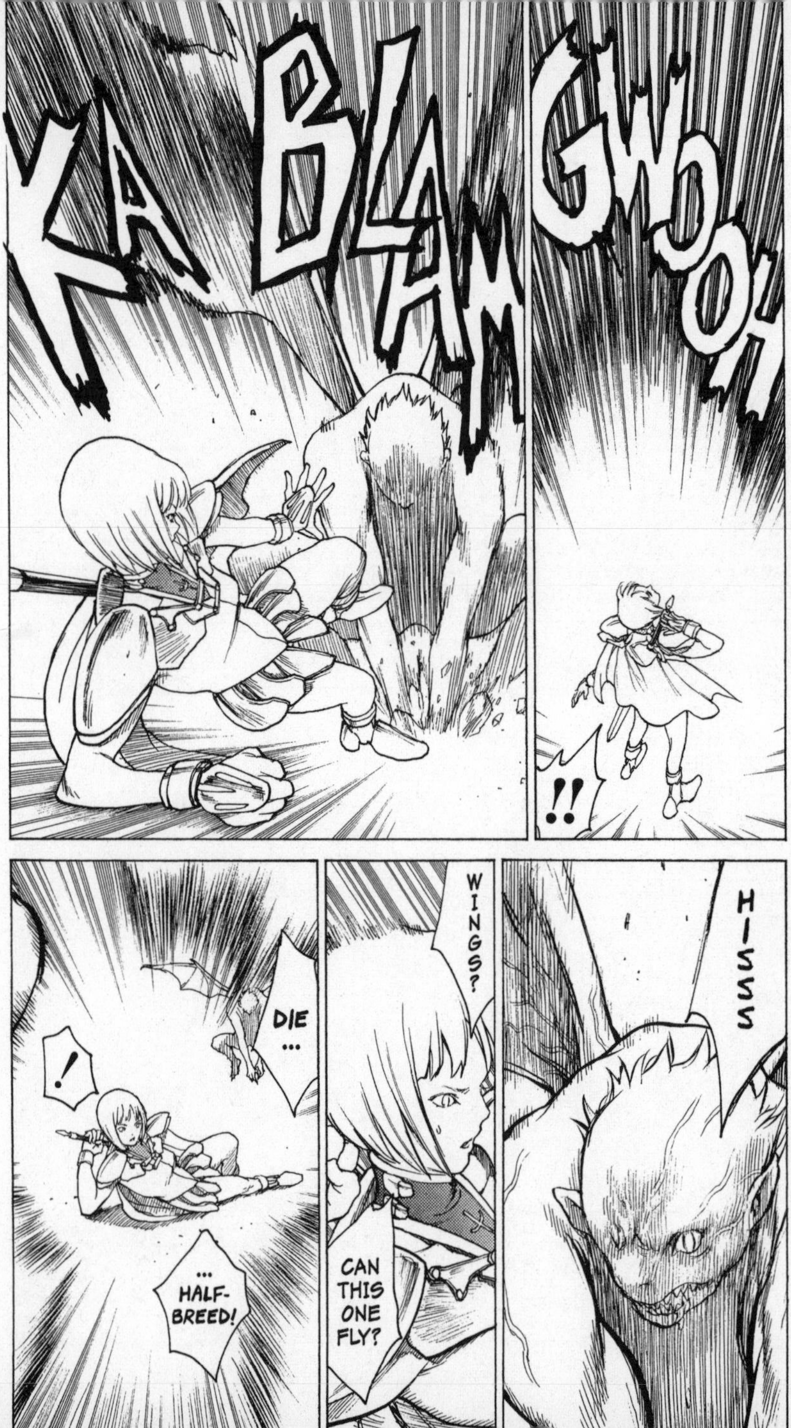
GWOOOH
!!
KA BLAM
HISSS
WINGS?
CAN THIS ONE FLY?
DIE ...
!
... HALF-BREED!

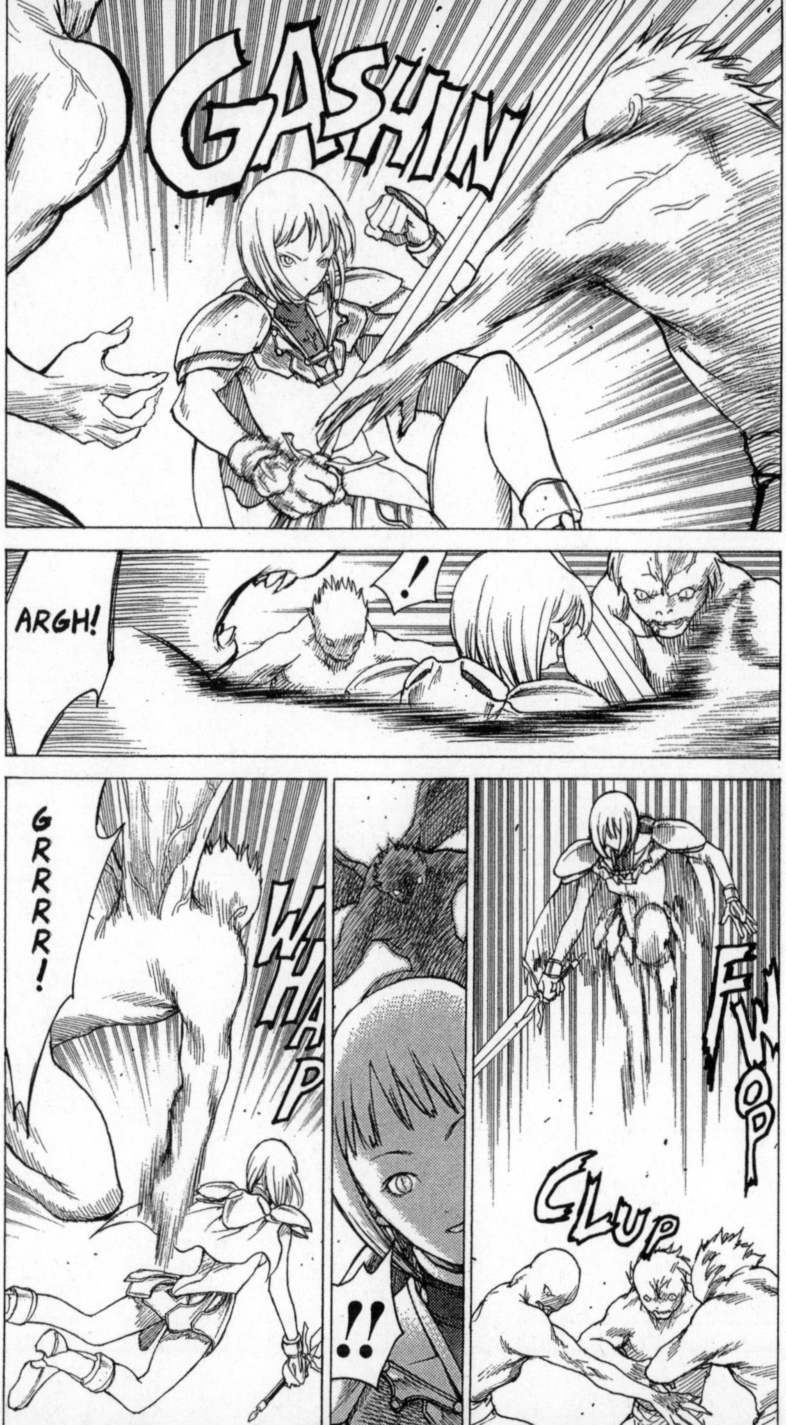
GASHIN
!
ARGH!
FWOP
CLUP
WHAP
!!
GRRRRR!

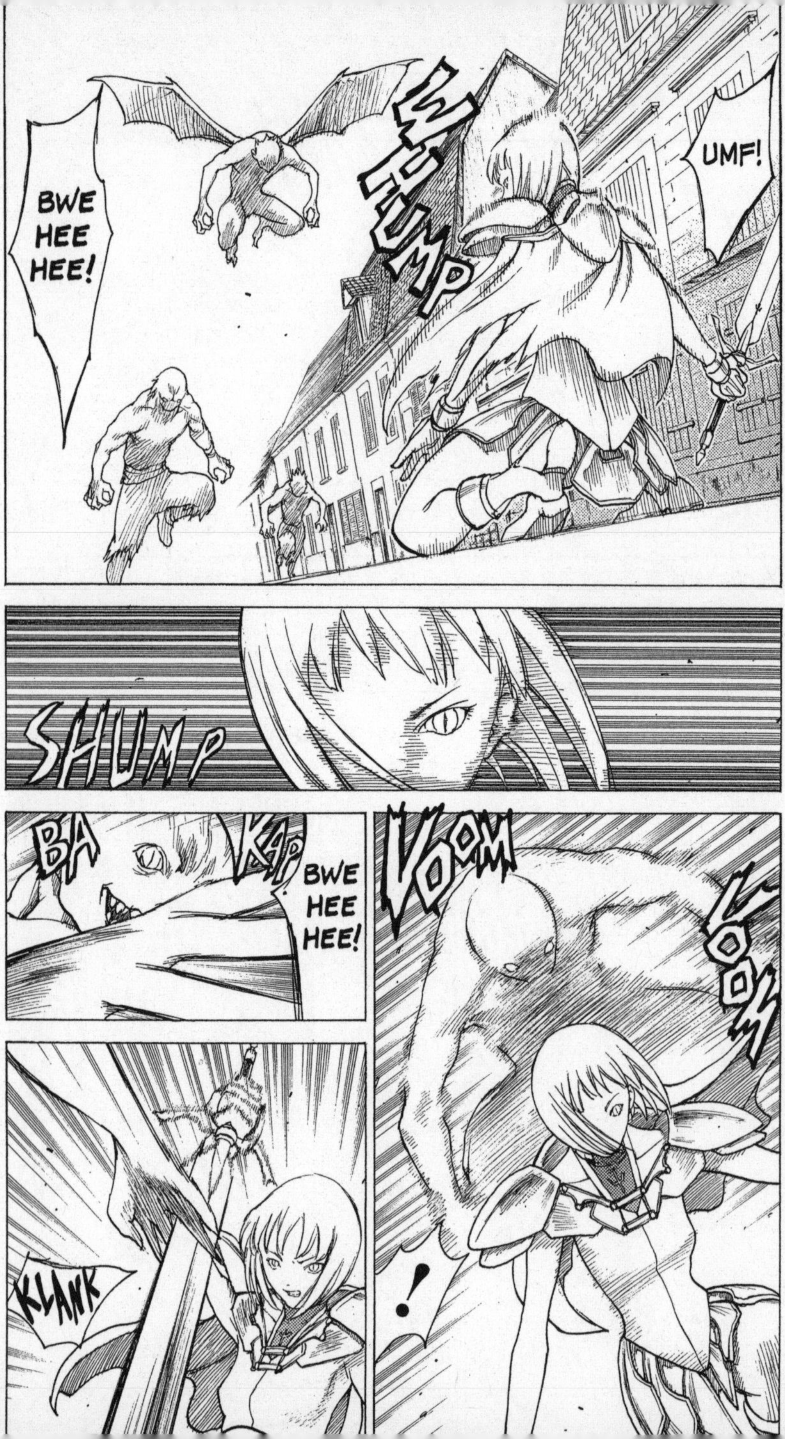
UMF!
WHUMP
BWE HEE HEE!
SHUMP
VOOM
VOOM
!
BA KAP
BWE HEE HEE!
KLANK

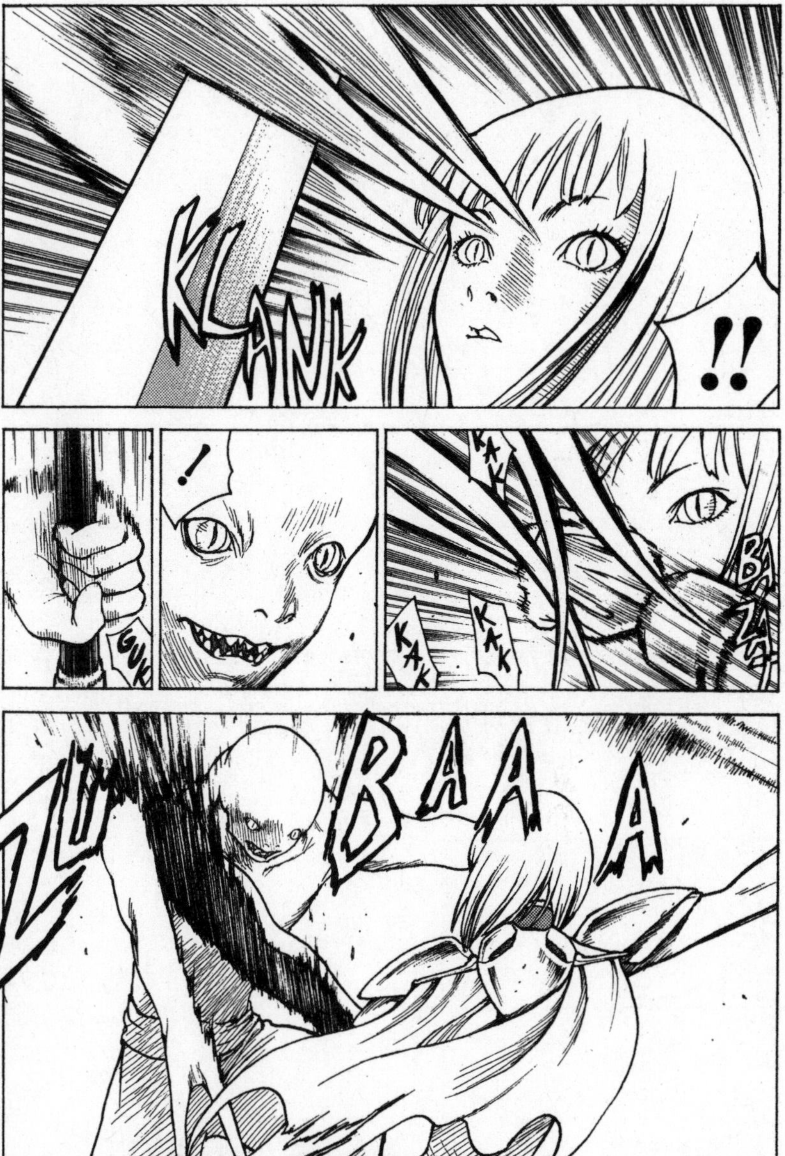
!!
KLANK
BAZA
KAK
KAK
KAK
!
GUK
ZUBAAA

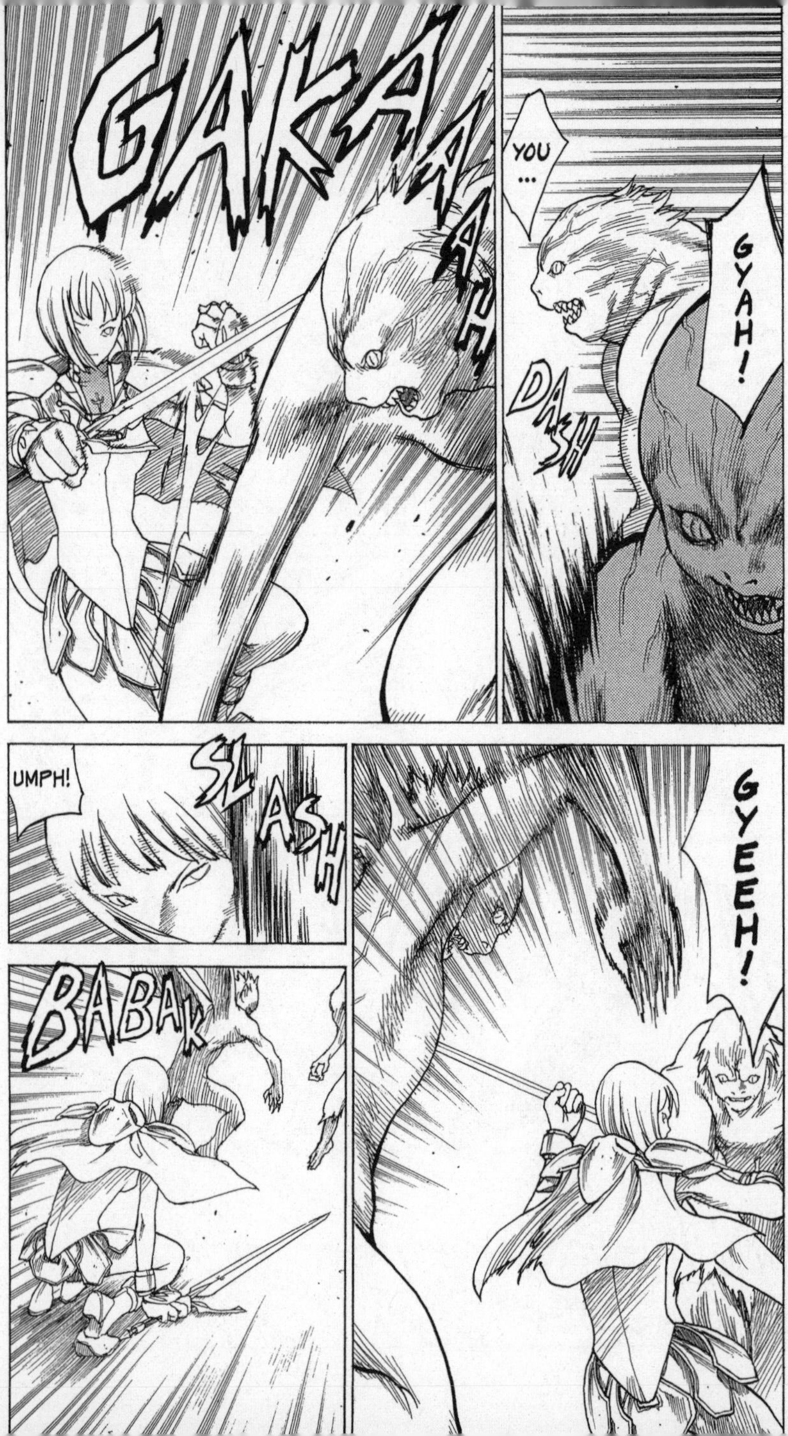
GYAH!
YOU ...
DASH
GAKAAAH
GYEEEH!
SLASH
UMPH!
BABAK

READ THIS WAY

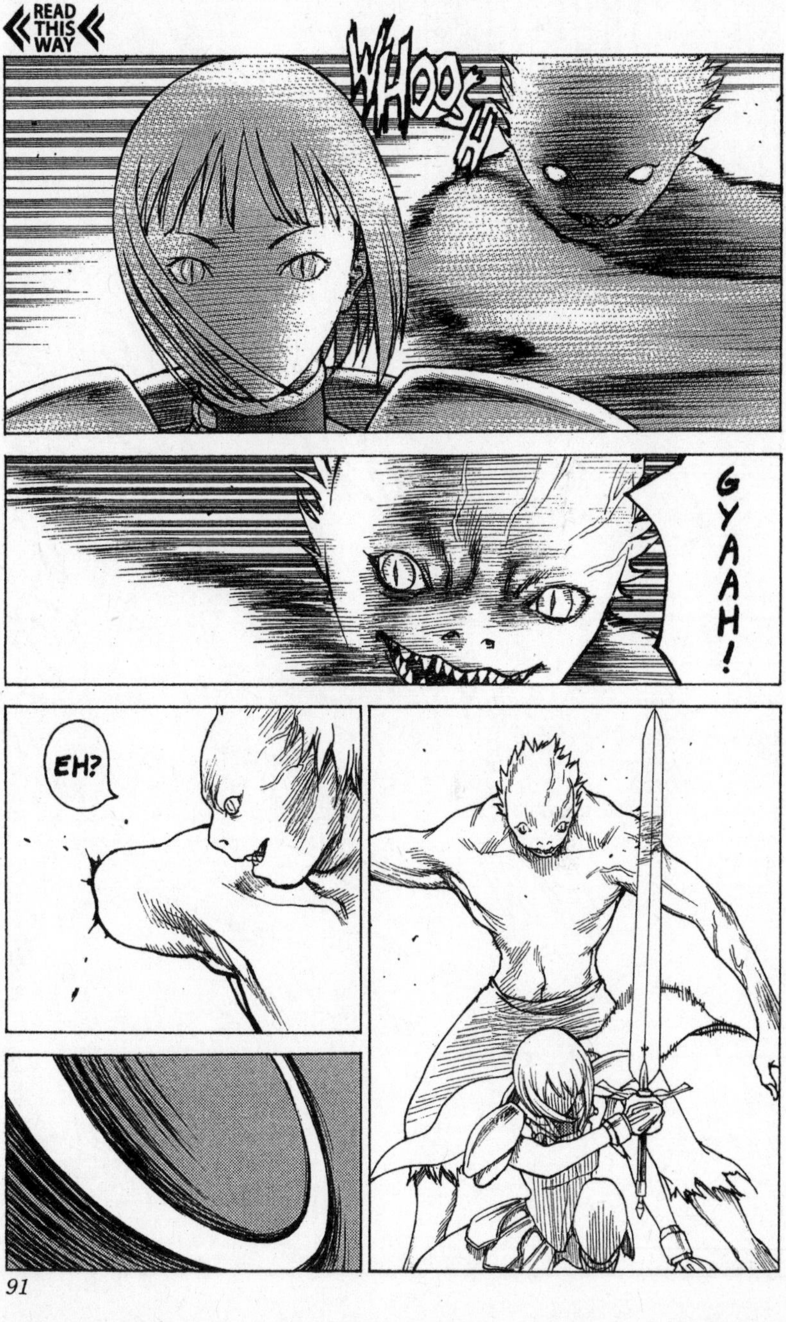
WHOOSH
GYAAH!
EH?

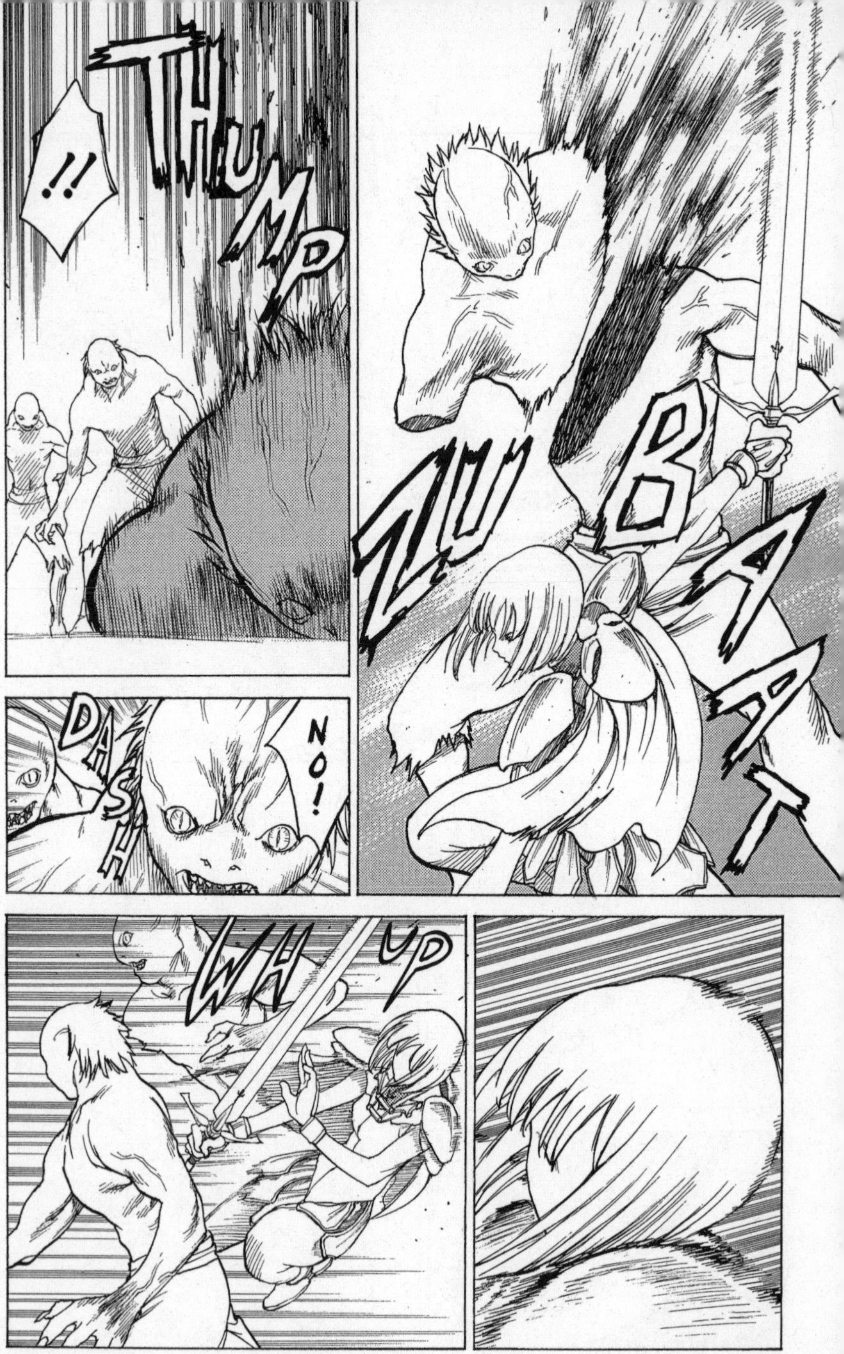
ZUBAAT
THUMP
!!
NO!
DASH
WHUP

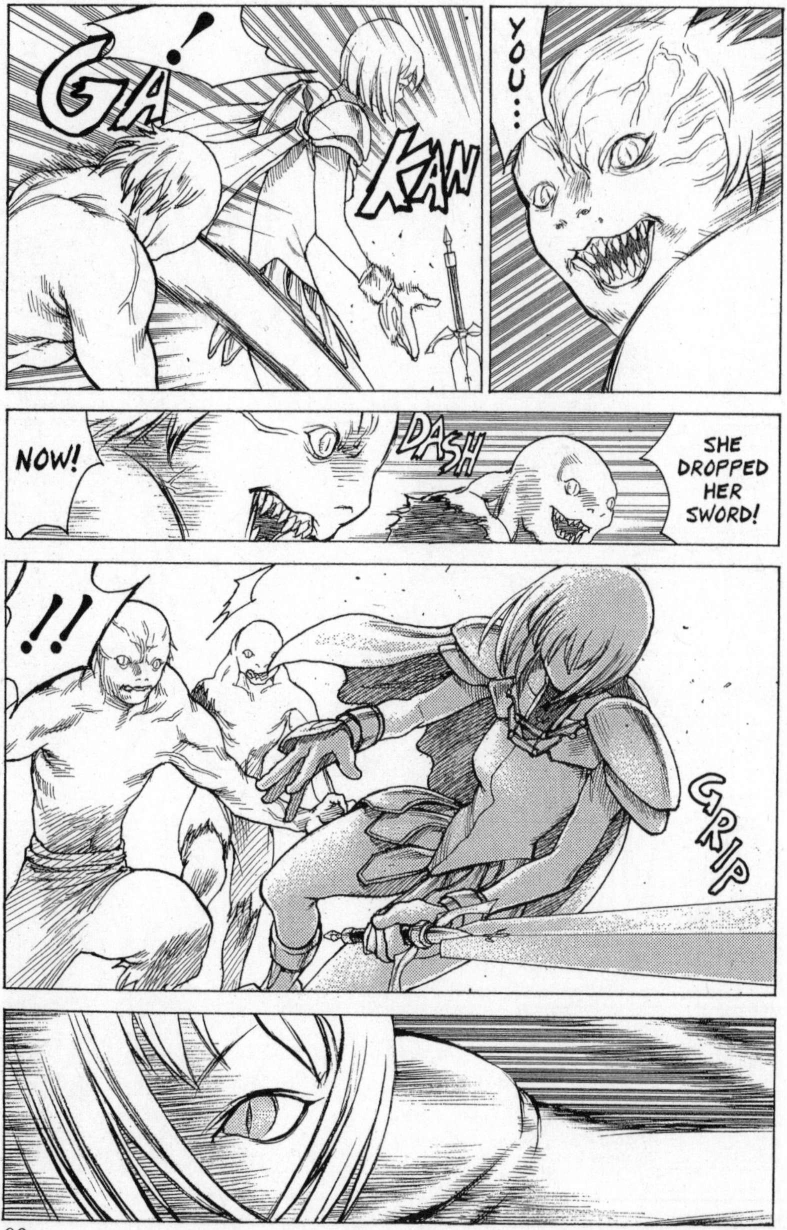
YOU...
GA!
KAN
SHE DROPPED HER SWORD!
DASH
NOW!
!!
GRIP

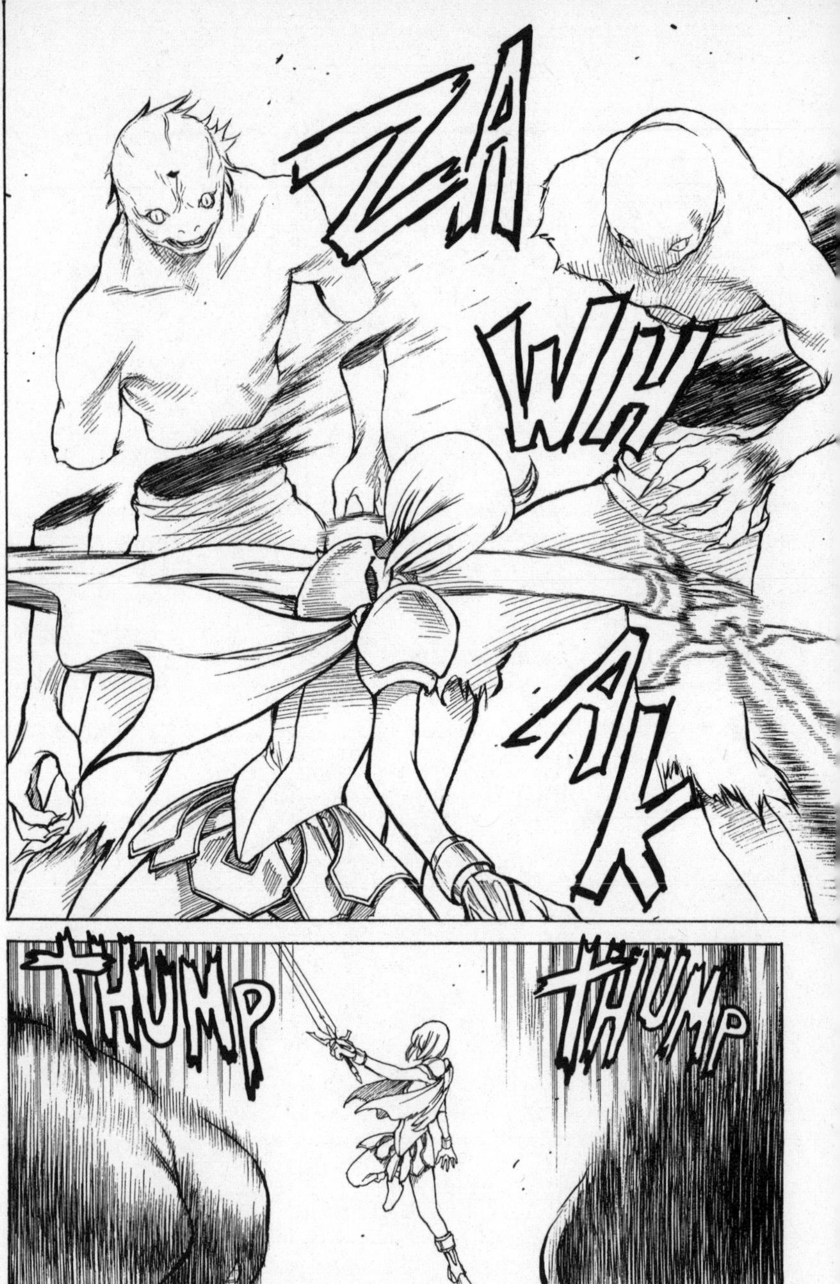
ZA WHAK
THUMP
THUMP

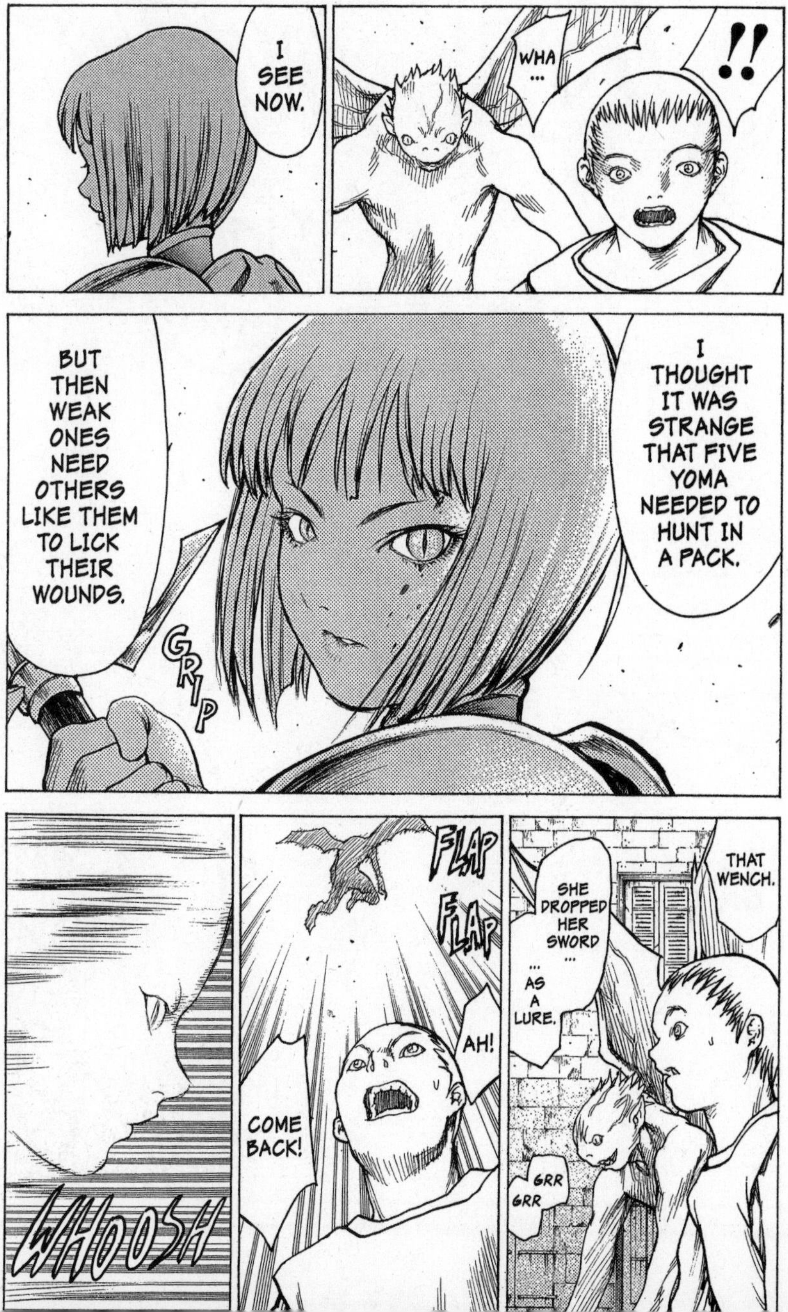
!!
WHA ...
I SEE NOW.
I THOUGHT IT WAS STRANGE THAT FIVE YOMA NEEDED TO HUNT IN A PACK.
BUT THEN WEAK ONES NEED OTHERS LIKE THEM TO LICK THEIR WOUNDS.
GRIP
THAT WENCH.
SHE DROPPED HER SWORD ...
... AS A LURE.
GRR
GRR
FLAP
FLAP
AH!
COME BACK!
WHOOSH

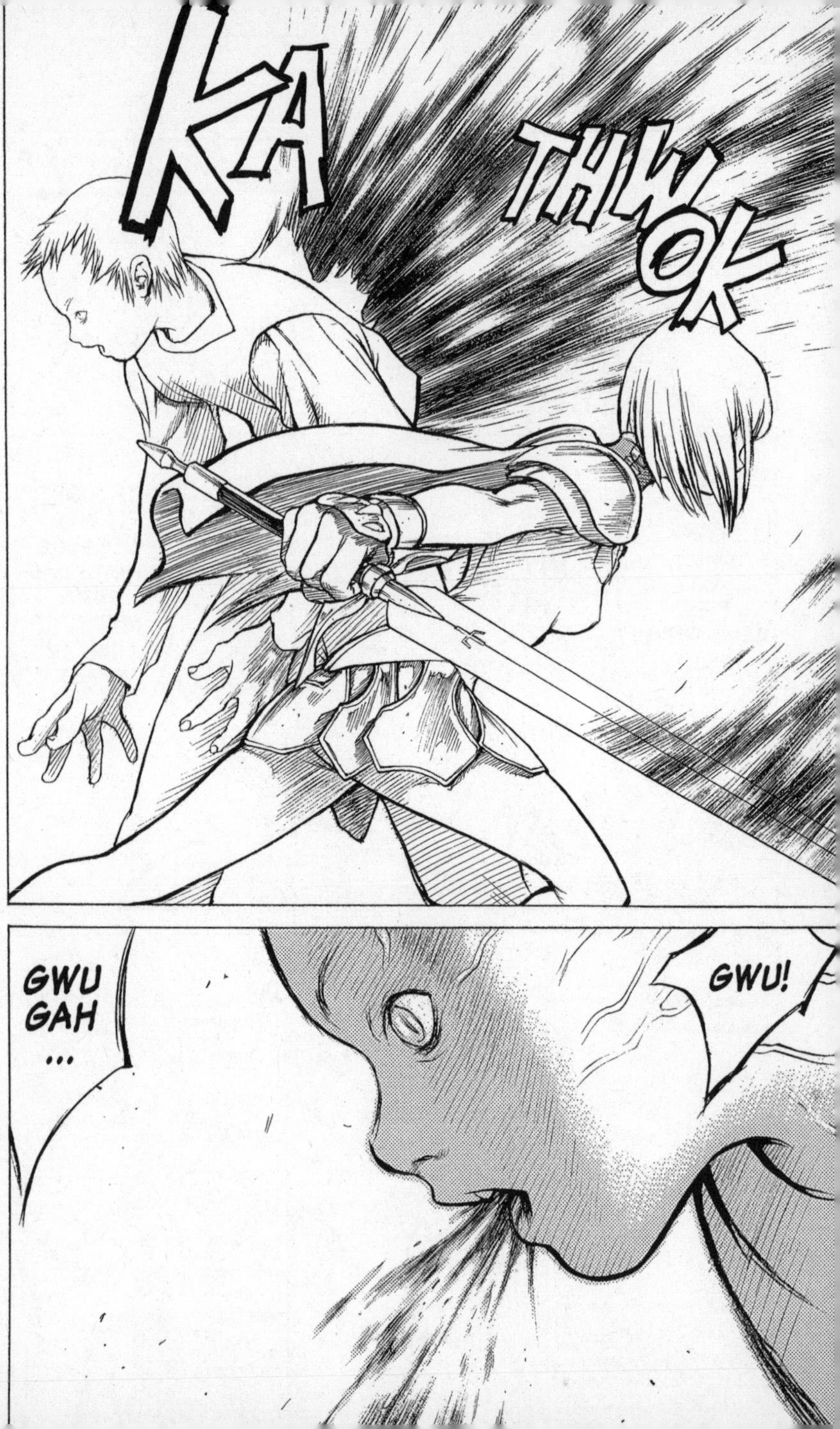
KA
THWOK
GWU!
GWU GAH ...

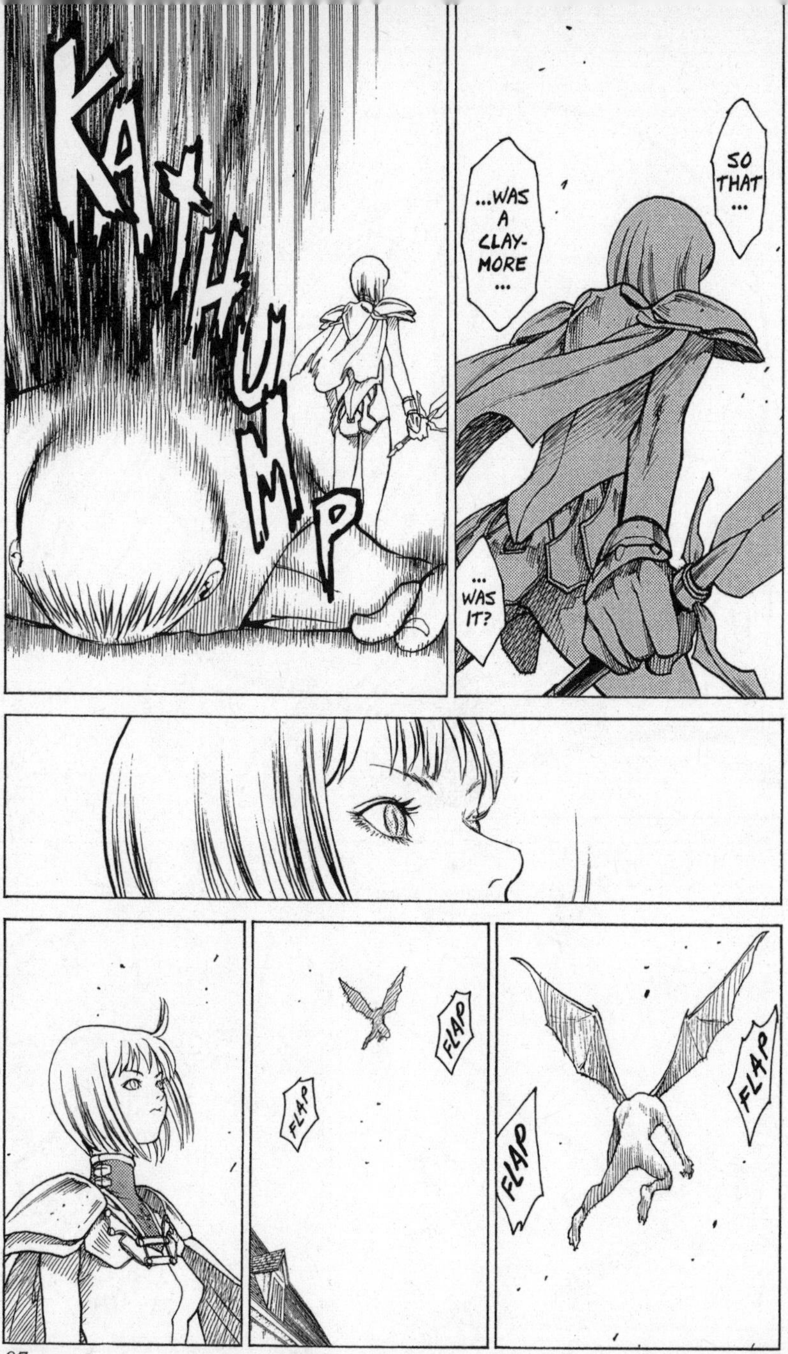
SO THAT...
...WAS A CLAYMORE...
...WAS IT?
KATHUMP
FLAP
FLAP
FLAP
FLAP
FLAP

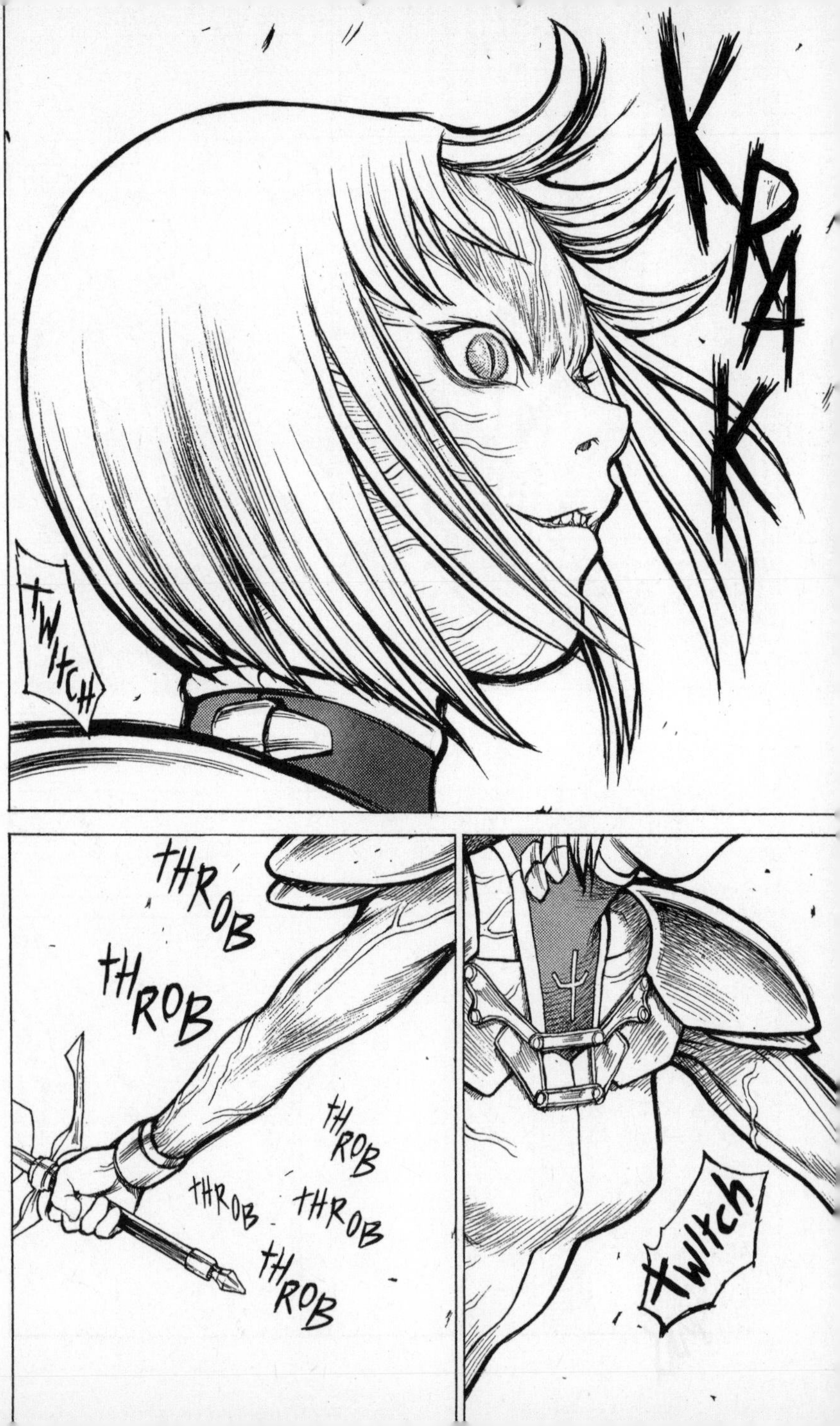
KRAK
TWITCH
TWITCH
THROB
THROB
THROB
THROB
THROB
THROB

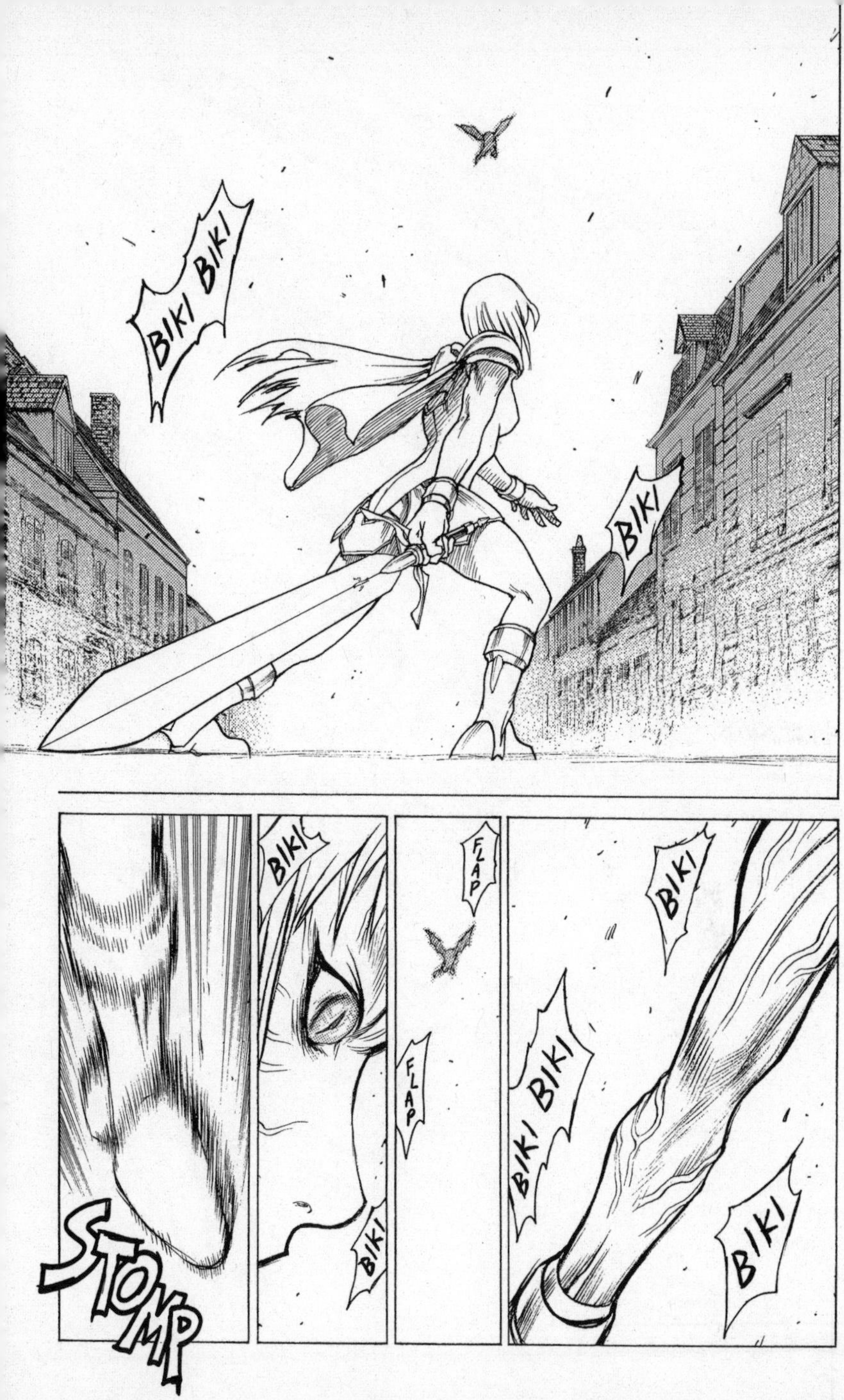
BIKI BIKI
BIKI
BIKI
BIKI BIKI
BIKI
FLAP
FLAP
BIKI
BIKI
STOMP

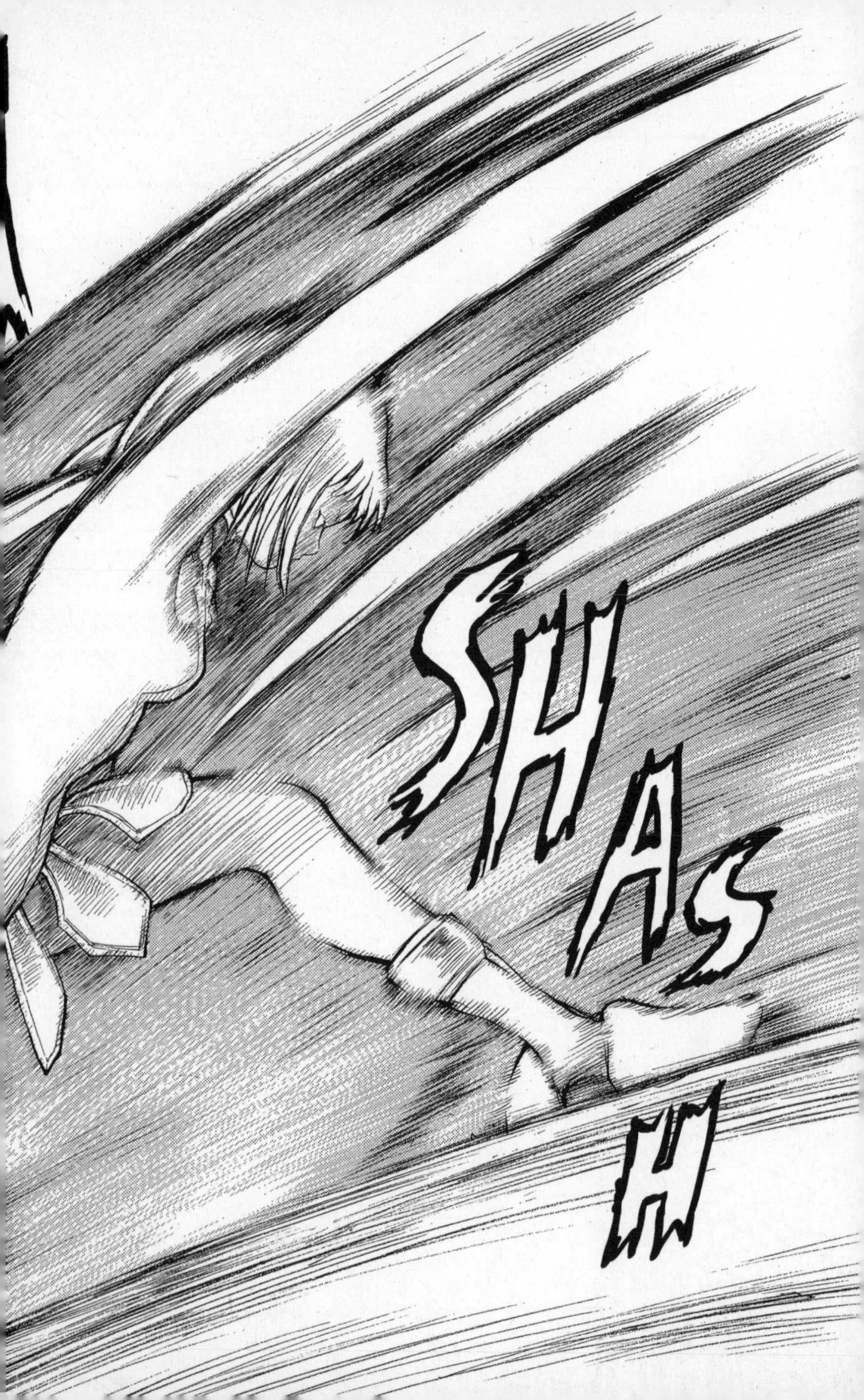
SHASH

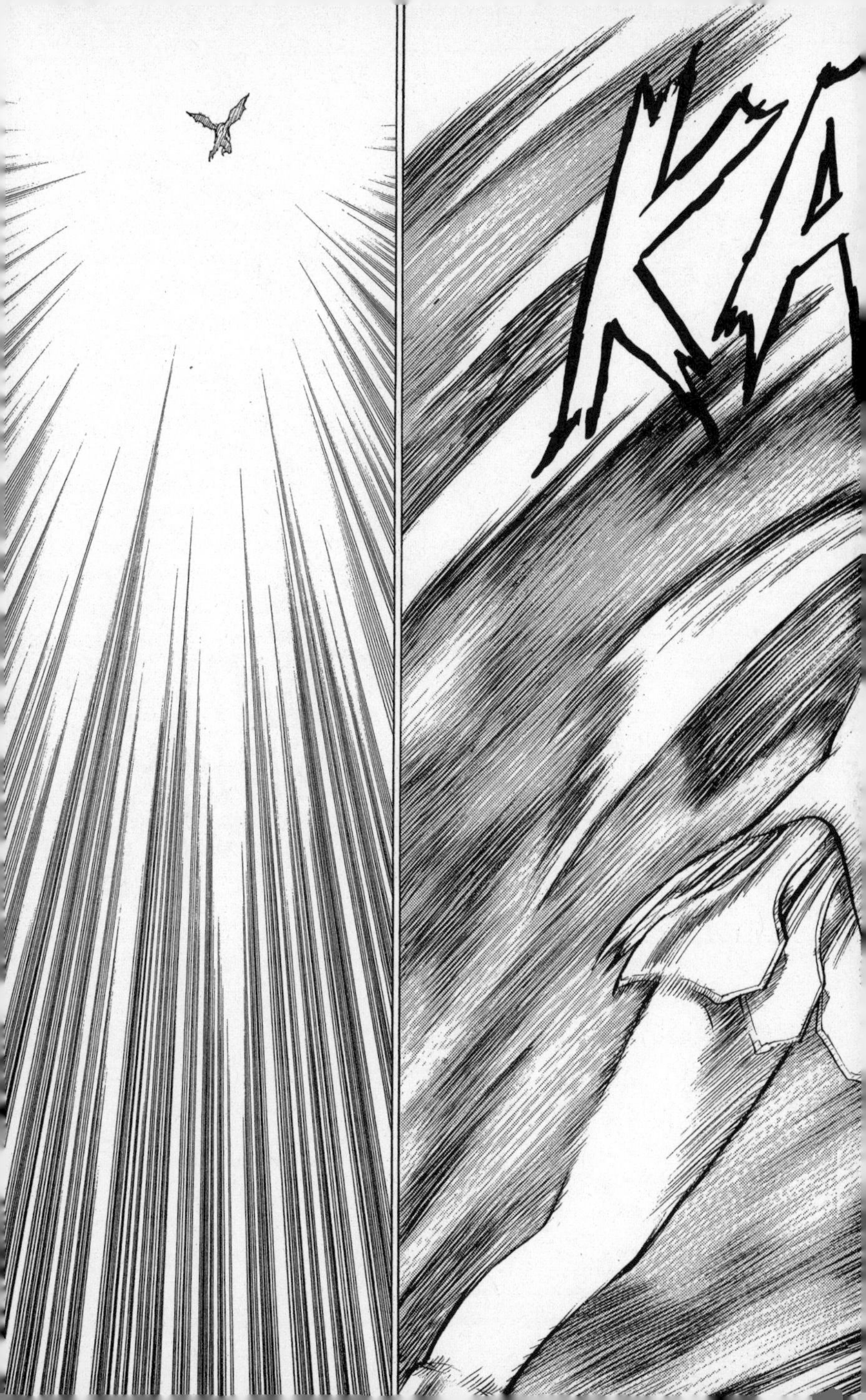
KA

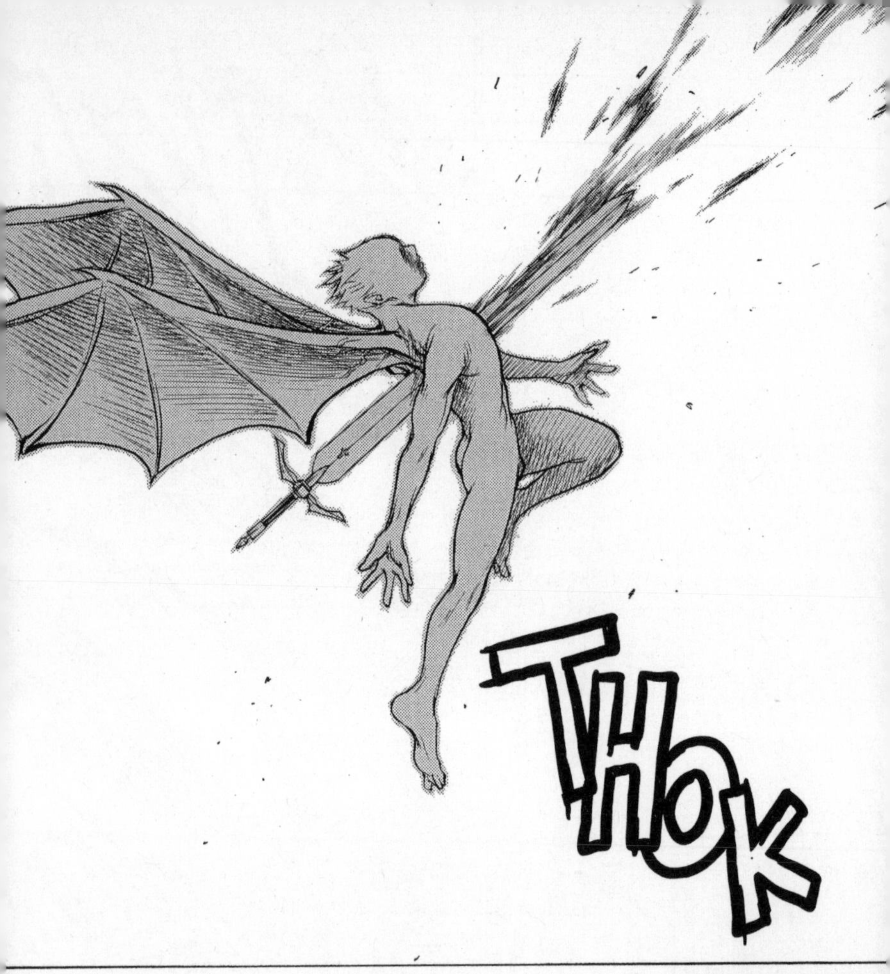
THOK
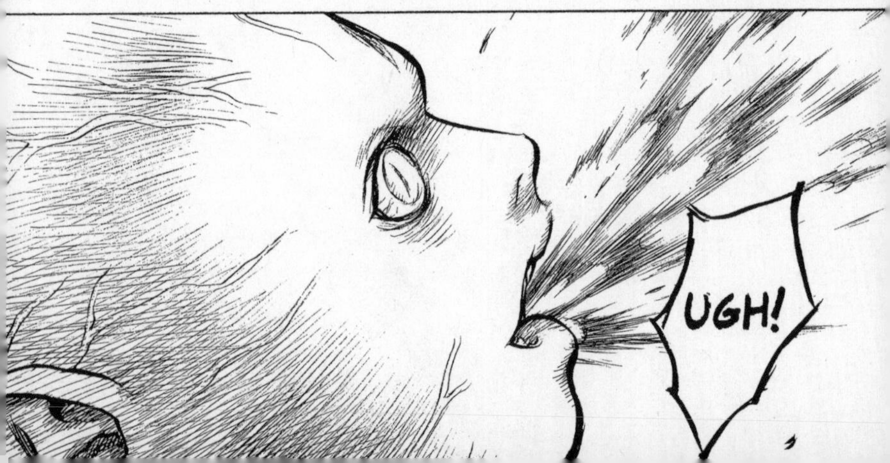
UGH!

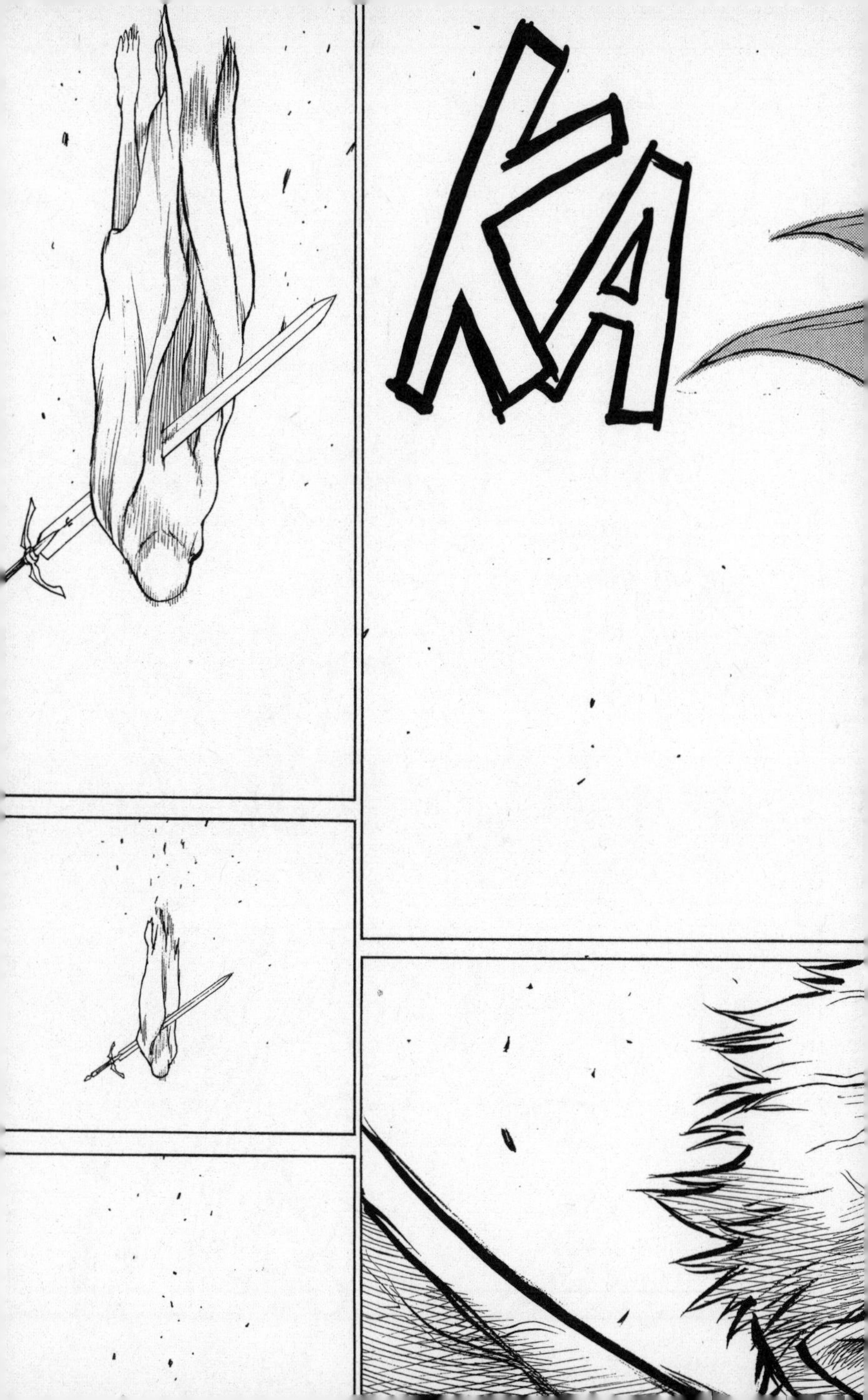
KA

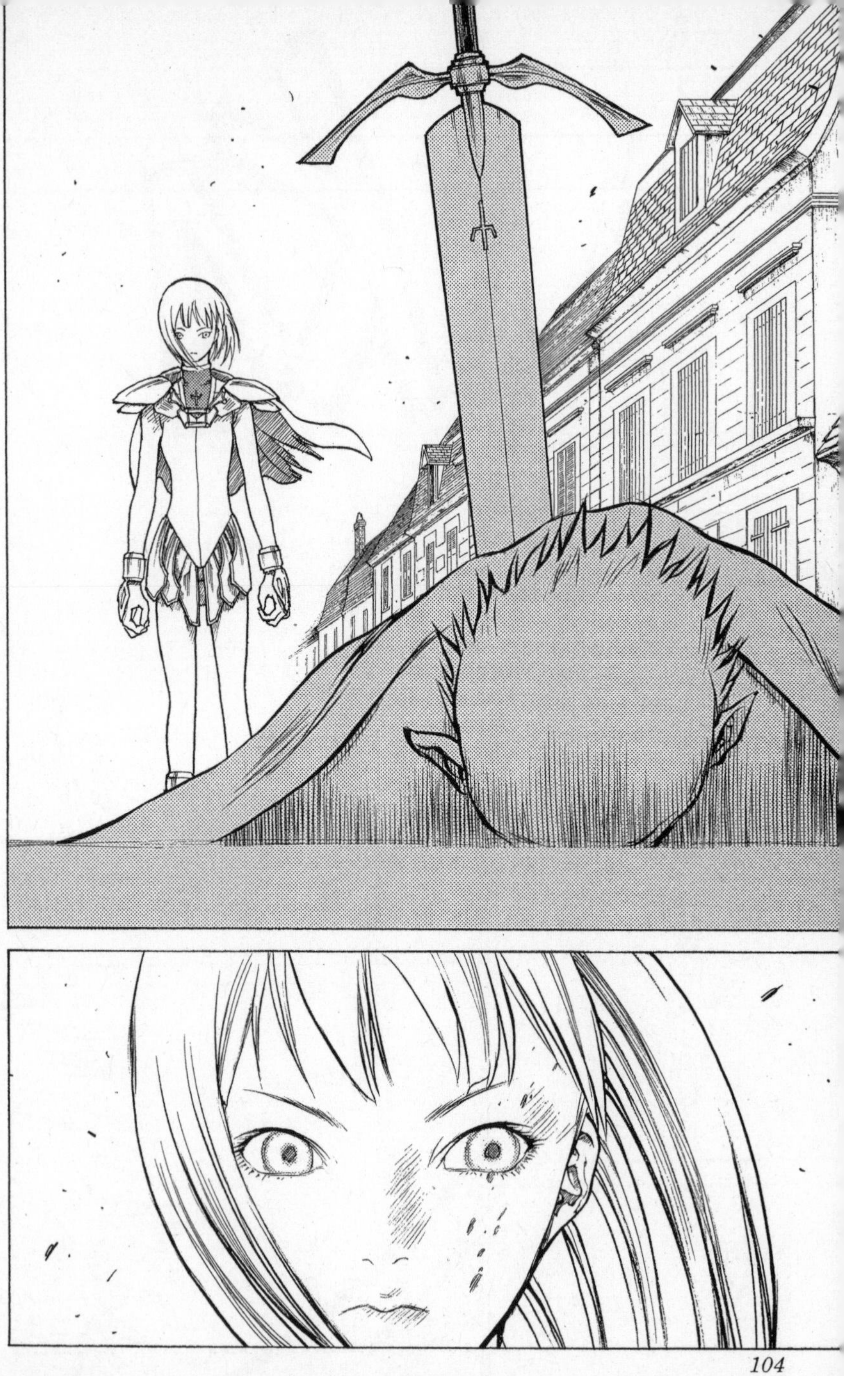

READ THIS WAY

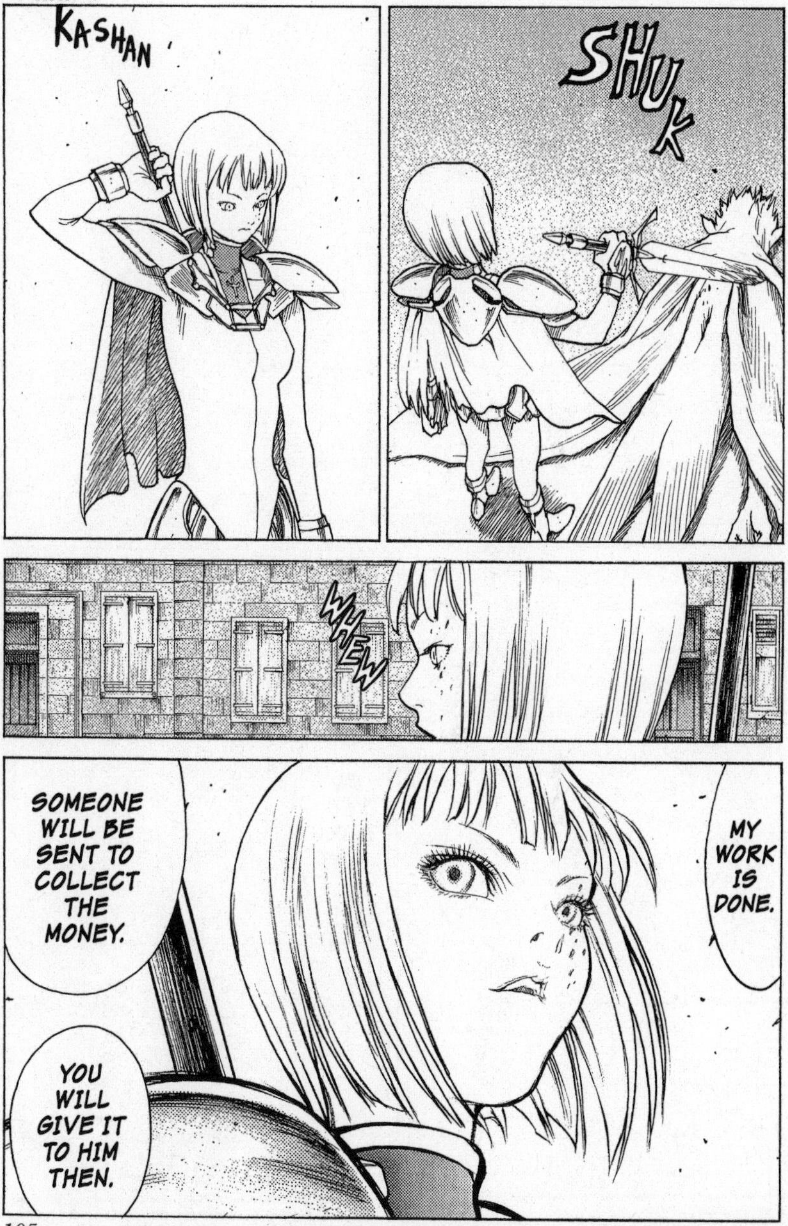
SHUK
KASHAN
WHEW
MY WORK IS DONE.
SOMEONE WILL BE SENT TO COLLECT THE MONEY.
YOU WILL GIVE IT TO HIM THEN.

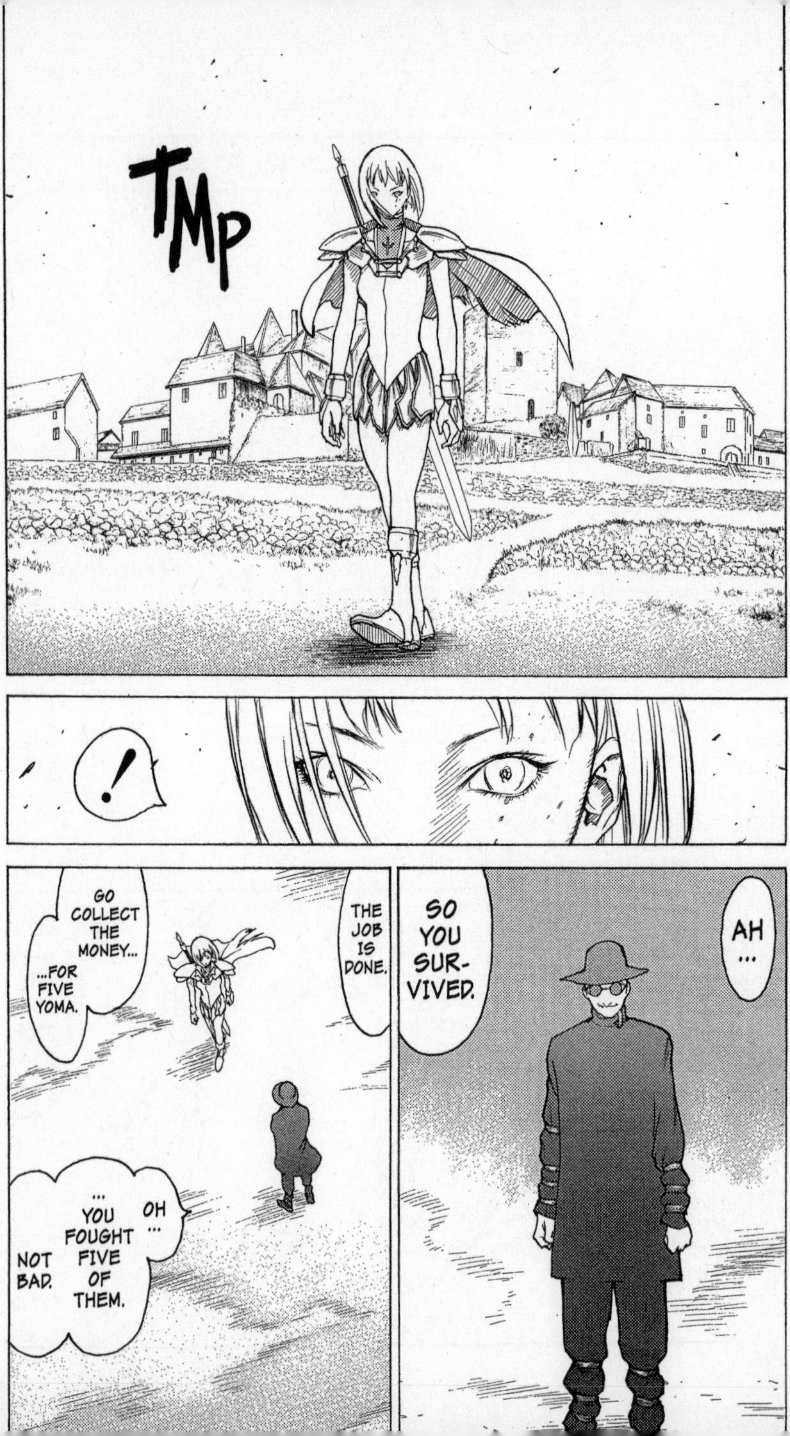
TMP
!
AH ...
SO YOU SUR-VIVED.
THE JOB IS DONE.
GO COLLECT THE MONEY... ...FOR FIVE YOMA.
OH ... ... YOU FOUGHT FIVE OF THEM. NOT BAD.

READ THIS WAY

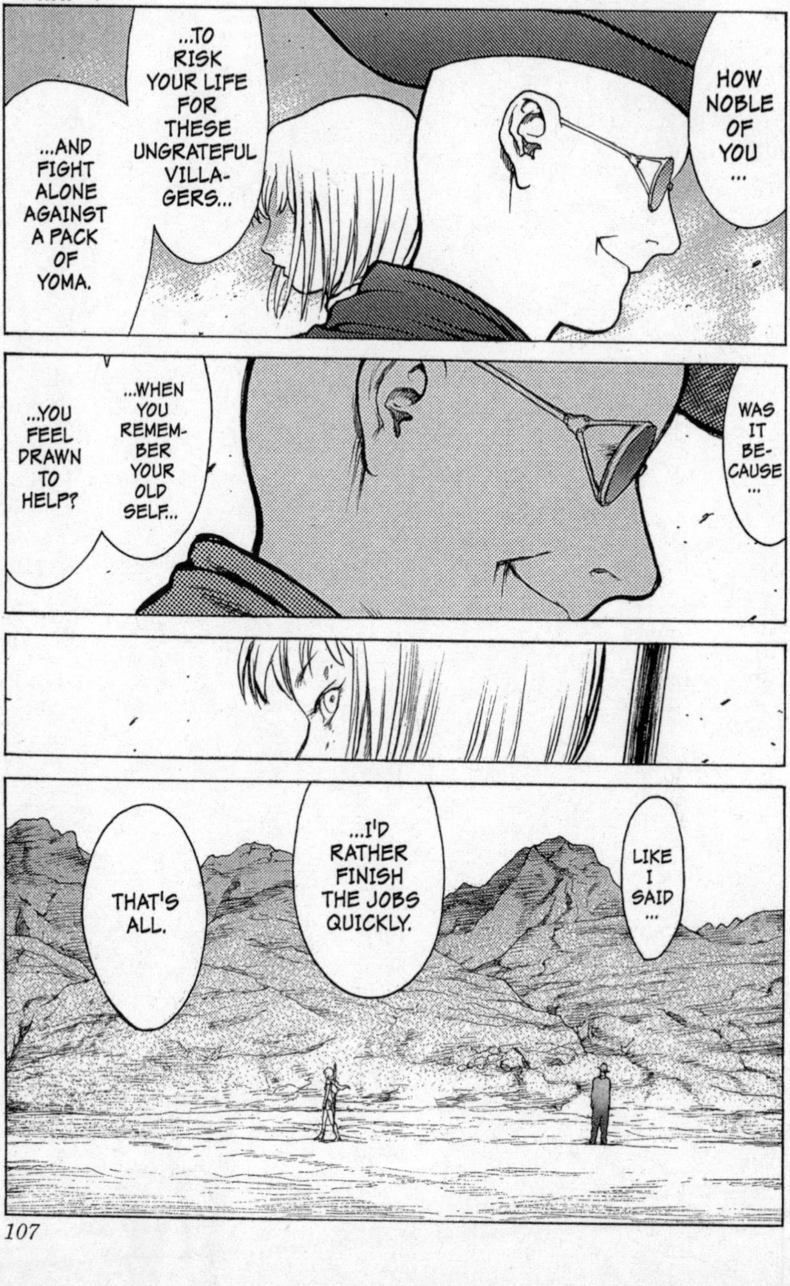
HOW NOBLE OF YOU...
...TO RISK YOUR LIFE FOR THESE UNGRATEFUL VILLAGERS...
...AND FIGHT ALONE AGAINST A PACK OF YOMA.
WAS IT BECAUSE...
...WHEN YOU REMEMBER YOUR OLD SELF...
...YOU FEEL DRAWN TO HELP?
LIKE I SAID...
...I'D RATHER FINISH THE JOBS QUICKLY.
THAT'S ALL.

クレイモア
Claymore

Scene 3: Memory of a Witch

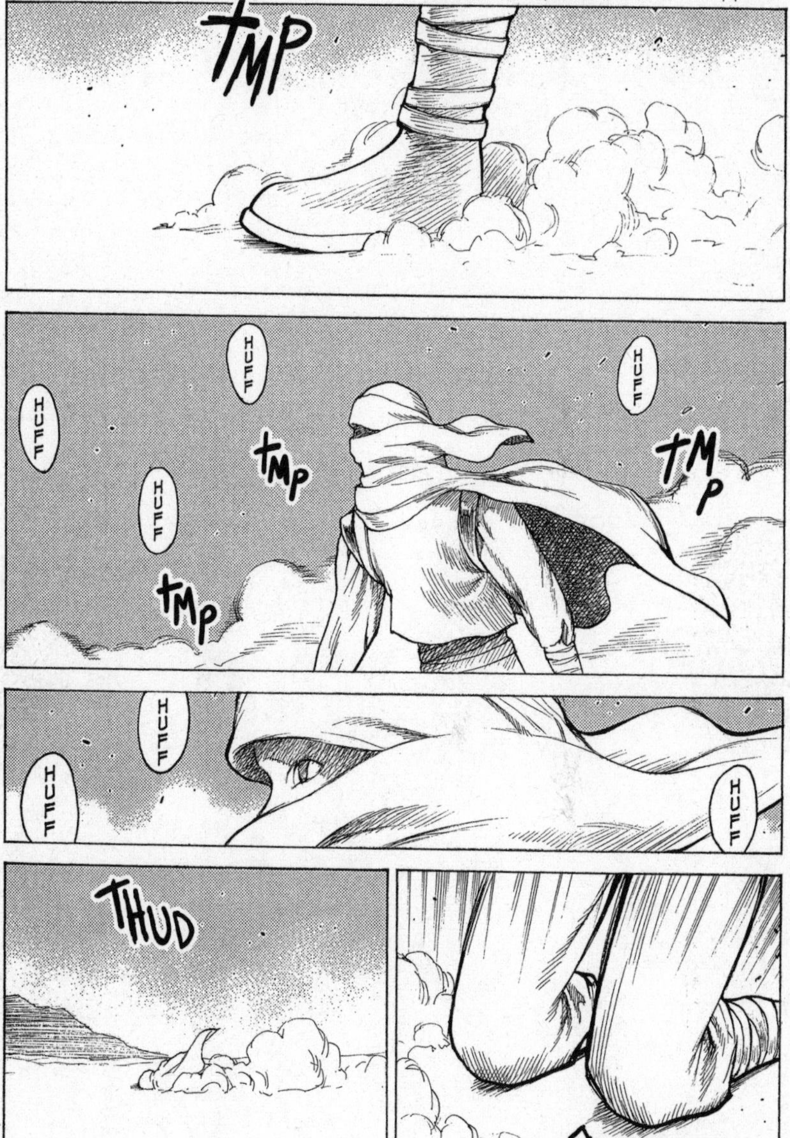
TMP
HUFF
TMP
HUFF
TMP
HUFF
TMP
HUFF
HUFF
HUFF
HUFF
SLUMP
THUD

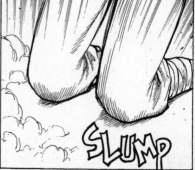

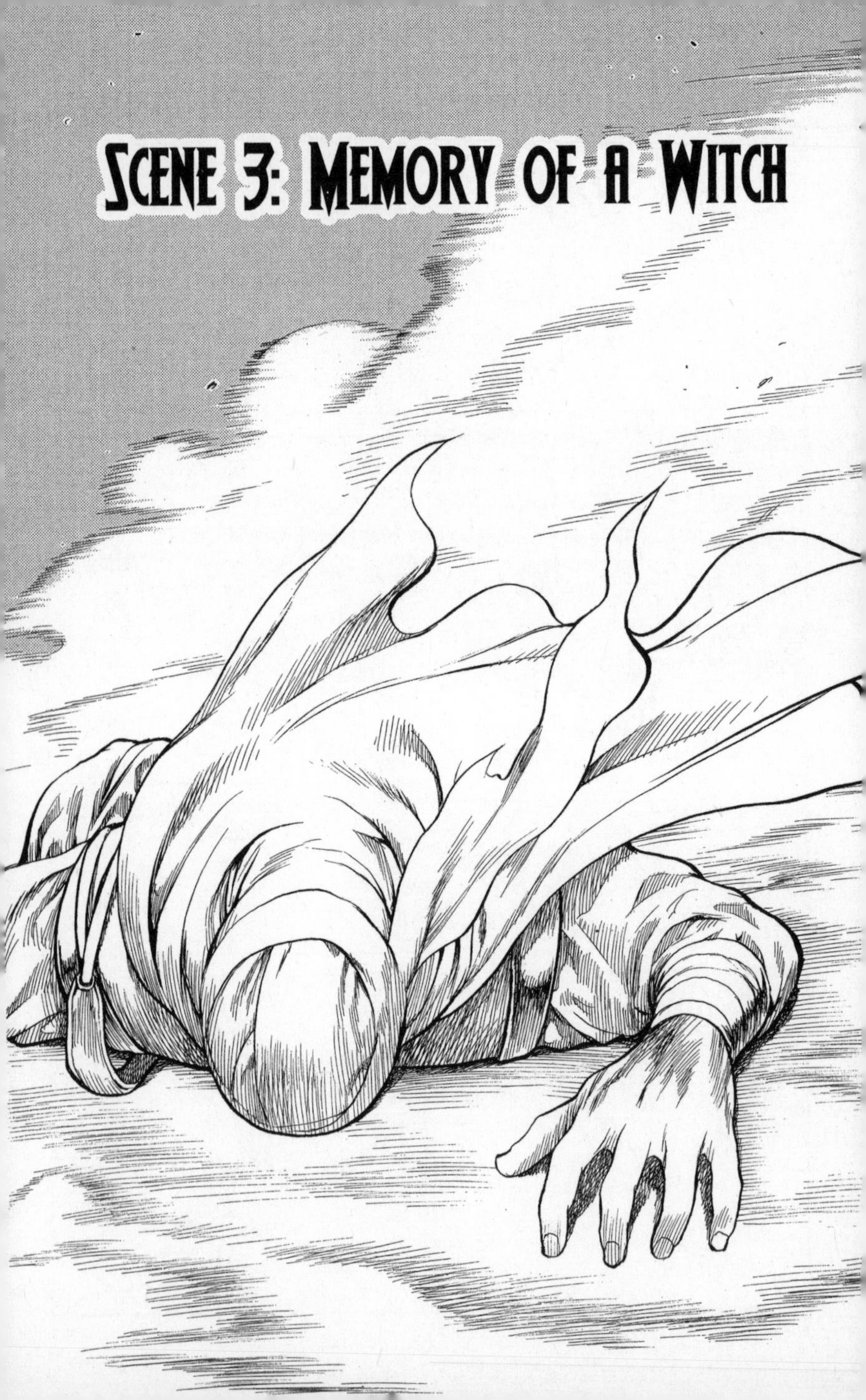
SCENE 3: MEMORY OF A WITCH

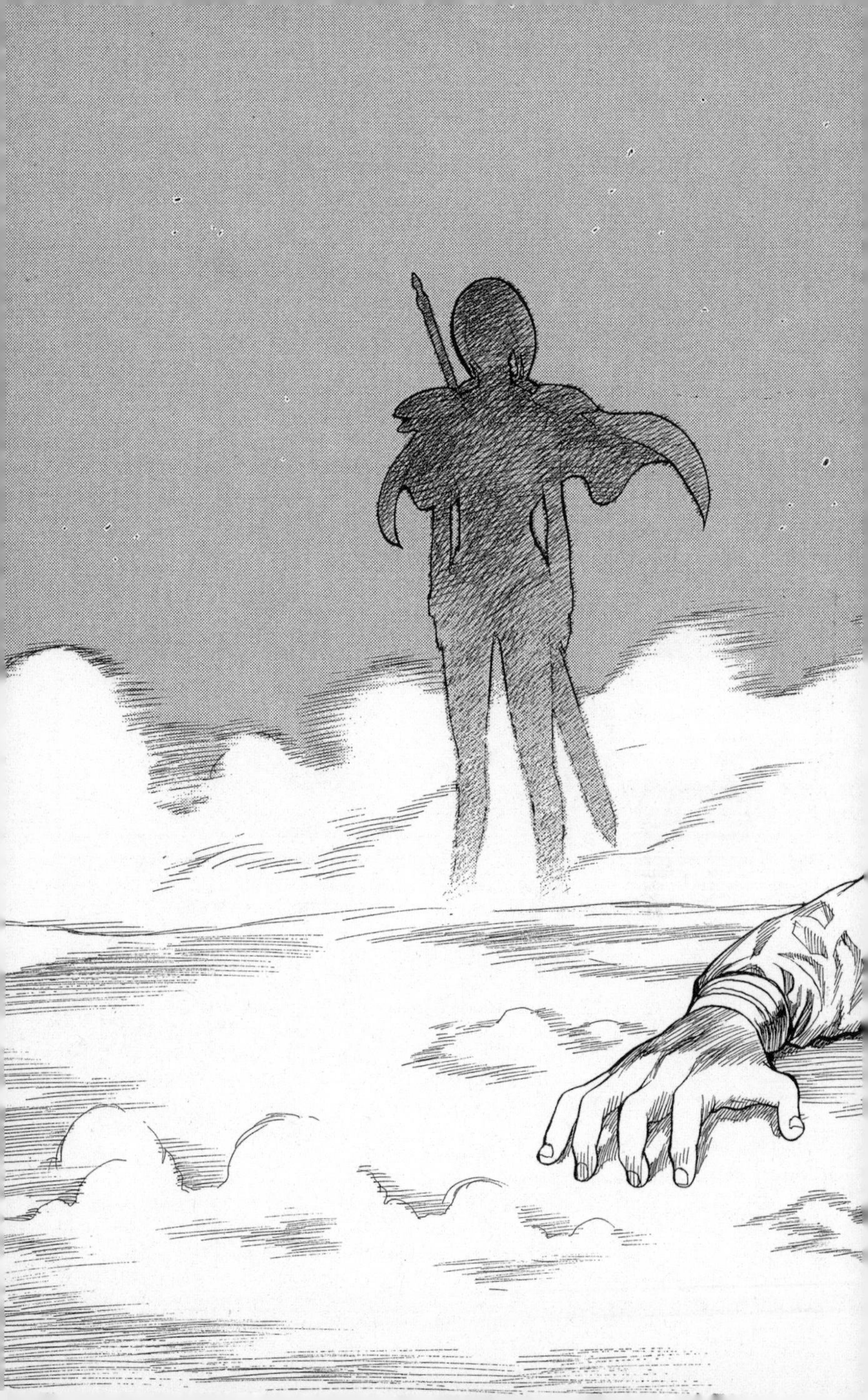

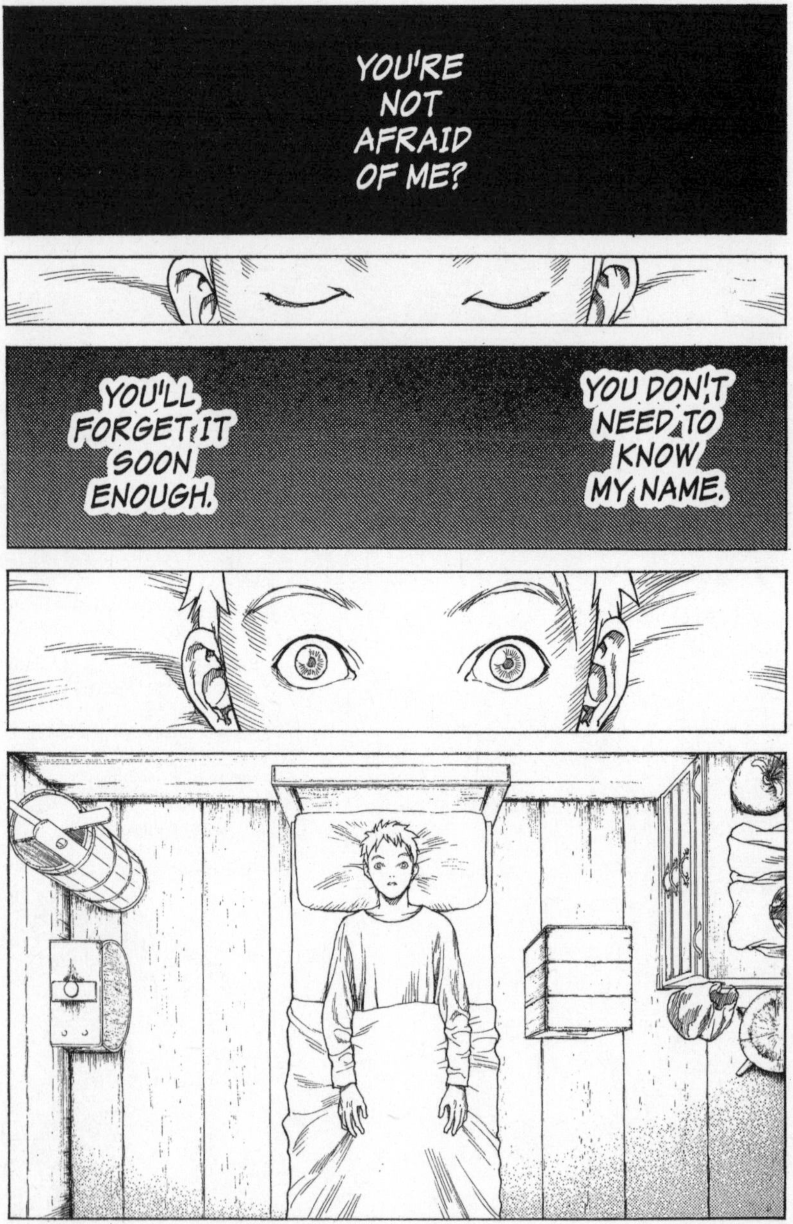
YOU'RE NOT AFRAID OF ME?
YOU DON'T NEED TO KNOW MY NAME.
YOU'LL FORGET IT SOON ENOUGH.

READ THIS WAY

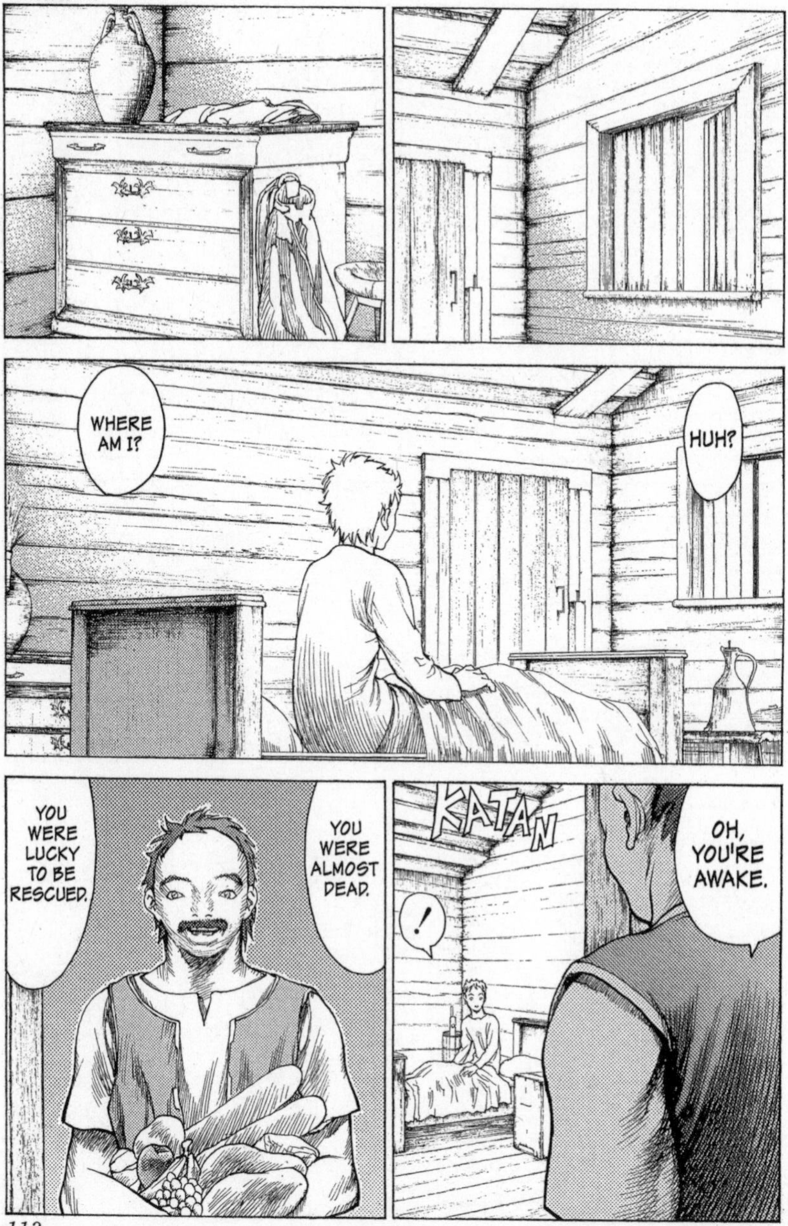
HUH?
WHERE AM I?
KATAN
OH, YOU'RE AWAKE.
!
YOU WERE ALMOST DEAD.
YOU WERE LUCKY TO BE RESCUED.

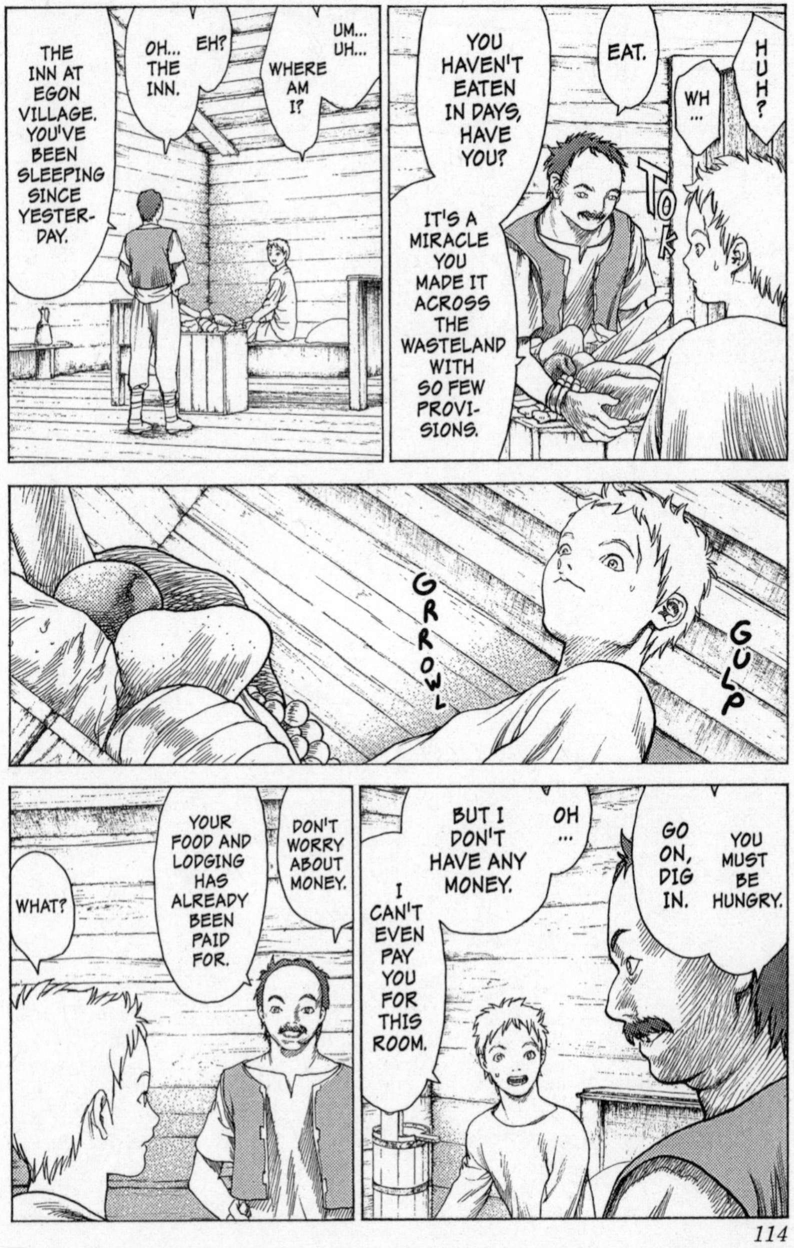
HUH?
WH...
EAT.
YOU HAVEN'T EATEN IN DAYS, HAVE YOU?
TOK
IT'S A MIRACLE YOU MADE IT ACROSS THE WASTELAND WITH SO FEW PROVISIONS.
UM... UH...
WHERE AM I?
EH?
OH... THE INN.
THE INN AT EGON VILLAGE. YOU'VE BEEN SLEEPING SINCE YESTERDAY.
GULP
GRROWL
YOU MUST BE HUNGRY.
GO ON, DIG IN.
OH...
BUT I DON'T HAVE ANY MONEY.
I CAN'T EVEN PAY YOU FOR THIS ROOM.
DON'T WORRY ABOUT MONEY.
YOUR FOOD AND LODGING HAS ALREADY BEEN PAID FOR.
WHAT?

READ THIS WAY

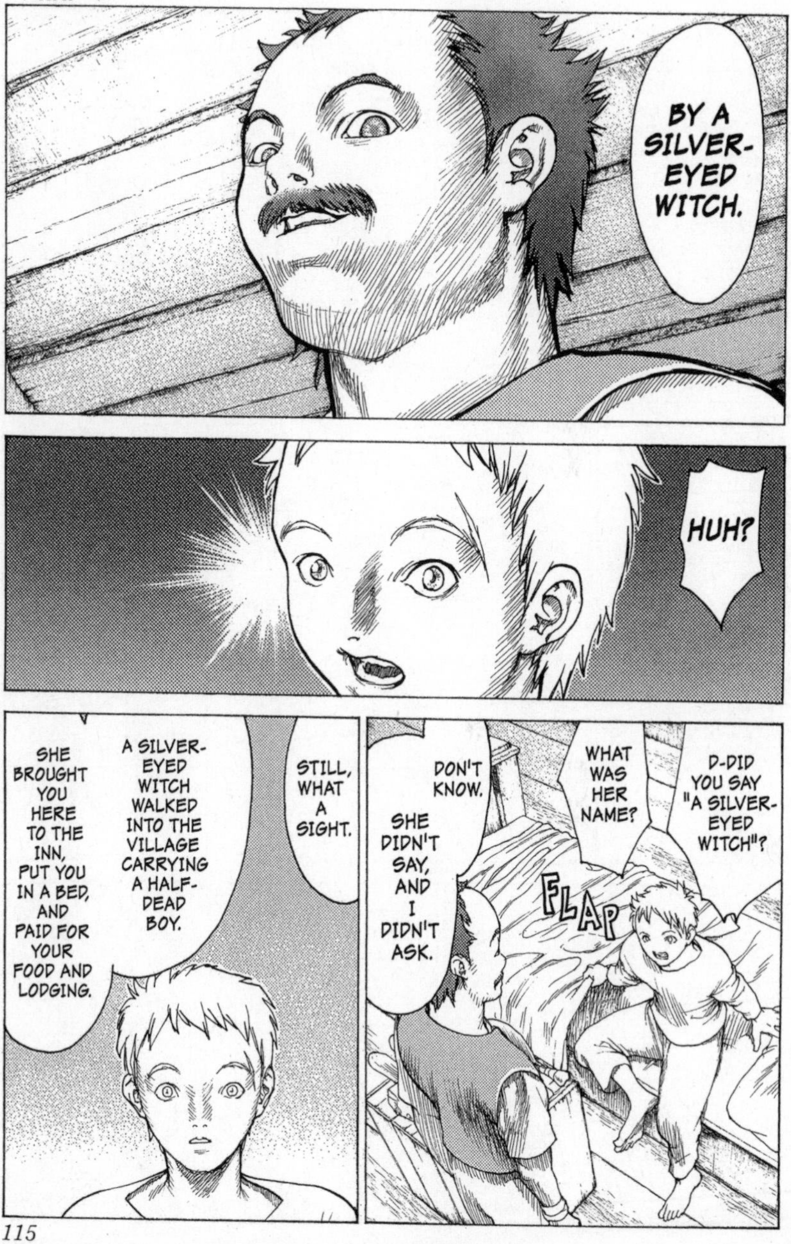
BY A SILVER-EYED WITCH.
HUH?
D-DID YOU SAY "A SILVER-EYED WITCH"?
WHAT WAS HER NAME?
FLAP
DON'T KNOW.
SHE DIDN'T SAY, AND I DIDN'T ASK.
STILL, WHAT A SIGHT.
A SILVER-EYED WITCH WALKED INTO THE VILLAGE CARRYING A HALF-DEAD BOY.
SHE BROUGHT YOU HERE TO THE INN, PUT YOU IN A BED, AND PAID FOR YOUR FOOD AND LODGING.

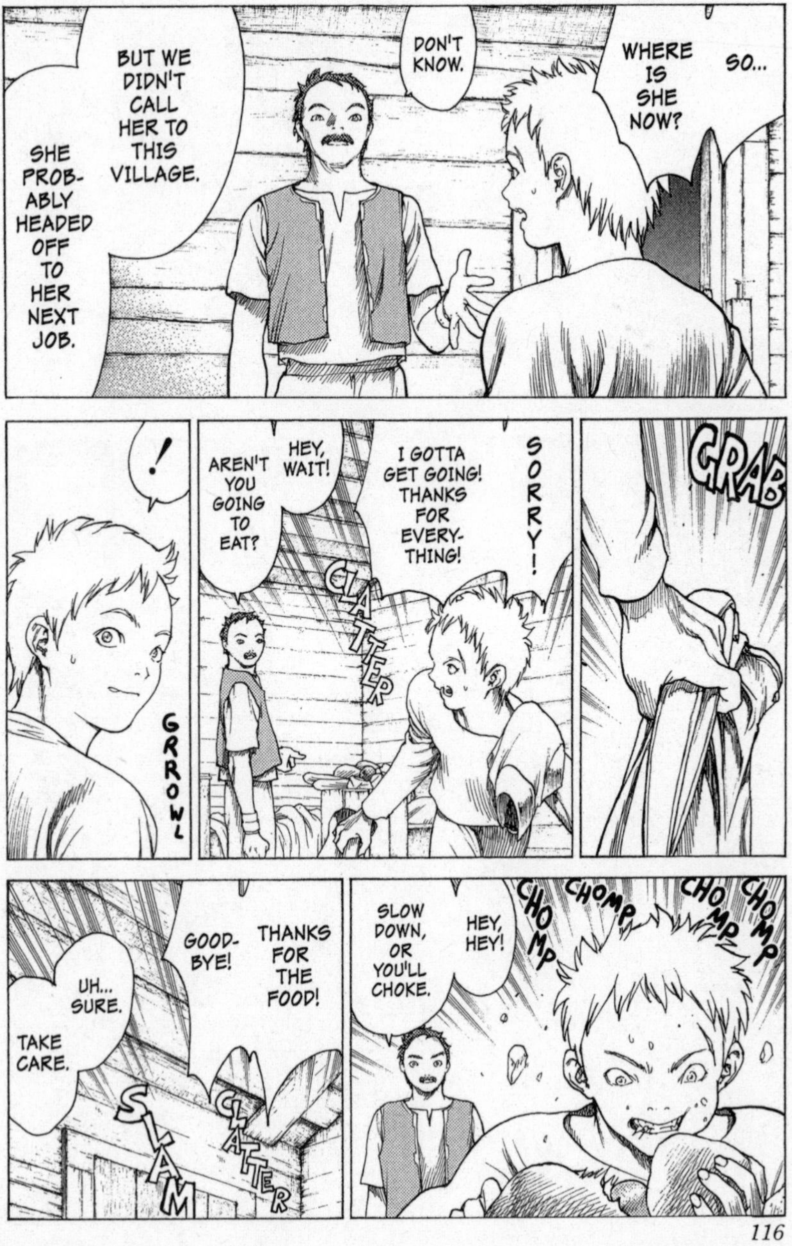

SO...
WHERE IS SHE NOW?
DON'T KNOW.
BUT WE DIDN'T CALL HER TO THIS VILLAGE.
SHE PROBABLY HEADED OFF TO HER NEXT JOB.
GRAB
SORRY!
I GOTTA GET GOING! THANKS FOR EVERYTHING!
CLATTER
HEY, WAIT!
AREN'T YOU GOING TO EAT?
!
GRROWL
CHOMP
CHOMP
CHOMP
CHOMP
HEY, HEY!
SLOW DOWN, OR YOU'LL CHOKE.
THANKS FOR THE FOOD!
GOOD-BYE!
CLATTER
SLAM
UH... SURE.
TAKE CARE.

READ THIS WAY

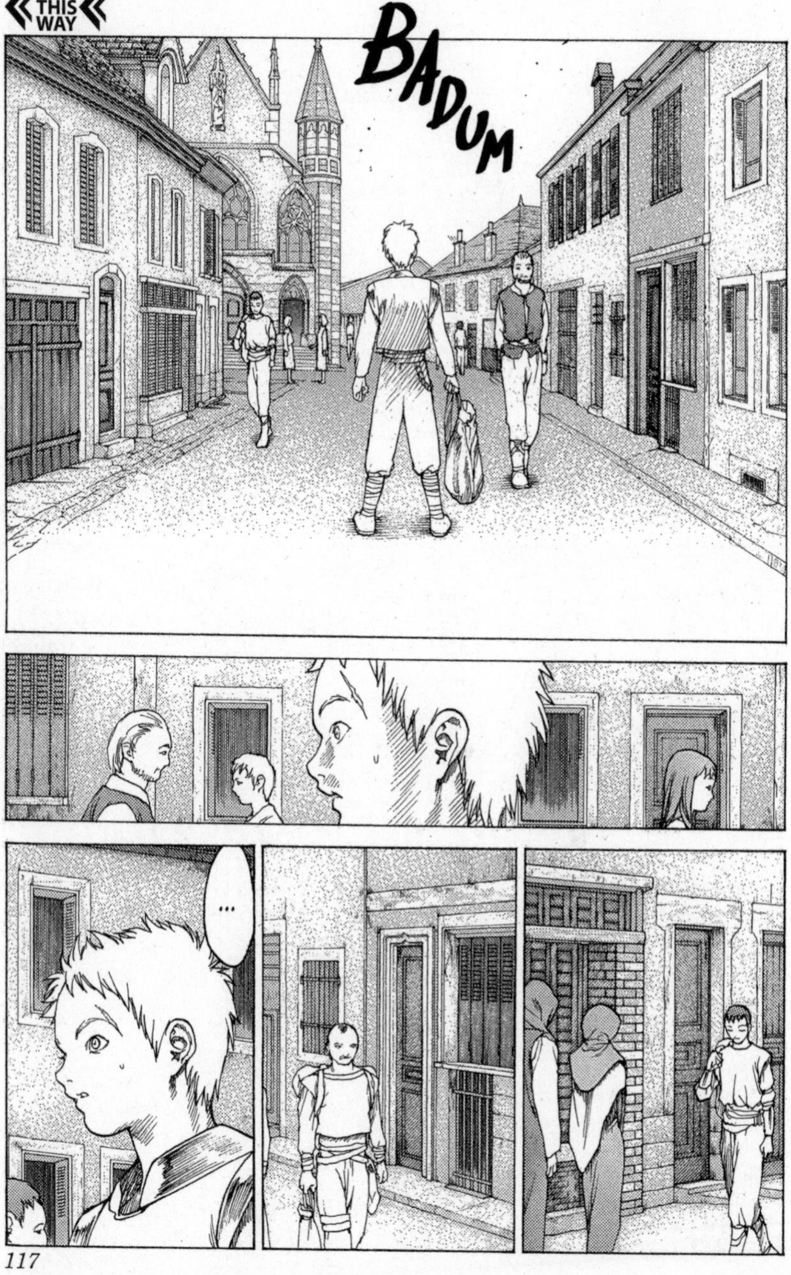
BADUM
...

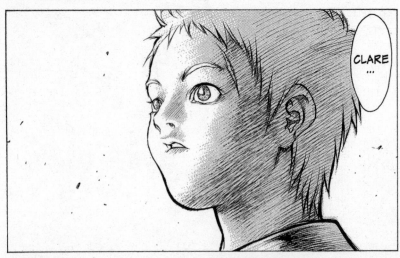

CLARE ...
YOU'RE NOT...
...AFRAID OF ME?
YOU DON'T NEED TO KNOW MY NAME.
YOU'LL FORGET IT SOON ENOUGH.
MY NAME'S CLARE.

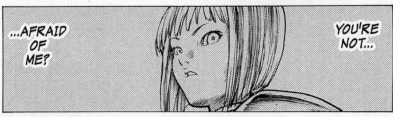

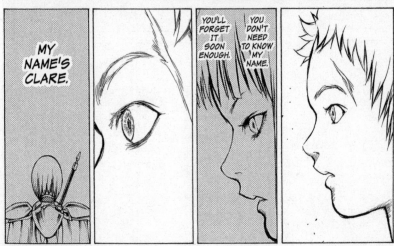

READ THIS WAY

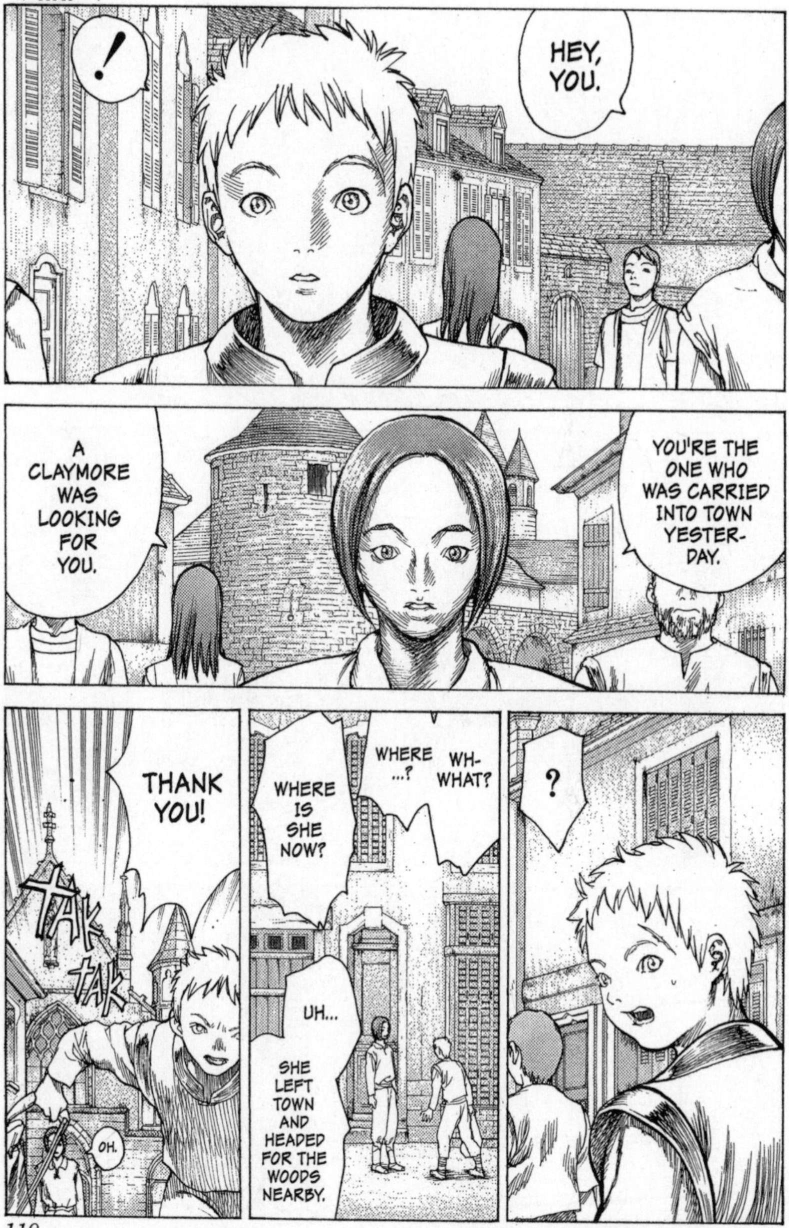
HEY, YOU.
!
YOU'RE THE ONE WHO WAS CARRIED INTO TOWN YESTER-DAY.
A CLAYMORE WAS LOOKING FOR YOU.
?
WH-WHAT?
WHERE ...?
WHERE IS SHE NOW?
UH...
SHE LEFT TOWN AND HEADED FOR THE WOODS NEARBY.
THANK YOU!
TAK TAK
OH.

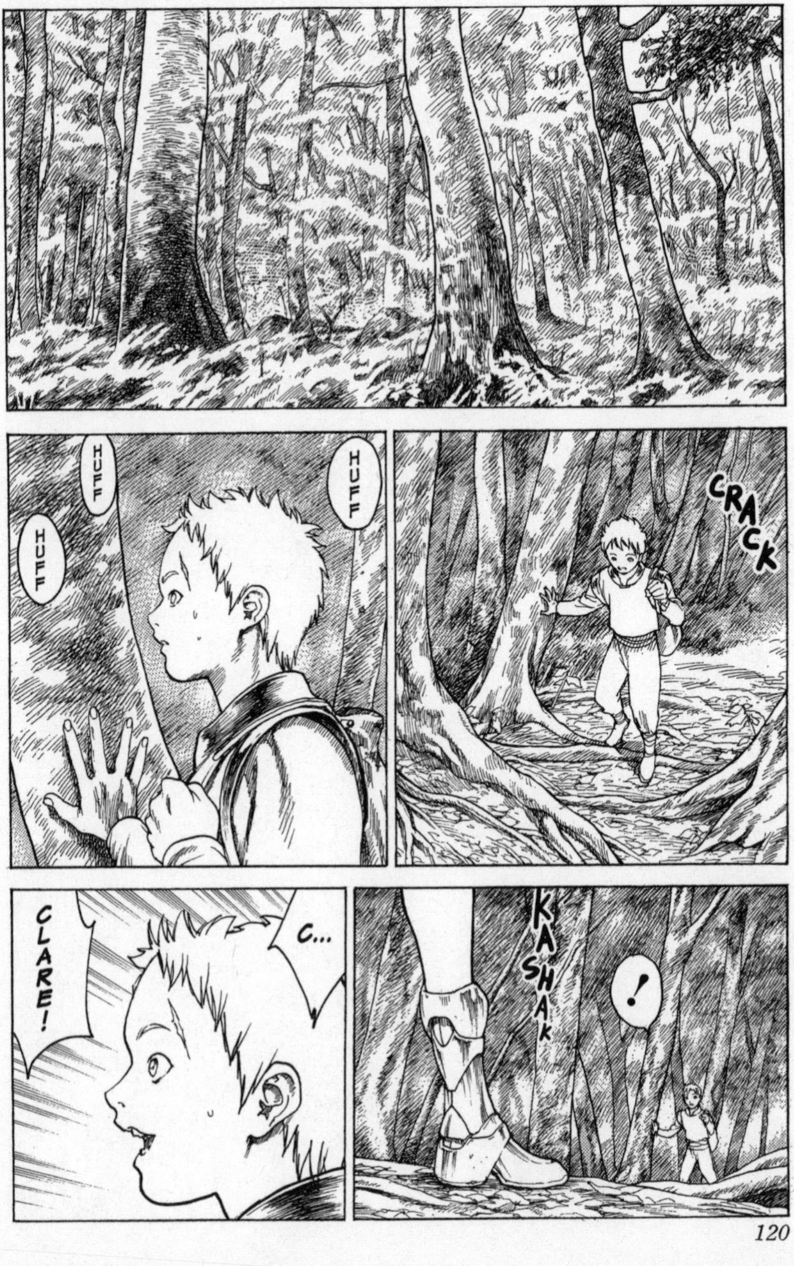
CRACK
HUFF
HUFF
HUFF
HUFF
KASHAK
!
C...
CLARE!

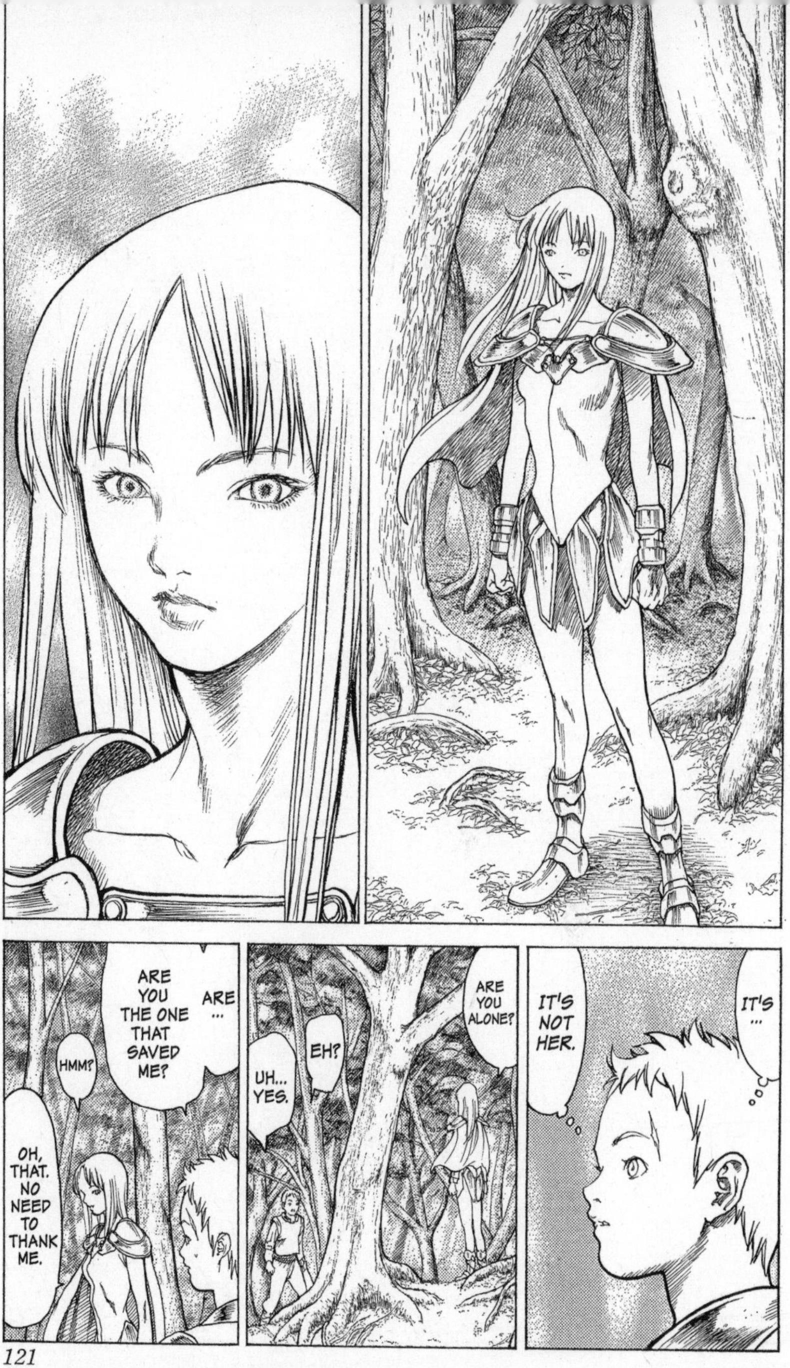
IT'S ...
IT'S NOT HER.
ARE YOU ALONE?
EH?
UH... YES.
ARE ...
ARE YOU THE ONE THAT SAVED ME?
HMM?
OH, THAT. NO NEED TO THANK ME.

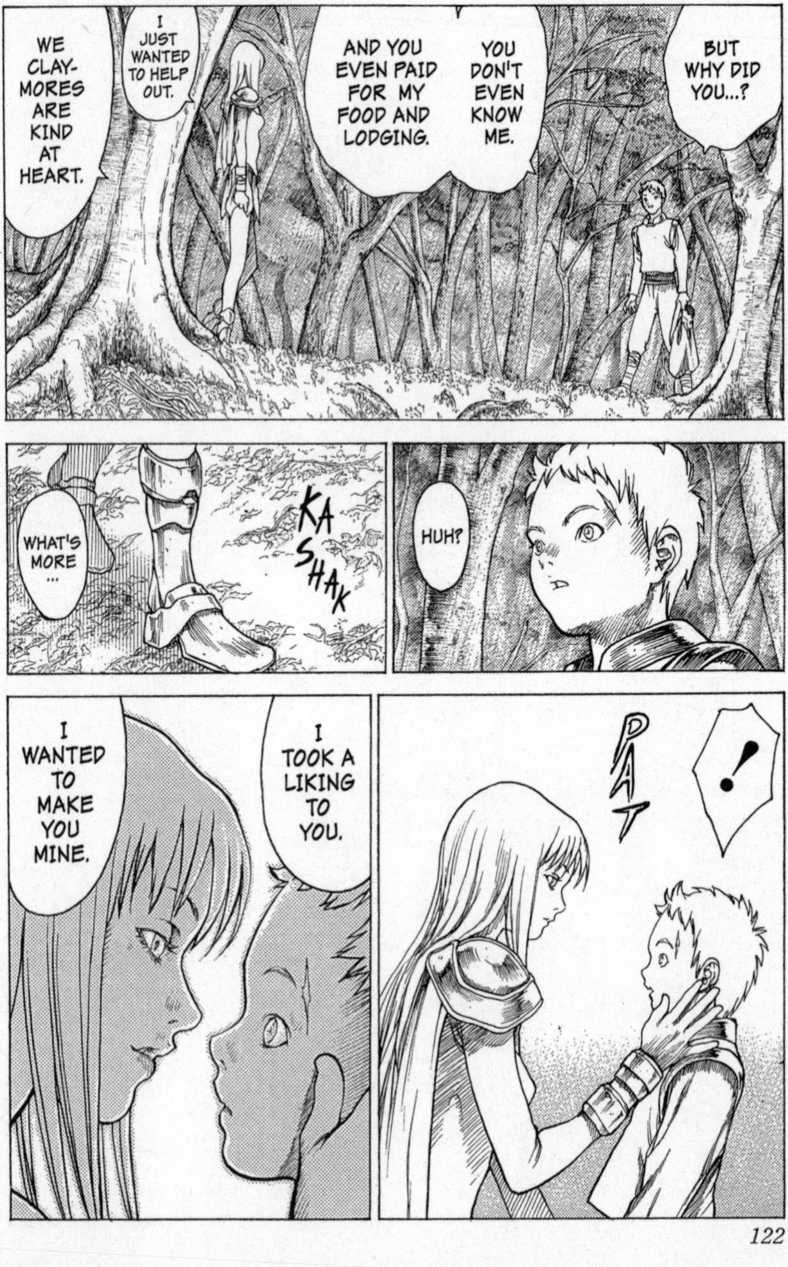
BUT WHY DID YOU...?
YOU DON'T EVEN KNOW ME.
AND YOU EVEN PAID FOR MY FOOD AND LODGING.
I JUST WANTED TO HELP OUT.
WE CLAYMORES ARE KIND AT HEART.
HUH?
KASHAK
WHAT'S MORE ...
PAT
!
I TOOK A LIKING TO YOU.
I WANTED TO MAKE YOU MINE.

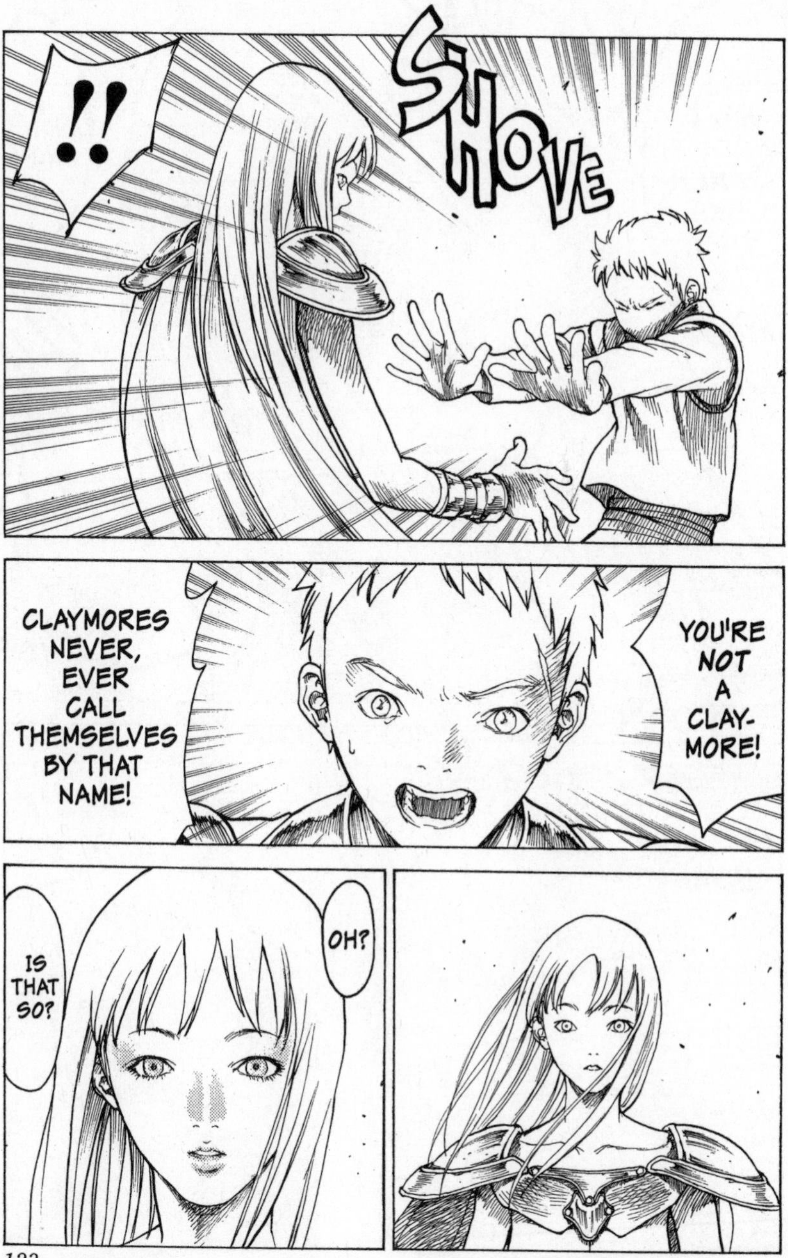
SHOVE
!!
YOU'RE NOT A CLAYMORE!
CLAYMORES NEVER, EVER CALL THEMSELVES BY THAT NAME!
OH?
IS THAT SO?

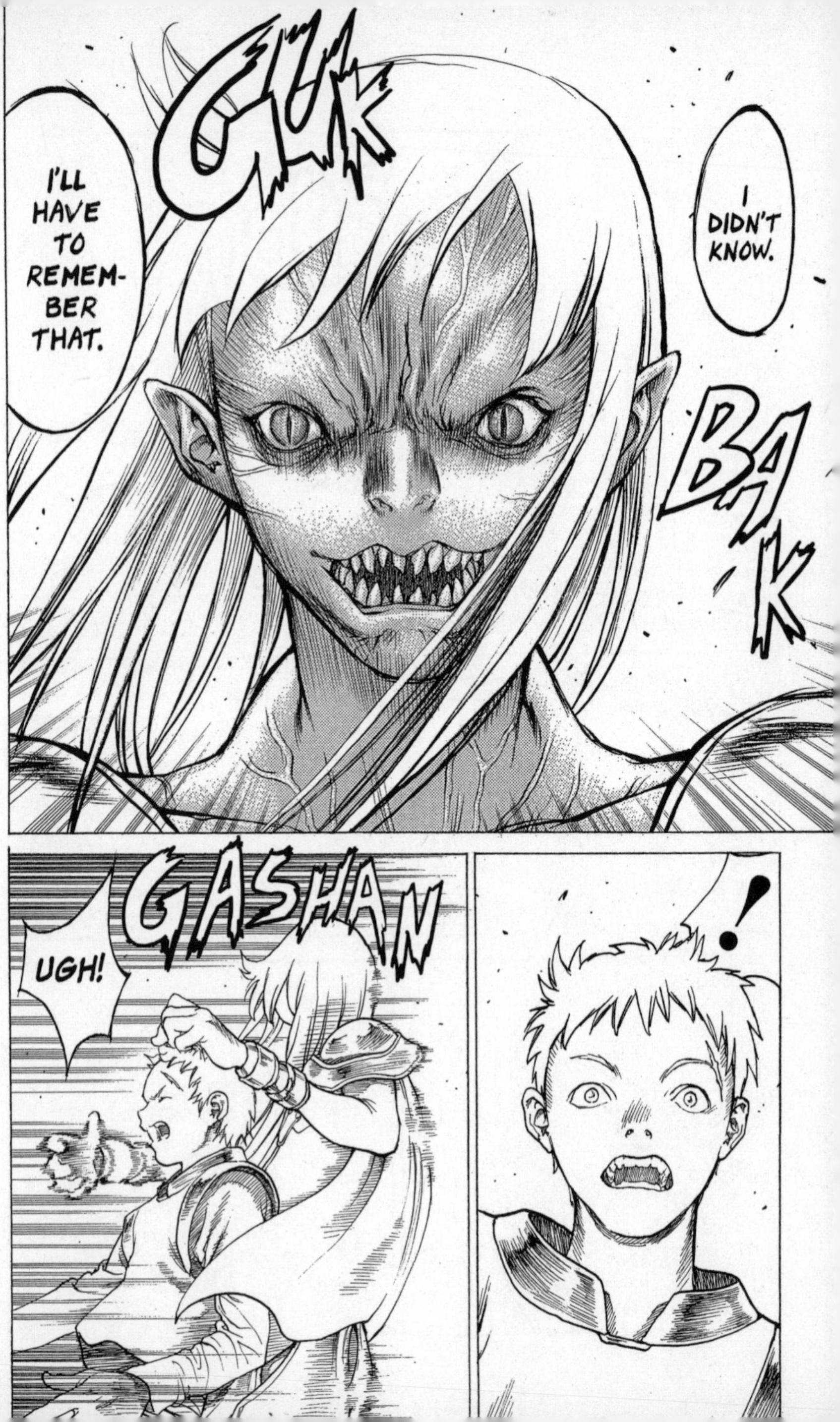
I DIDN'T KNOW.
GULK
I'LL HAVE TO REMEMBER THAT.
BAK
!
GASHAN
UGH!

READ THIS WAY

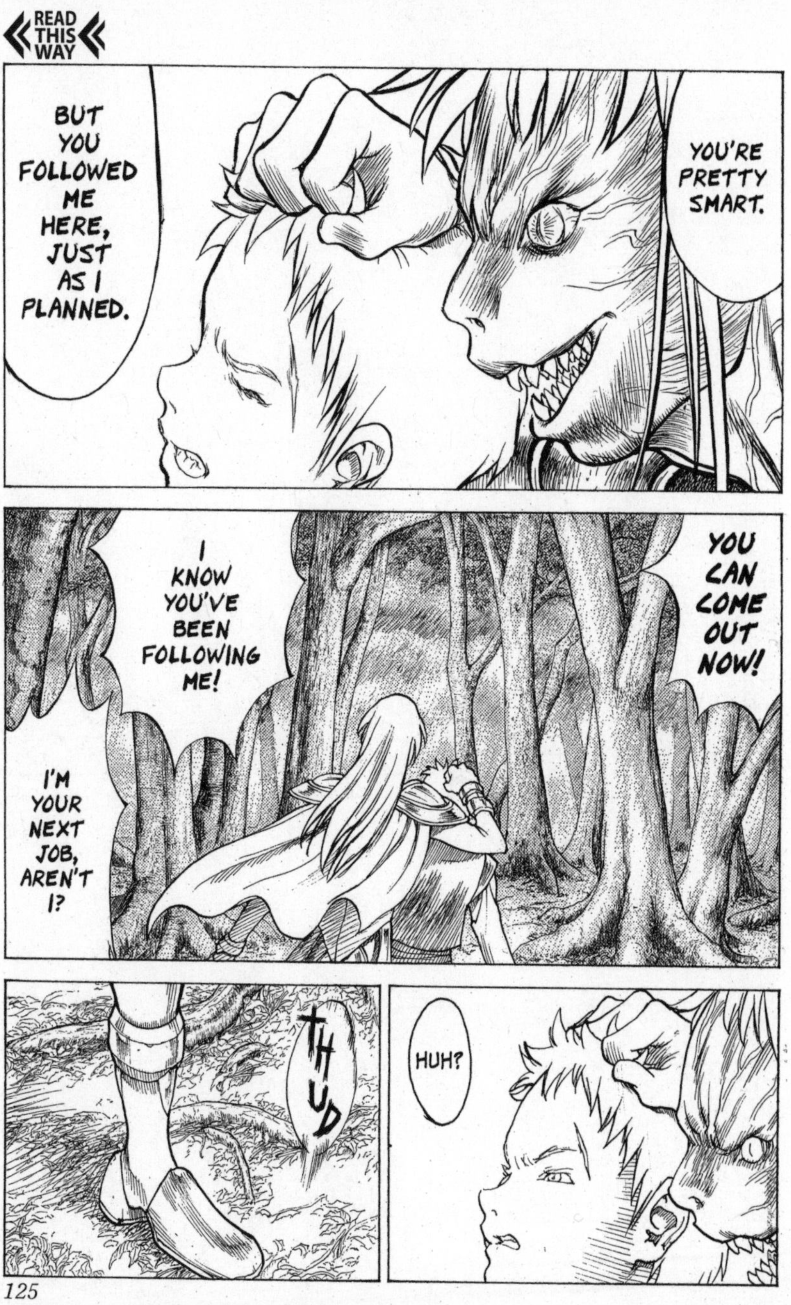
YOU'RE PRETTY SMART.
BUT YOU FOLLOWED ME HERE, JUST AS I PLANNED.
YOU CAN COME OUT NOW!
I KNOW YOU'VE BEEN FOLLOWING ME!
I'M YOUR NEXT JOB, AREN'T I?
HUH?
THUD

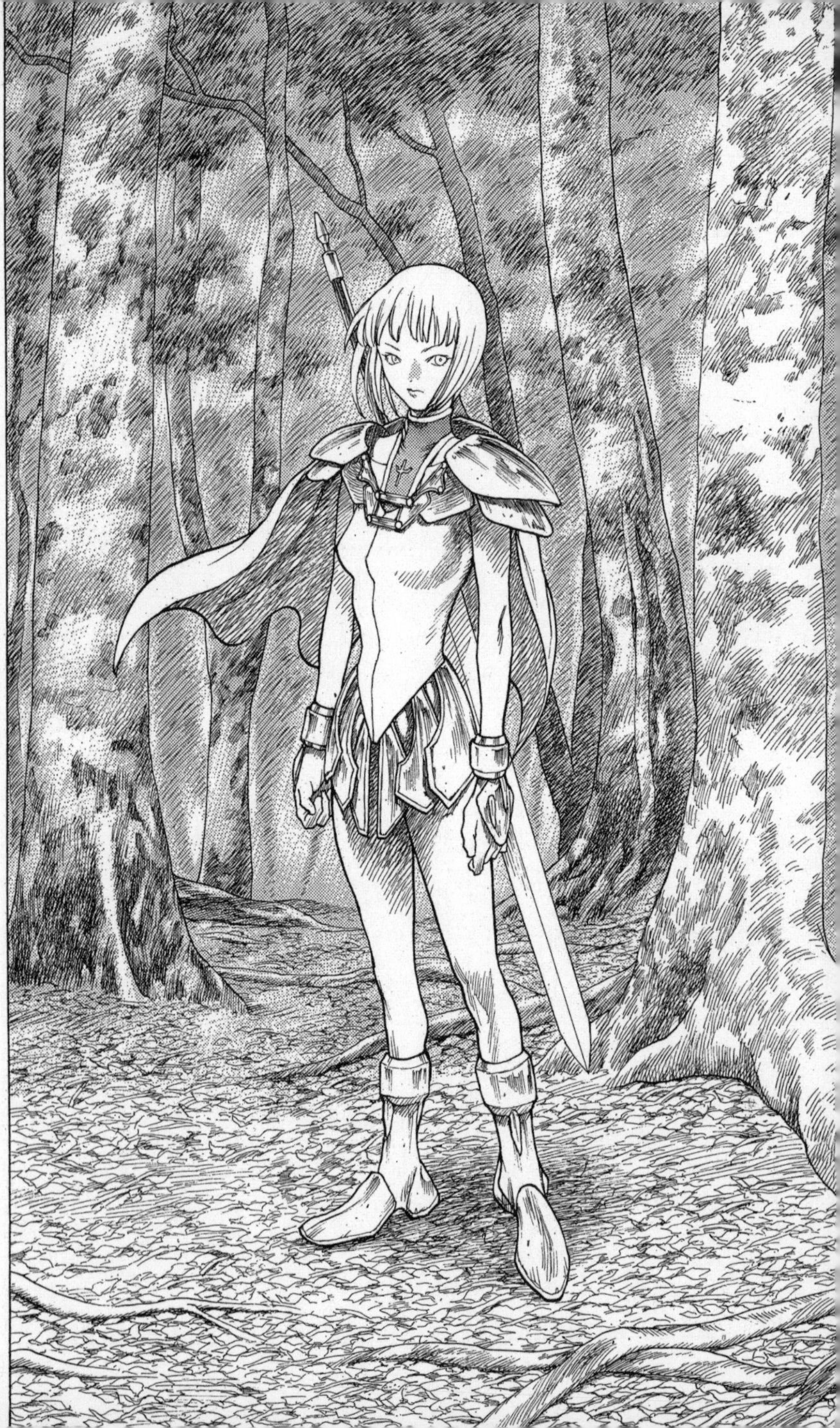

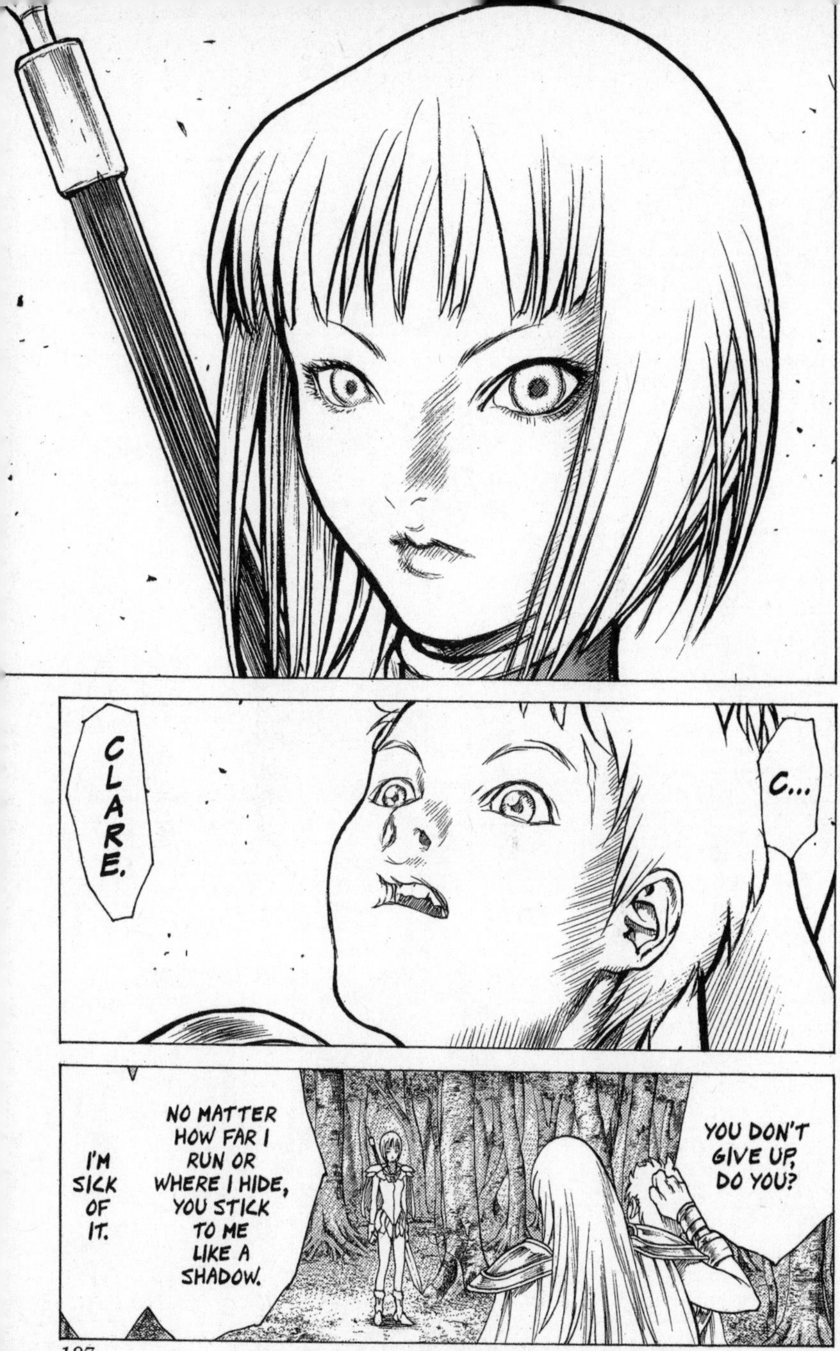
C...
CLARE.
YOU DON'T GIVE UP, DO YOU?
NO MATTER HOW FAR I RUN OR WHERE I HIDE, YOU STICK TO ME LIKE A SHADOW.
I'M SICK OF IT.

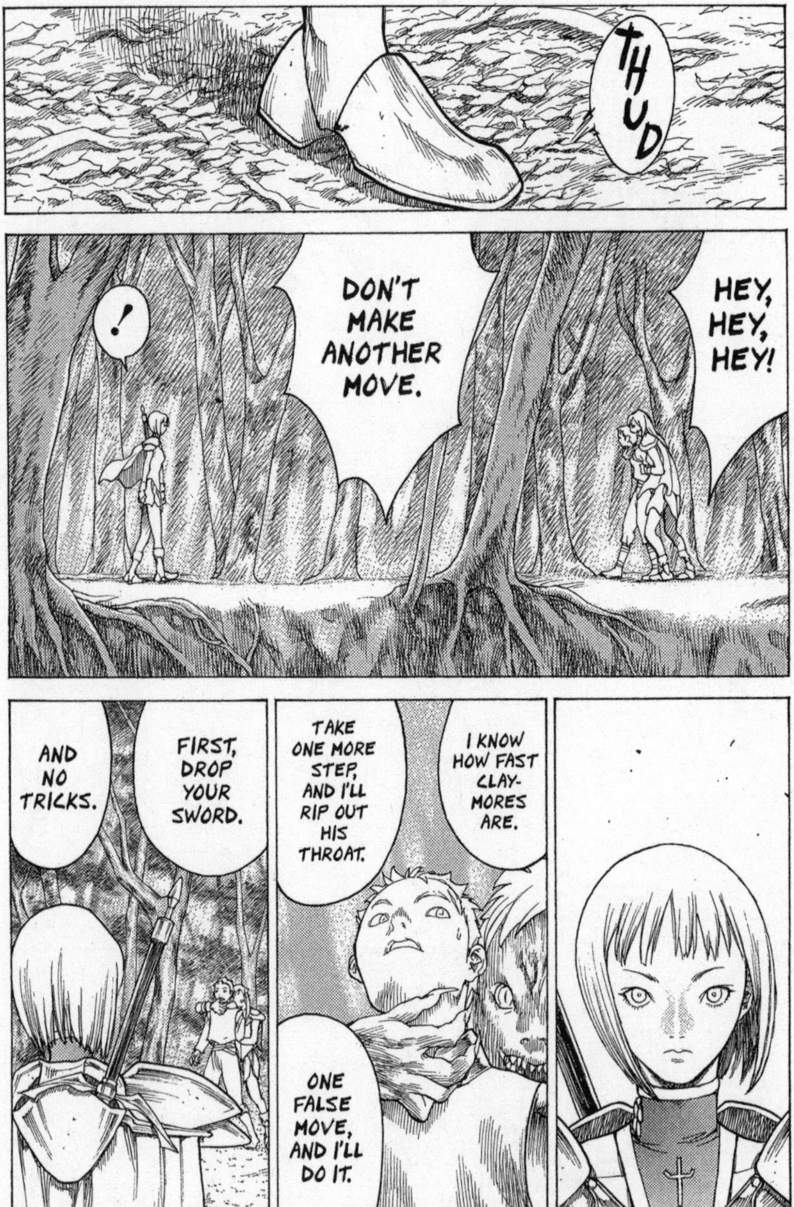
THUD
HEY, HEY, HEY!
DON'T MAKE ANOTHER MOVE.
!
I KNOW HOW FAST CLAY-MORES ARE.
TAKE ONE MORE STEP, AND I'LL RIP OUT HIS THROAT.
ONE FALSE MOVE, AND I'LL DO IT.
FIRST, DROP YOUR SWORD.
AND NO TRICKS.

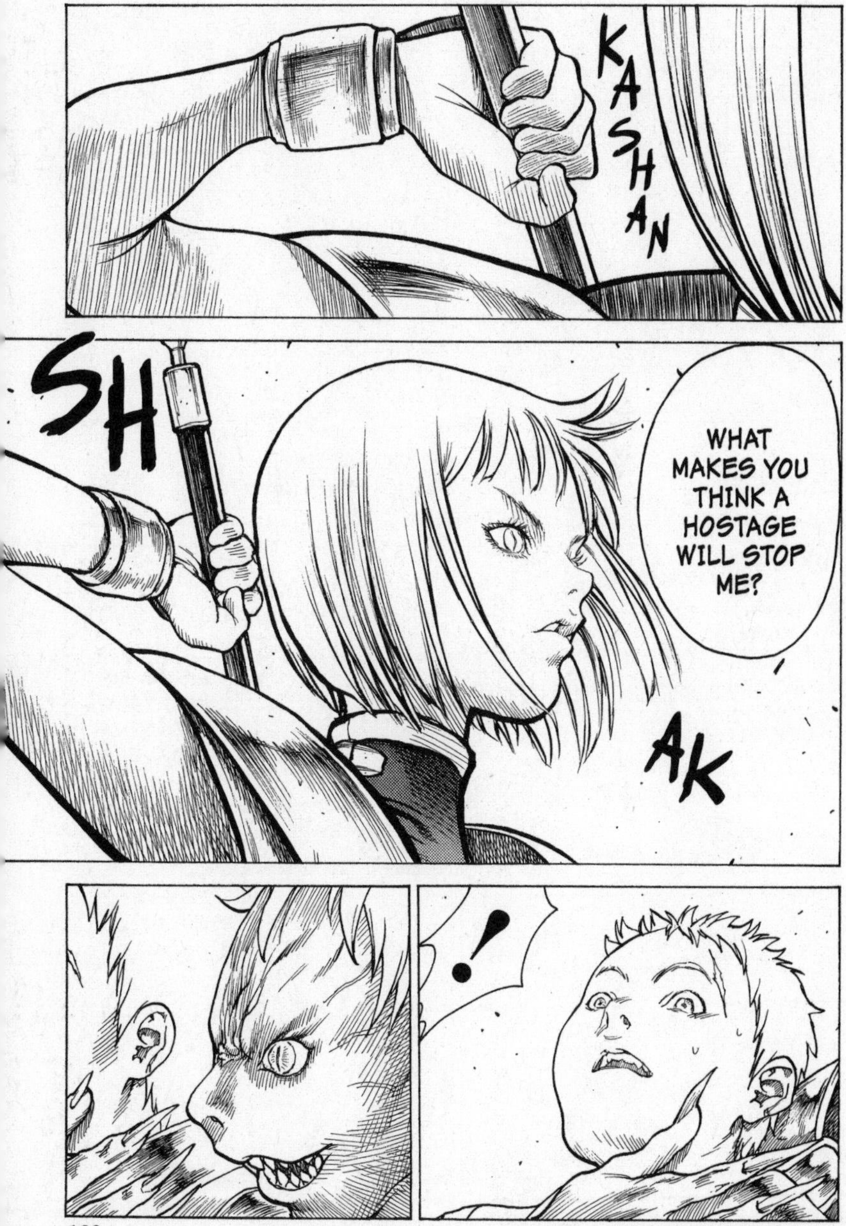
KASHAN
WHAT MAKES YOU THINK A HOSTAGE WILL STOP ME?
SH
AK
!

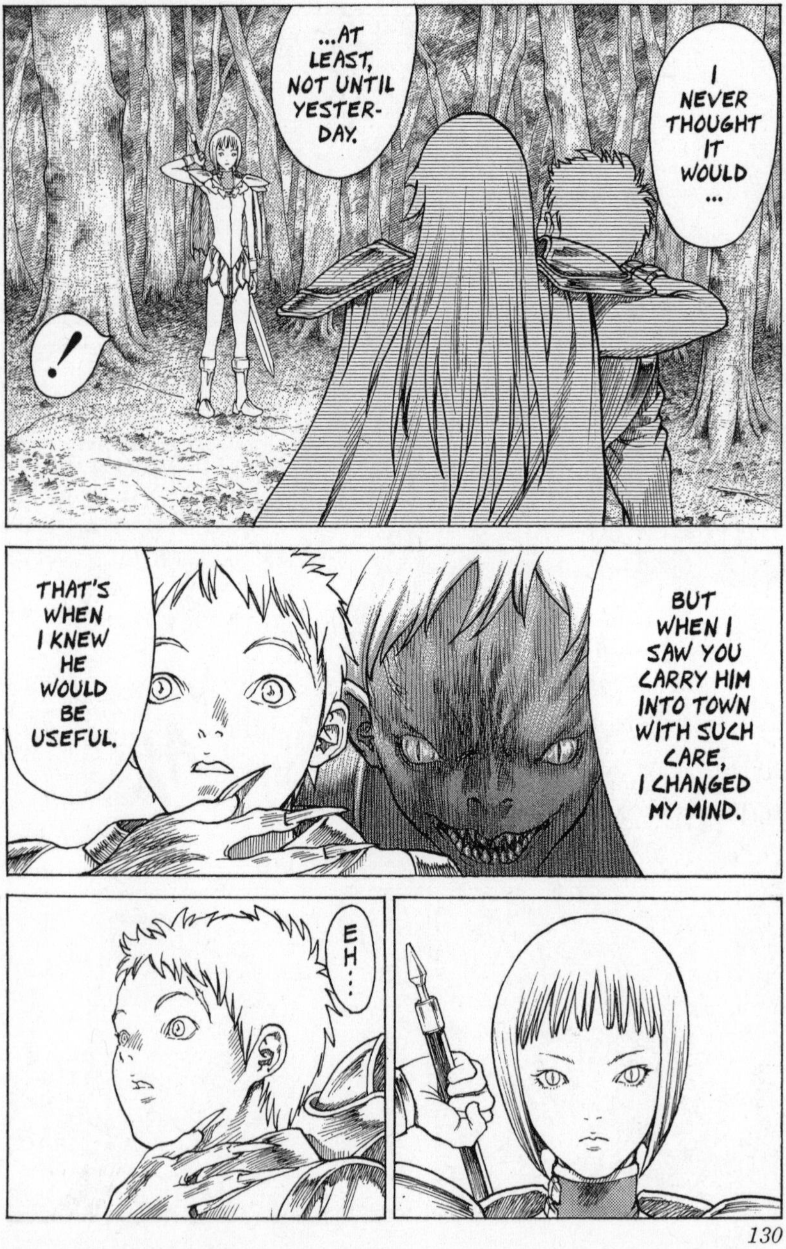
I NEVER THOUGHT IT WOULD...
...AT LEAST, NOT UNTIL YESTER-DAY.
!
BUT WHEN I SAW YOU CARRY HIM INTO TOWN WITH SUCH CARE, I CHANGED MY MIND.
THAT'S WHEN I KNEW HE WOULD BE USEFUL.
EH...

READ THIS WAY

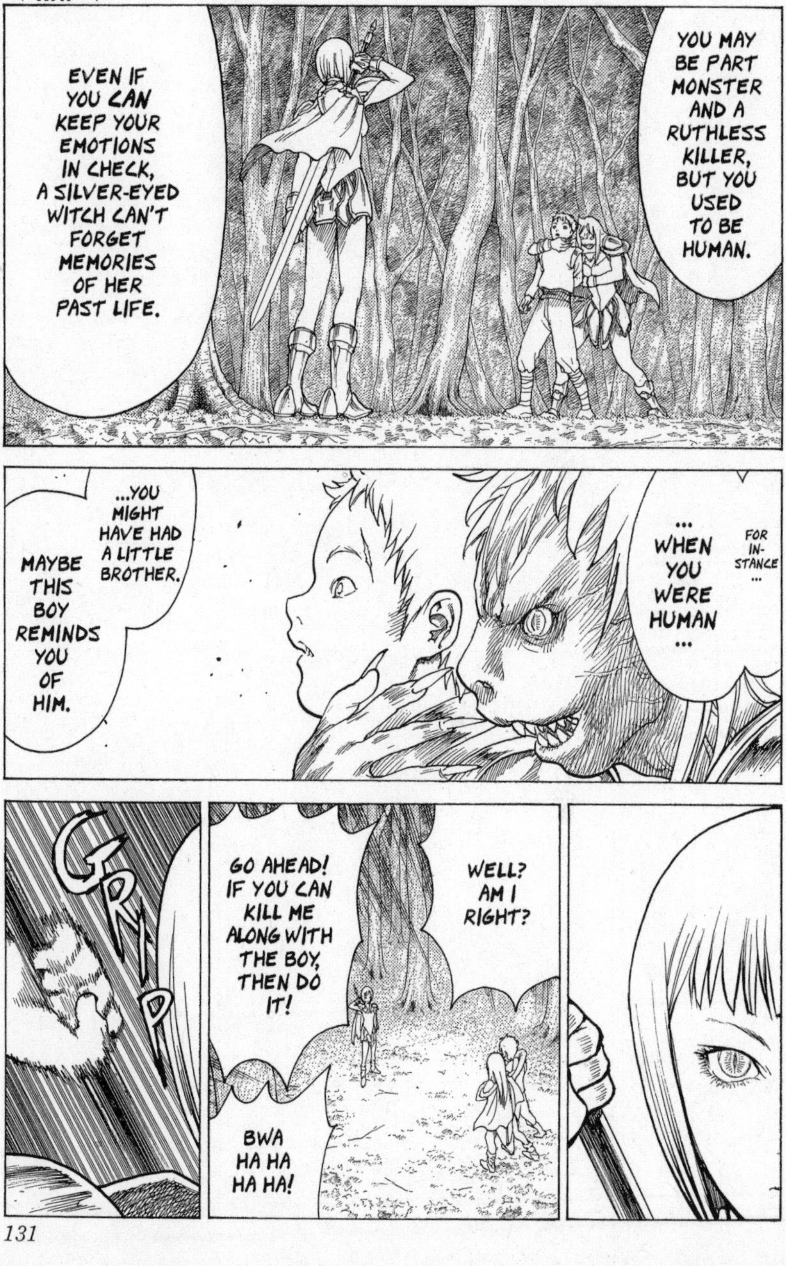

YOU MAY BE PART MONSTER AND A RUTHLESS KILLER, BUT YOU USED TO BE HUMAN.
EVEN IF YOU CAN KEEP YOUR EMOTIONS IN CHECK, A SILVER-EYED WITCH CAN'T FORGET MEMORIES OF HER PAST LIFE.
FOR INSTANCE...
...WHEN YOU WERE HUMAN...
...YOU MIGHT HAVE HAD A LITTLE BROTHER.
MAYBE THIS BOY REMINDS YOU OF HIM.
WELL? AM I RIGHT?
GO AHEAD! IF YOU CAN KILL ME ALONG WITH THE BOY, THEN DO IT!
BWA HA HA HA HA!
GRIP

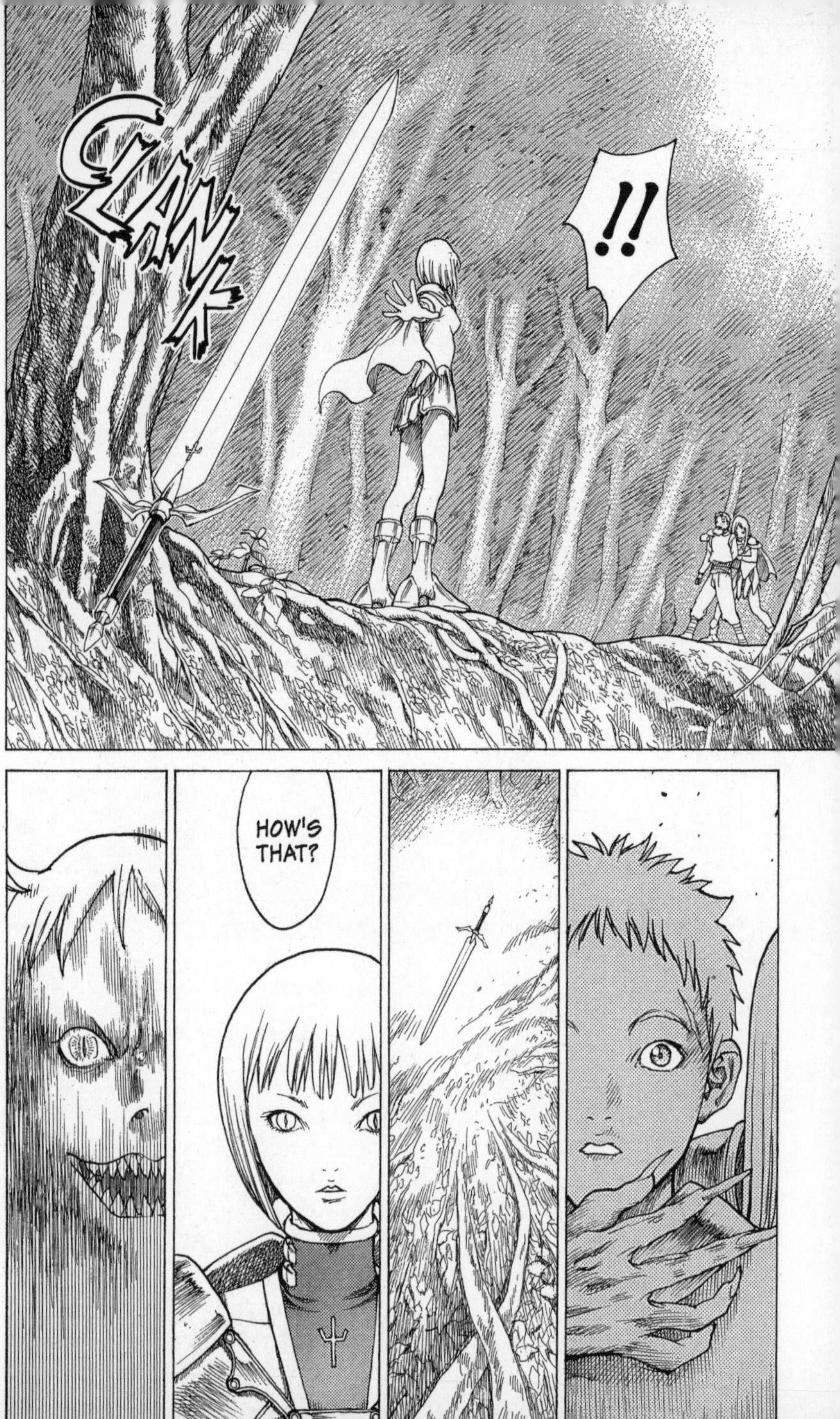
!!
CLANK
HOW'S THAT?

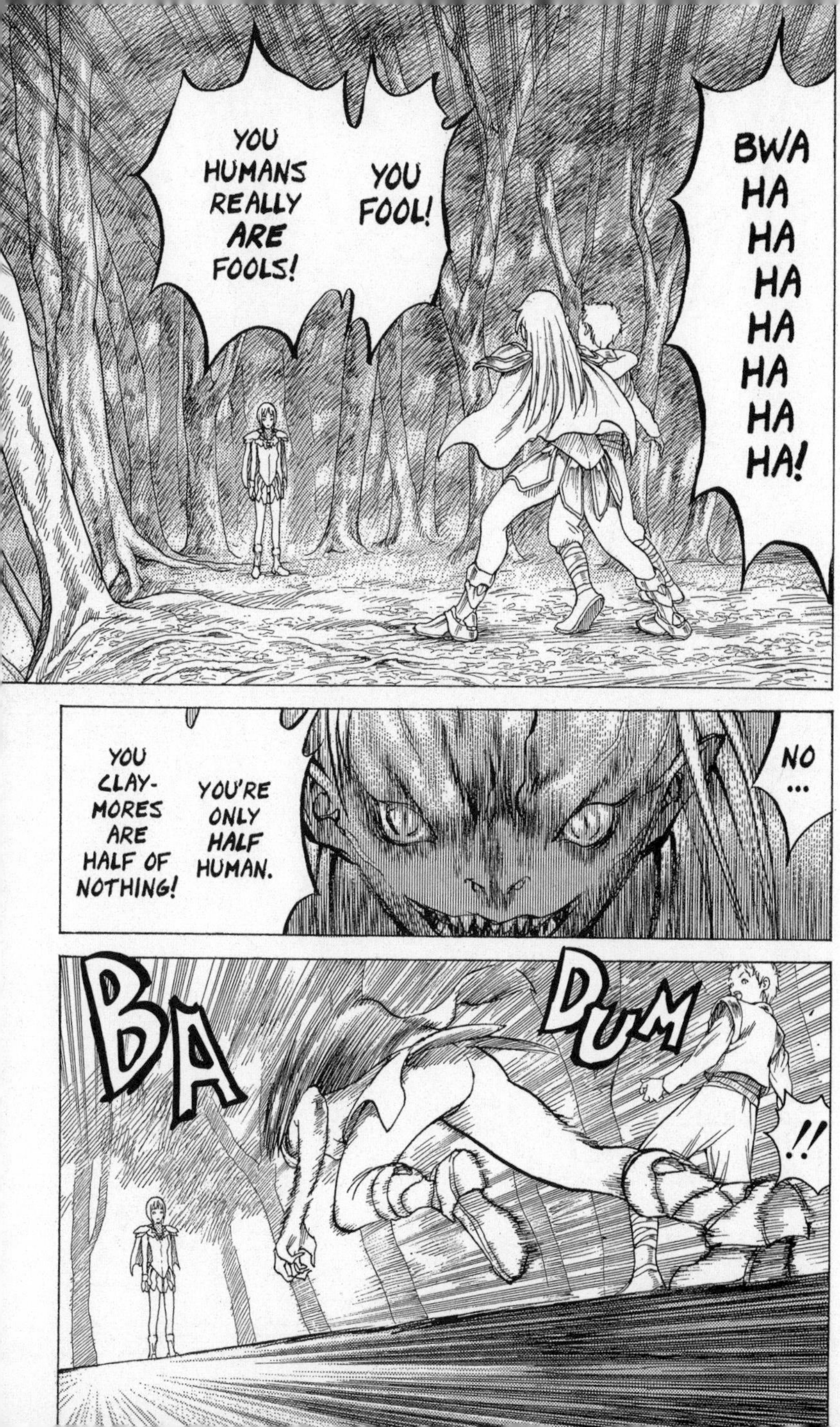
BWA HA HA HA HA HA HA HA!
YOU FOOL!
YOU HUMANS REALLY ARE FOOLS!
NO...
YOU'RE ONLY HALF HUMAN.
YOU CLAY-MORES ARE HALF OF NOTHING!
BA DUM
!!

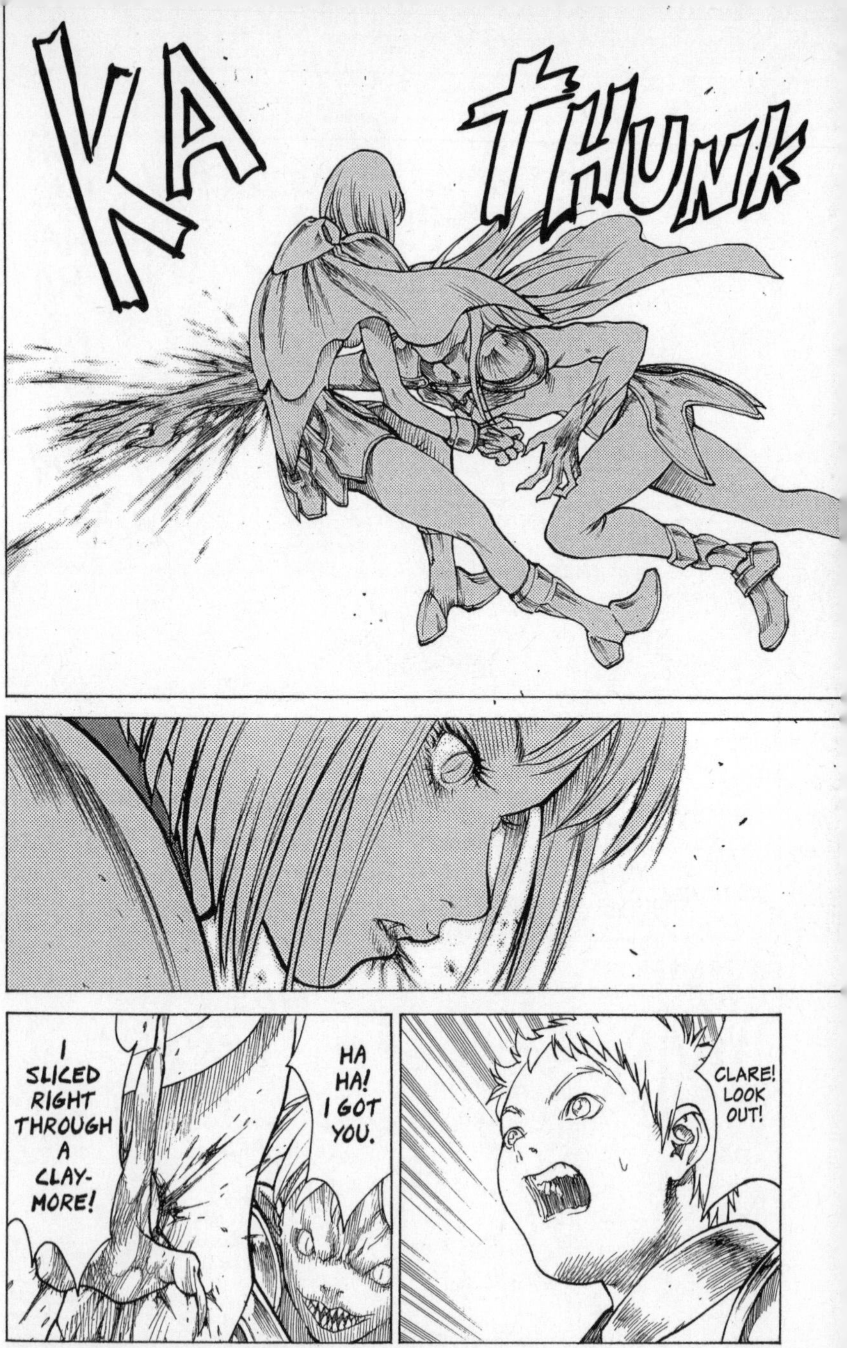
KA THUNK
CLARE! LOOK OUT!
HA HA! I GOT YOU.
I SLICED RIGHT THROUGH A CLAY-MORE!

READ THIS WAY

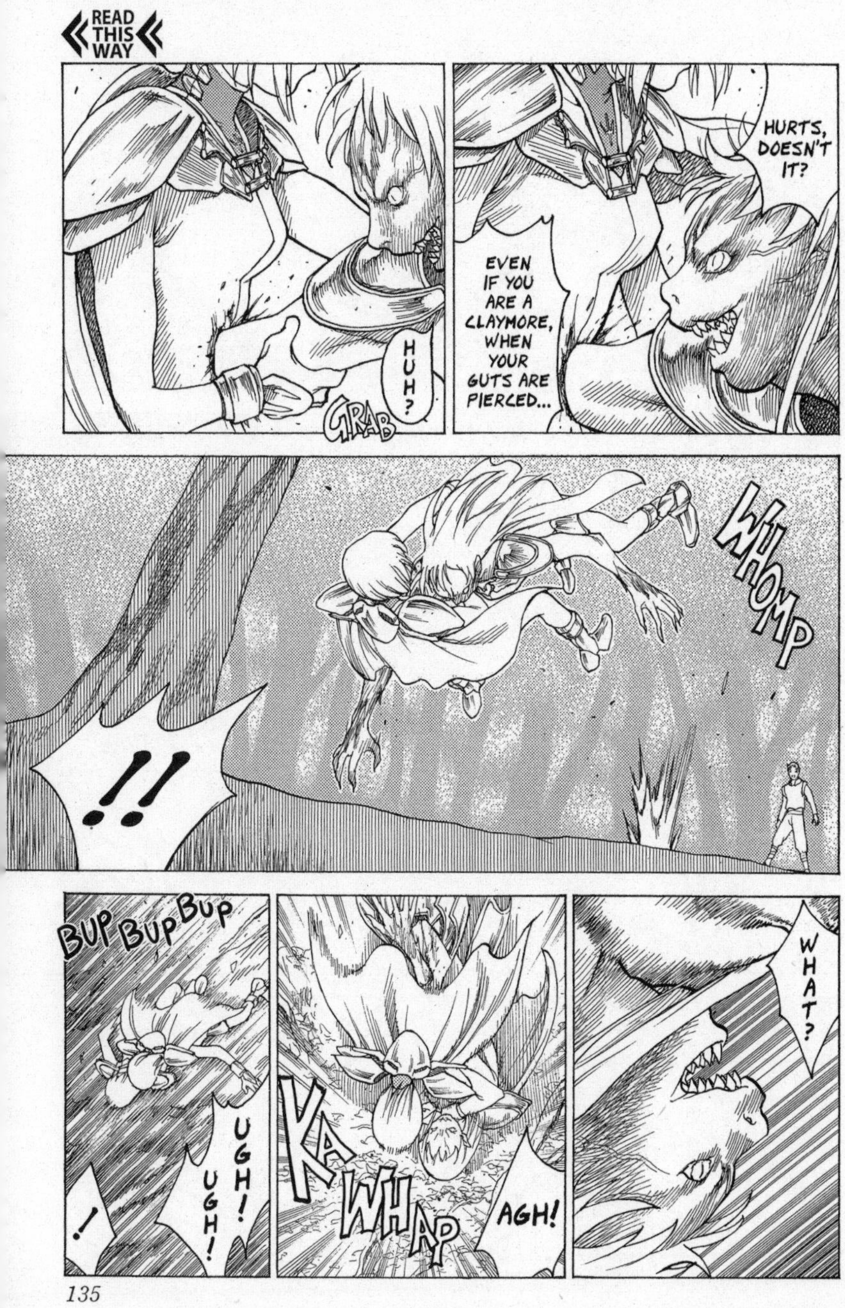
HURTS, DOESN'T IT?
EVEN IF YOU ARE A CLAYMORE, WHEN YOUR GUTS ARE PIERCED...
HUH?
GRAB
WHOMP
!!
WHAT?
AGH!
KA WHAP
BUP BUP BUP
UGH!
UGH!
!

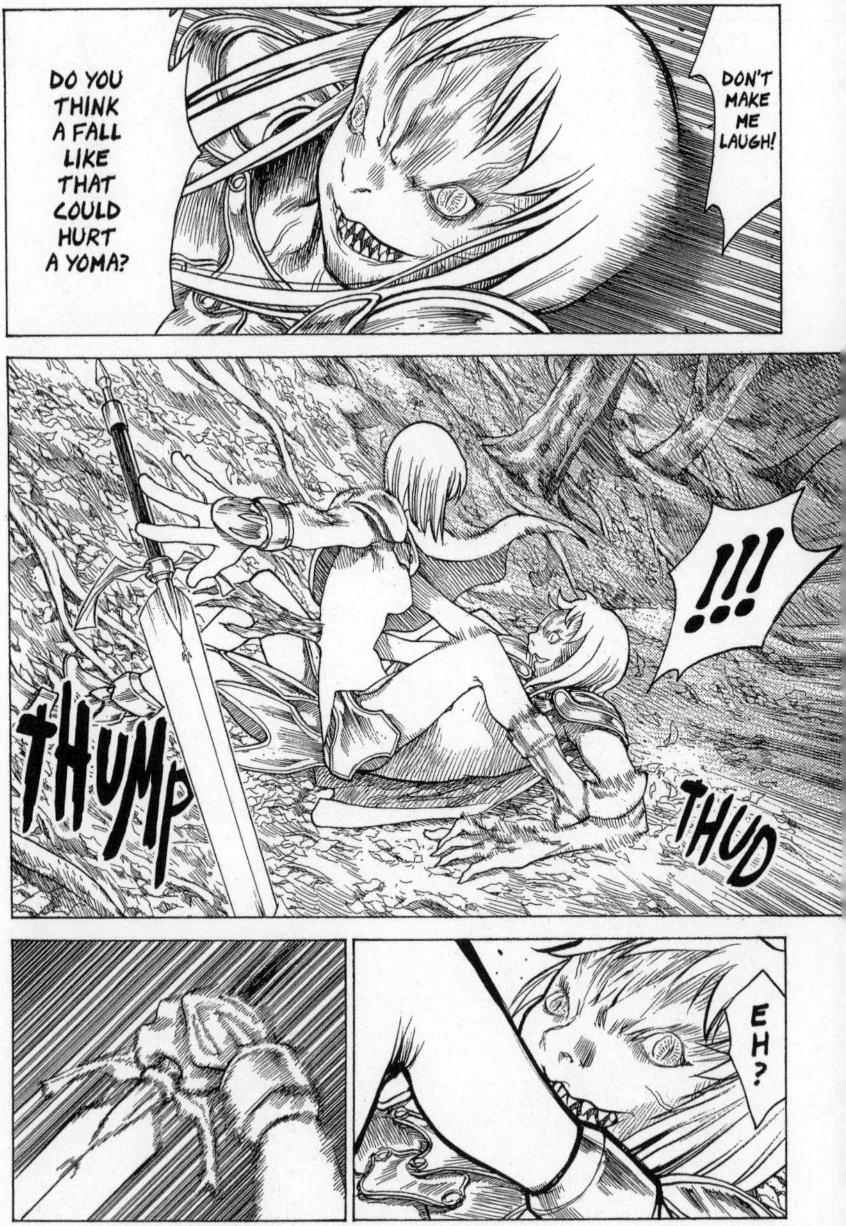
DON'T MAKE ME LAUGH!
DO YOU THINK A FALL LIKE THAT COULD HURT A YOMA?
!!!
THUD
THUMP
EH?

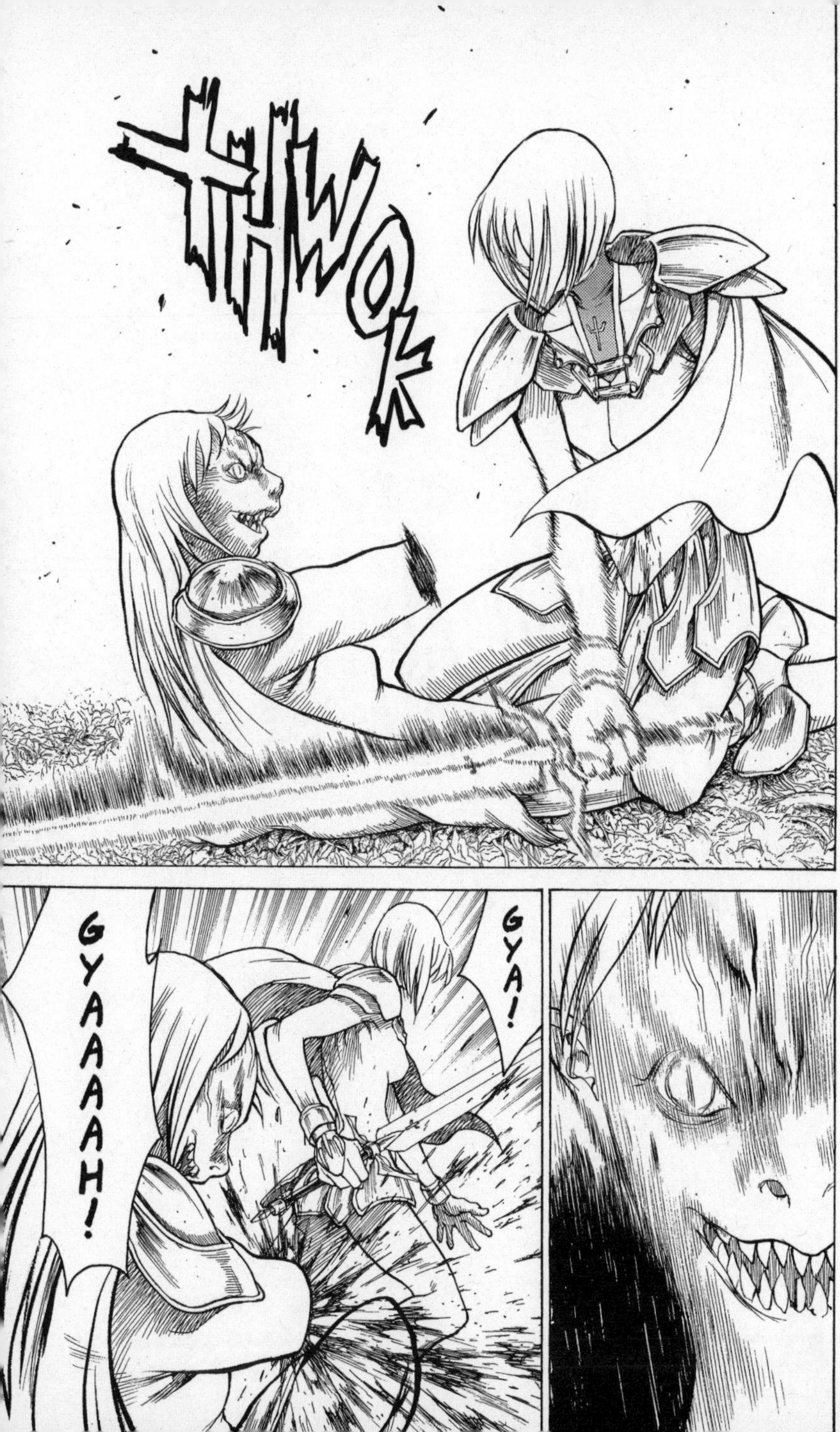
THWOK
GYA!
GYAAAAAH!

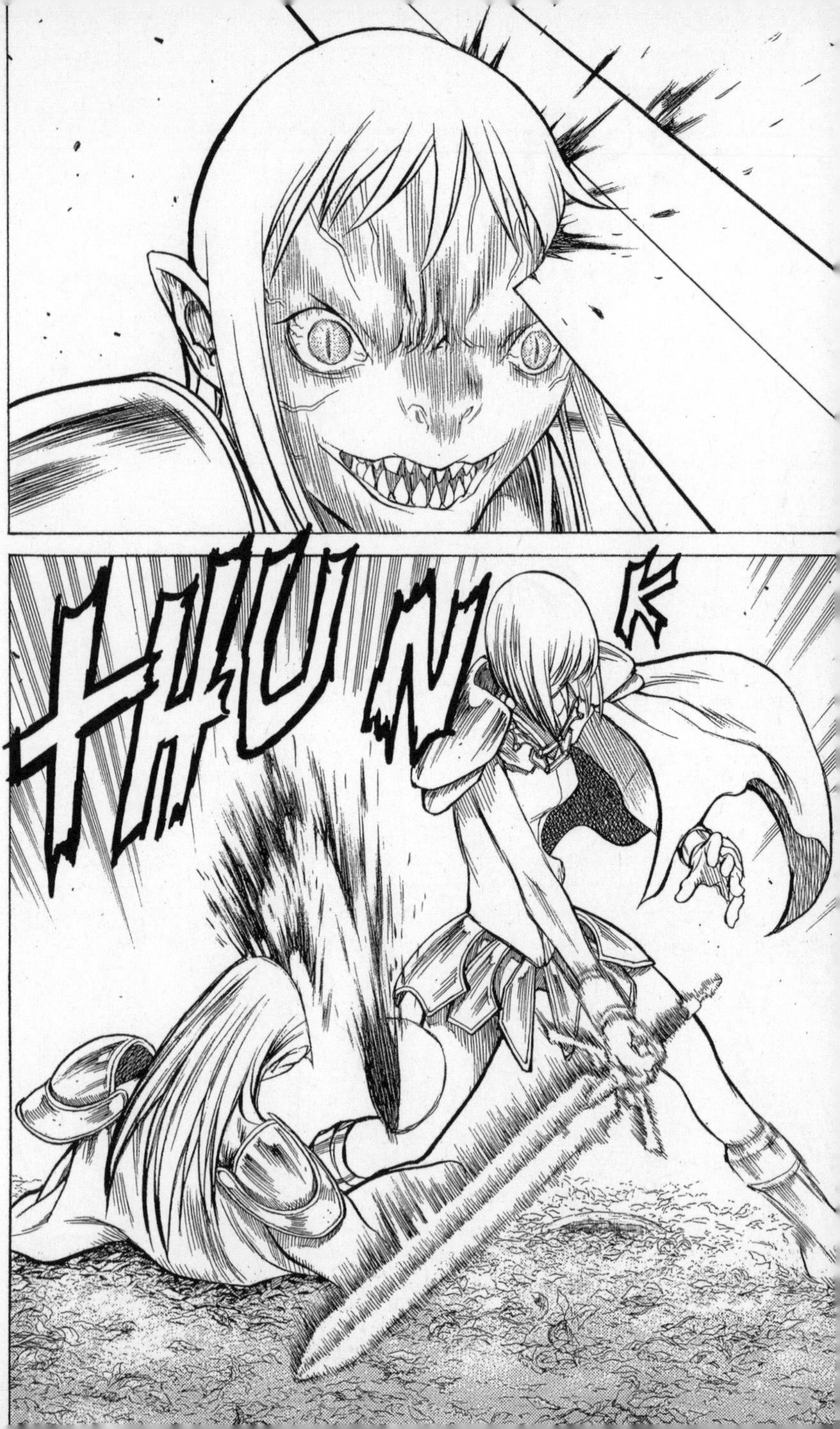
THUNK

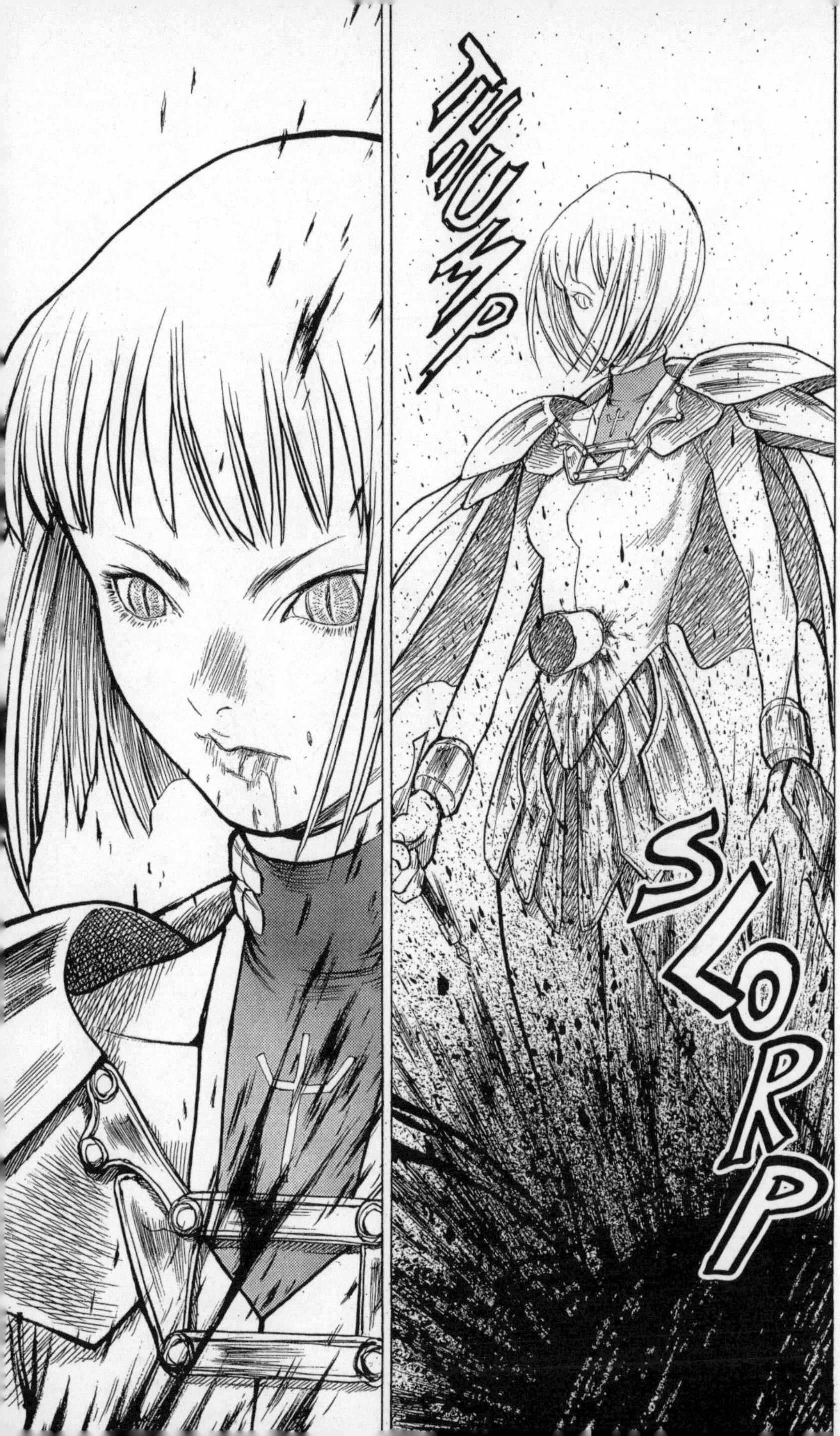
THUMP
SLORP

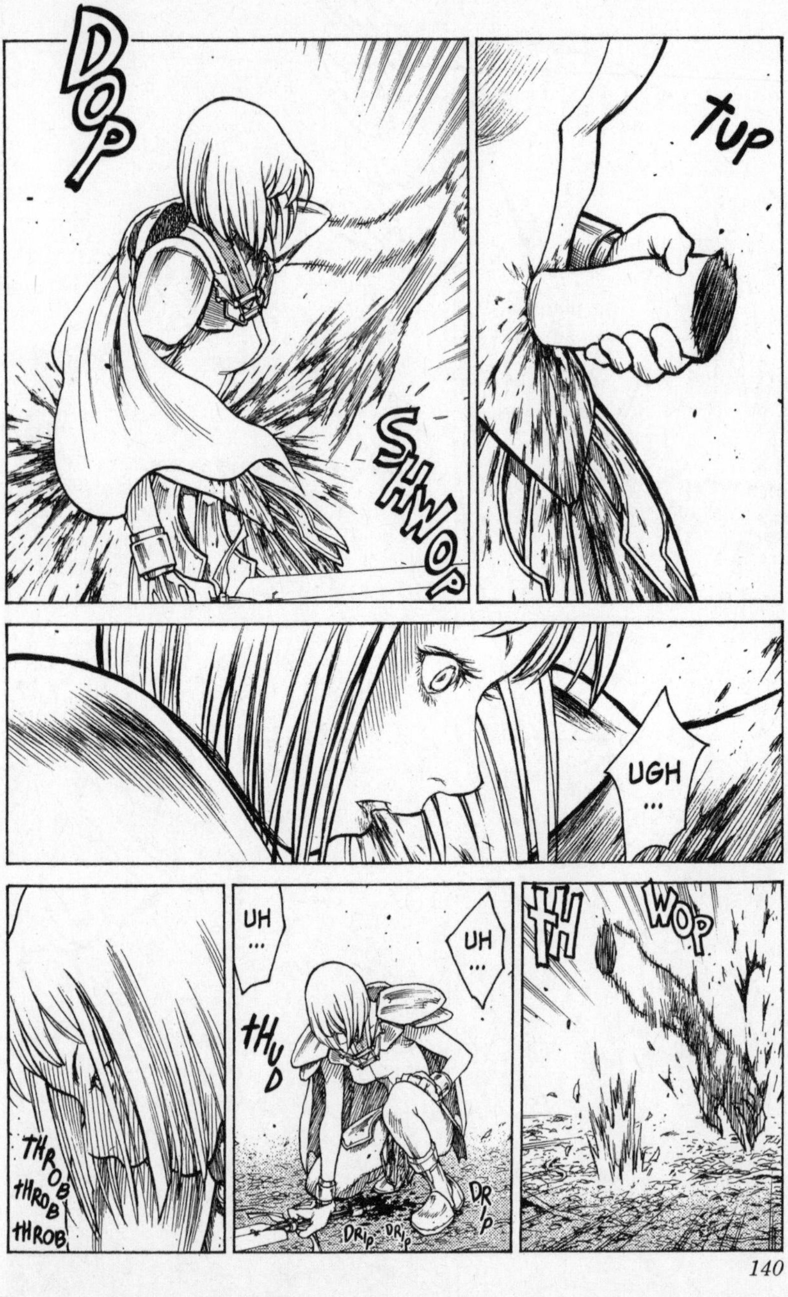
TUP
DOP
SHWOP
UGH ...
THWOP
UH ...
UH ...
THUD
DRIP
DRIP
DRIP
THROB
THROB
THROB

THAK

THAK

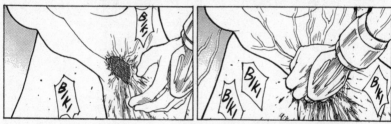

BIKI

BIKI

BIKI

BIKI

I'M SORRY, CLARE! IT'S MY FAULT!

I'M SORRY!

IT'S ALL MY FAULT!

CLARE!

ARE YOU OKAY?

!

CLARE!

KRAK

KRAK

KRAK

KRAK

KRAK

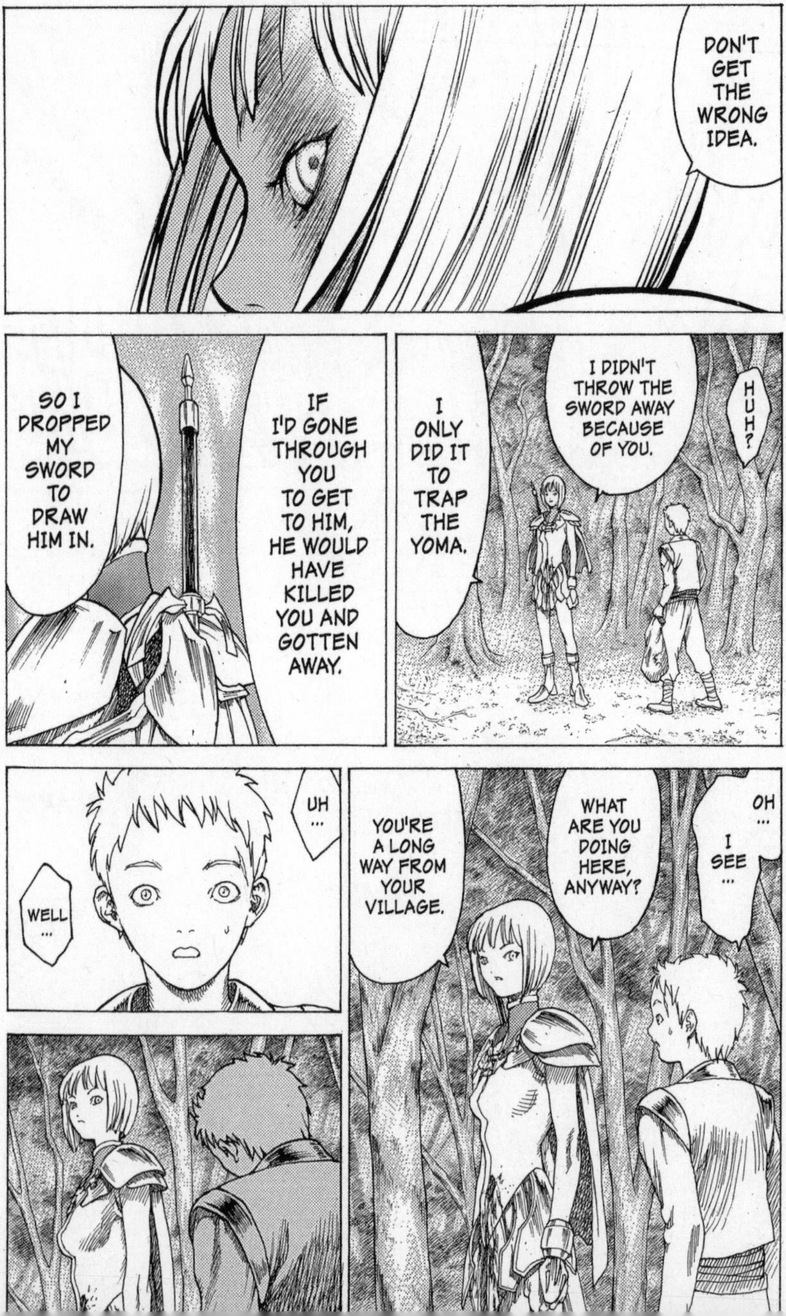
DON'T GET THE WRONG IDEA.
HUH?
I DIDN'T THROW THE SWORD AWAY BECAUSE OF YOU.
I ONLY DID IT TO TRAP THE YOMA.
IF I'D GONE THROUGH YOU TO GET TO HIM, HE WOULD HAVE KILLED YOU AND GOTTEN AWAY.
SO I DROPPED MY SWORD TO DRAW HIM IN.
OH ... I SEE ...
WHAT ARE YOU DOING HERE, ANYWAY?
YOU'RE A LONG WAY FROM YOUR VILLAGE.
UH ...
WELL ...

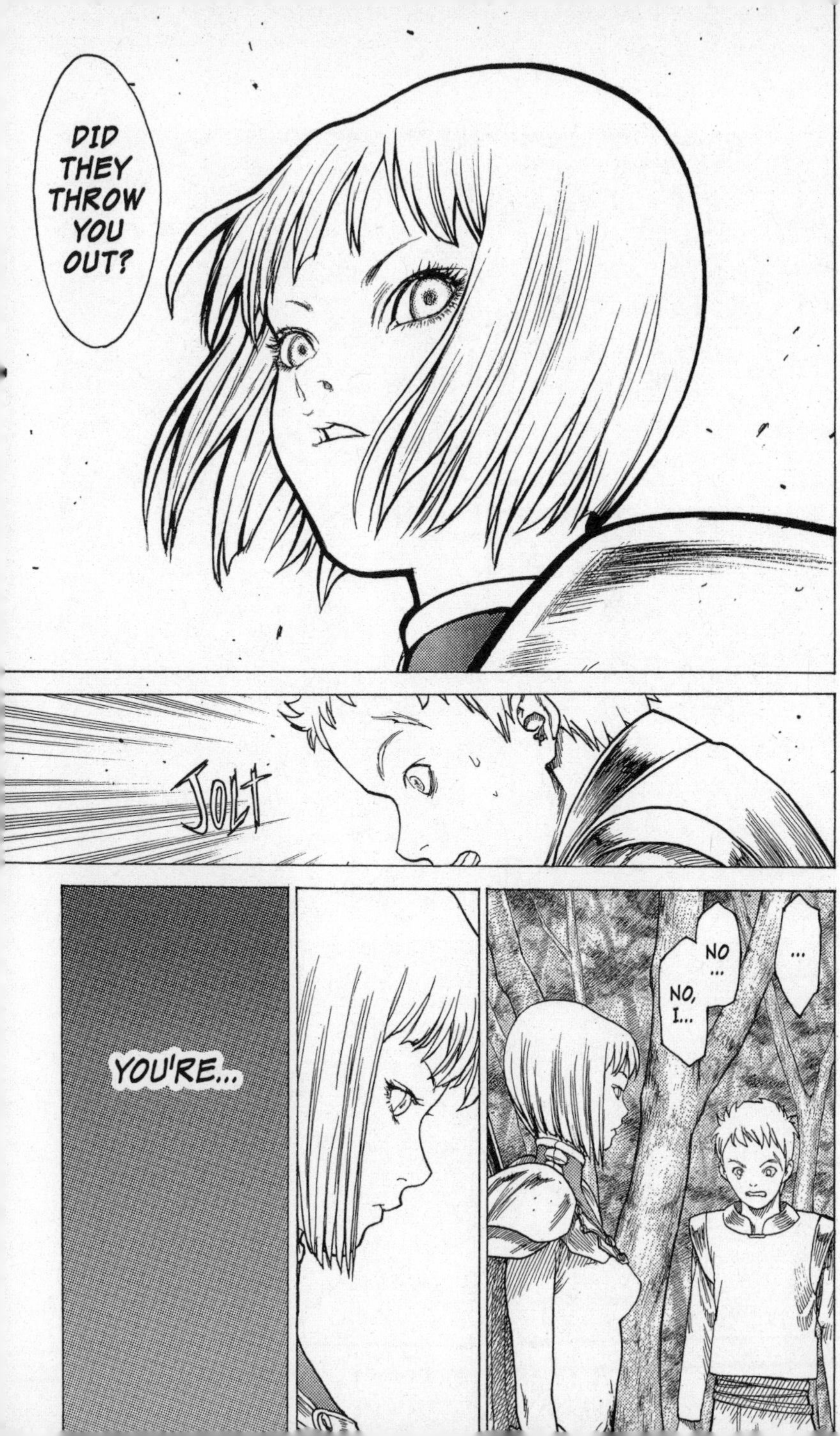
DID THEY THROW YOU OUT?
JOLT
...
NO ... NO, I...
YOU'RE...

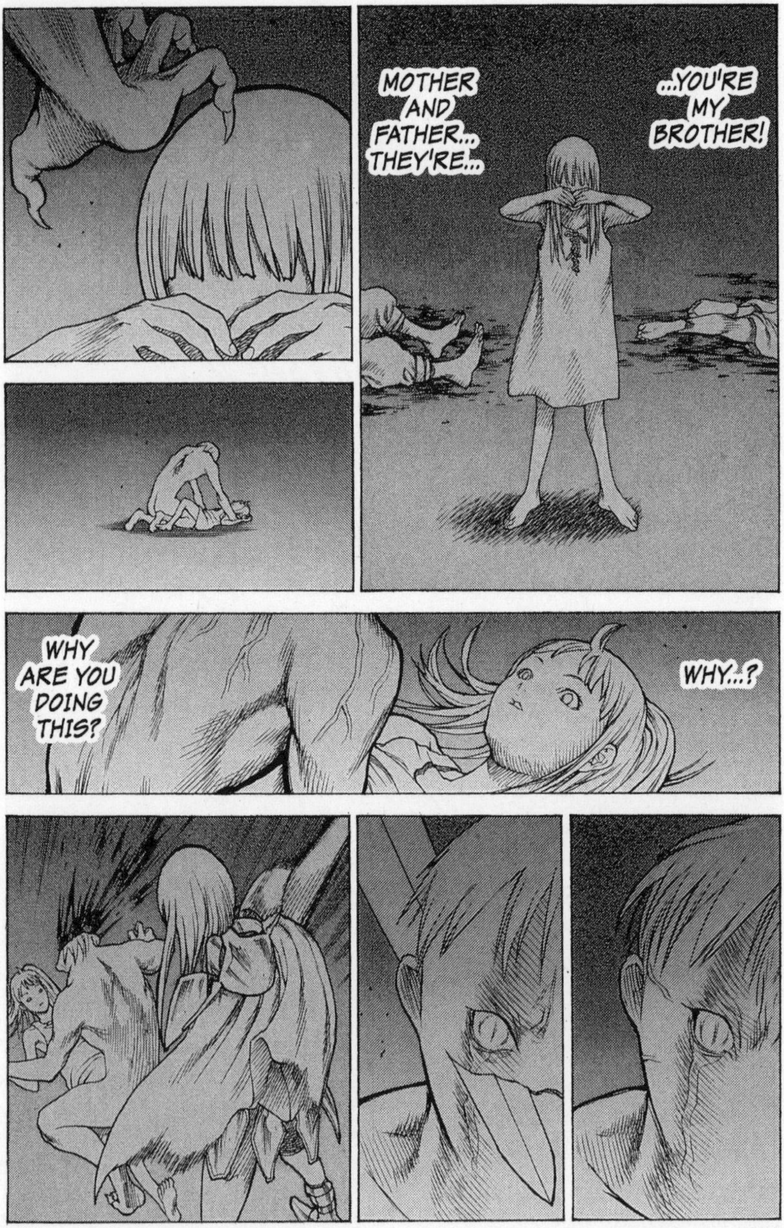
...YOU'RE MY BROTHER!
MOTHER AND FATHER... THEY'RE...
WHY...?
WHY ARE YOU DOING THIS?

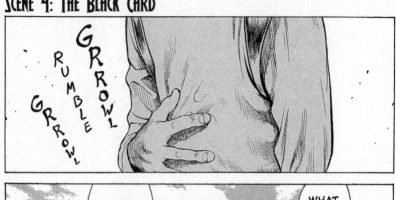

GRROWL
RUMBLE
GRROWL
GRROWL

ARE YOU HUNGRY?

WHAT IS IT?

WELL, YEAH.

UH...

KASHAN

!

WE HAVEN'T EATEN ANYTHING SINCE BREAKFAST, AND WE'VE BEEN WALKING ALL DAY.

I MEAN... UH...

IT'S KIND OF STRANGE YOU'RE NOT HUN—

Scene 4: The Black Card

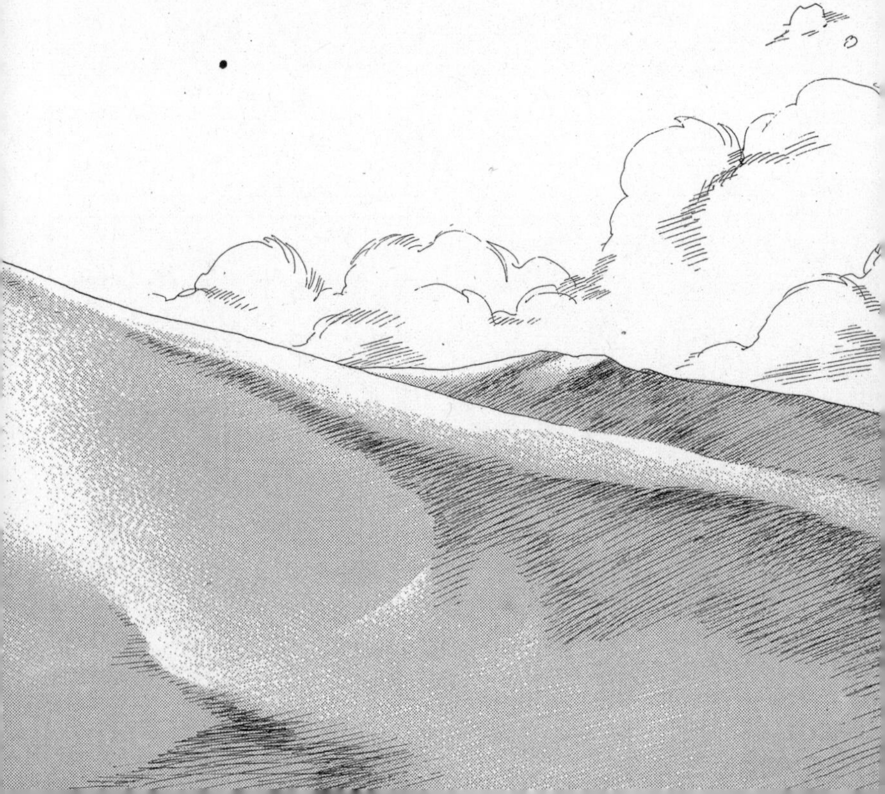

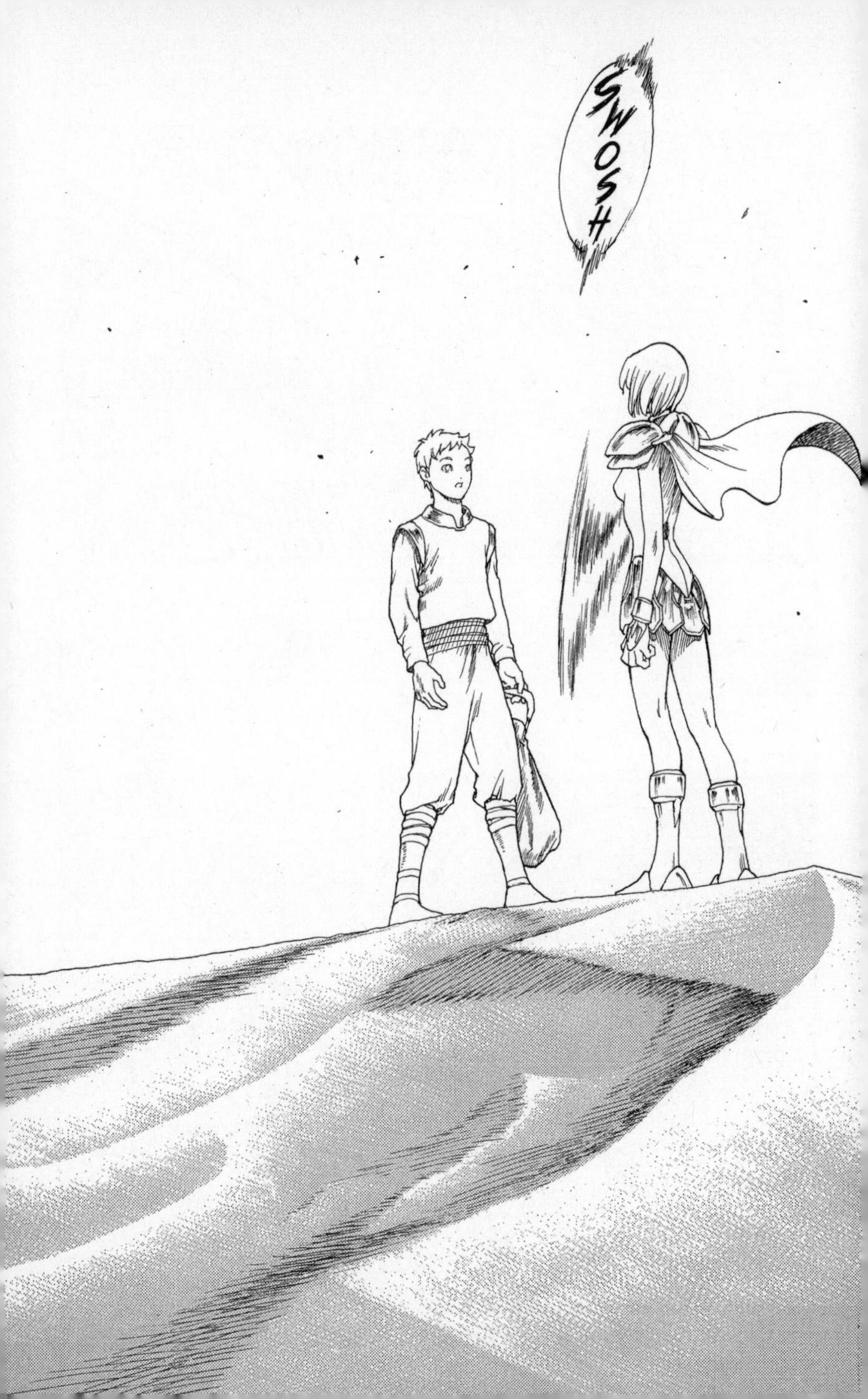
SWOSH

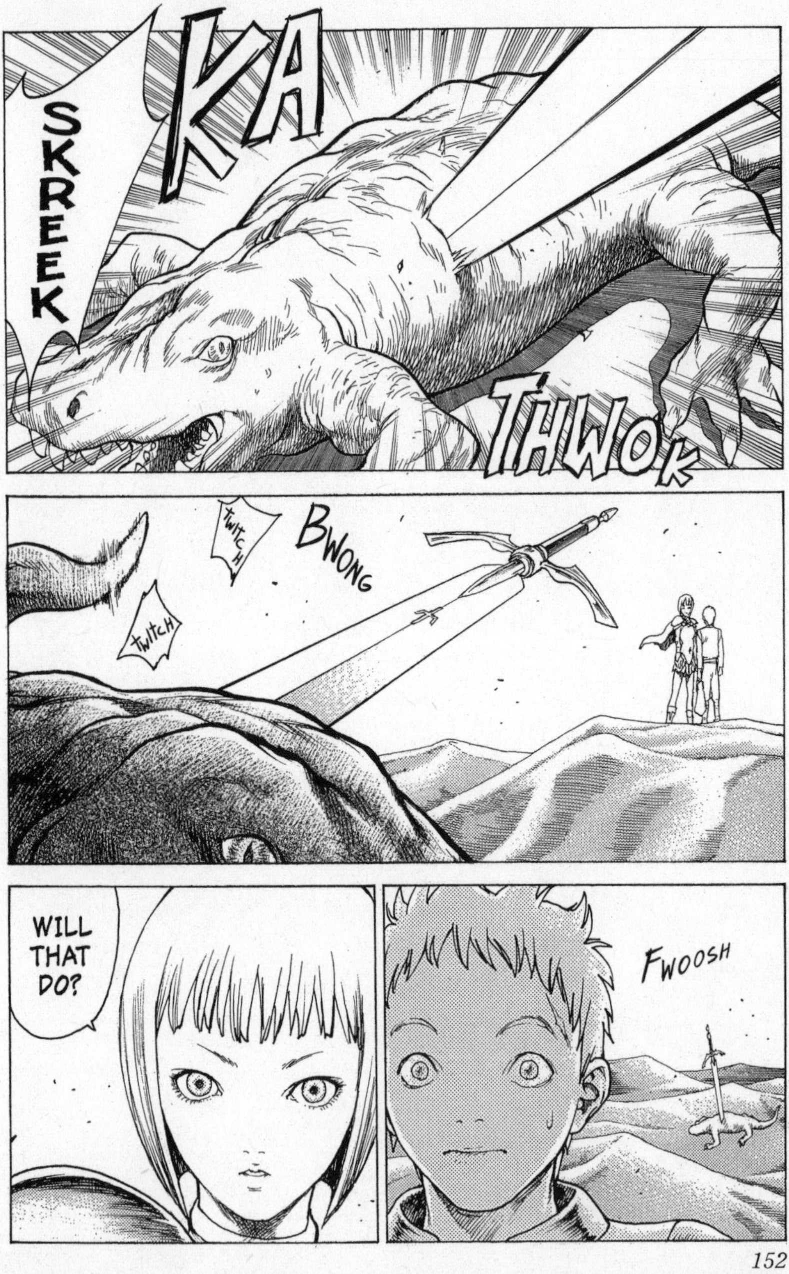
KA
SKREEK
THWOK
BWONG
TWITCH
TWITCH
FWOOSH
WILL THAT DO?

« READ THIS WAY «

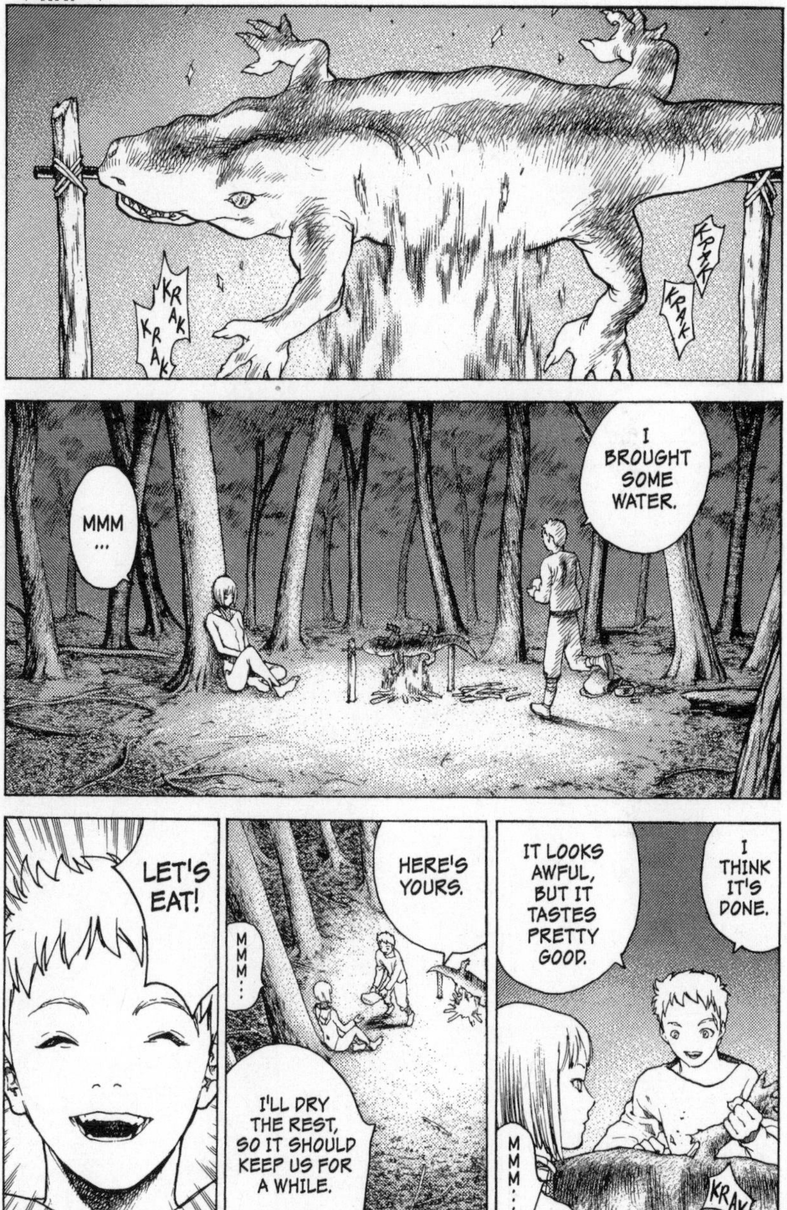
KRAK KRAK
KRAK KRAK
I BROUGHT SOME WATER.
MMM...
I THINK IT'S DONE.
IT LOOKS AWFUL, BUT IT TASTES PRETTY GOOD.
MMM...
KRAK
HERE'S YOURS.
MMM...
I'LL DRY THE REST, SO IT SHOULD KEEP US FOR A WHILE.
LET'S EAT!

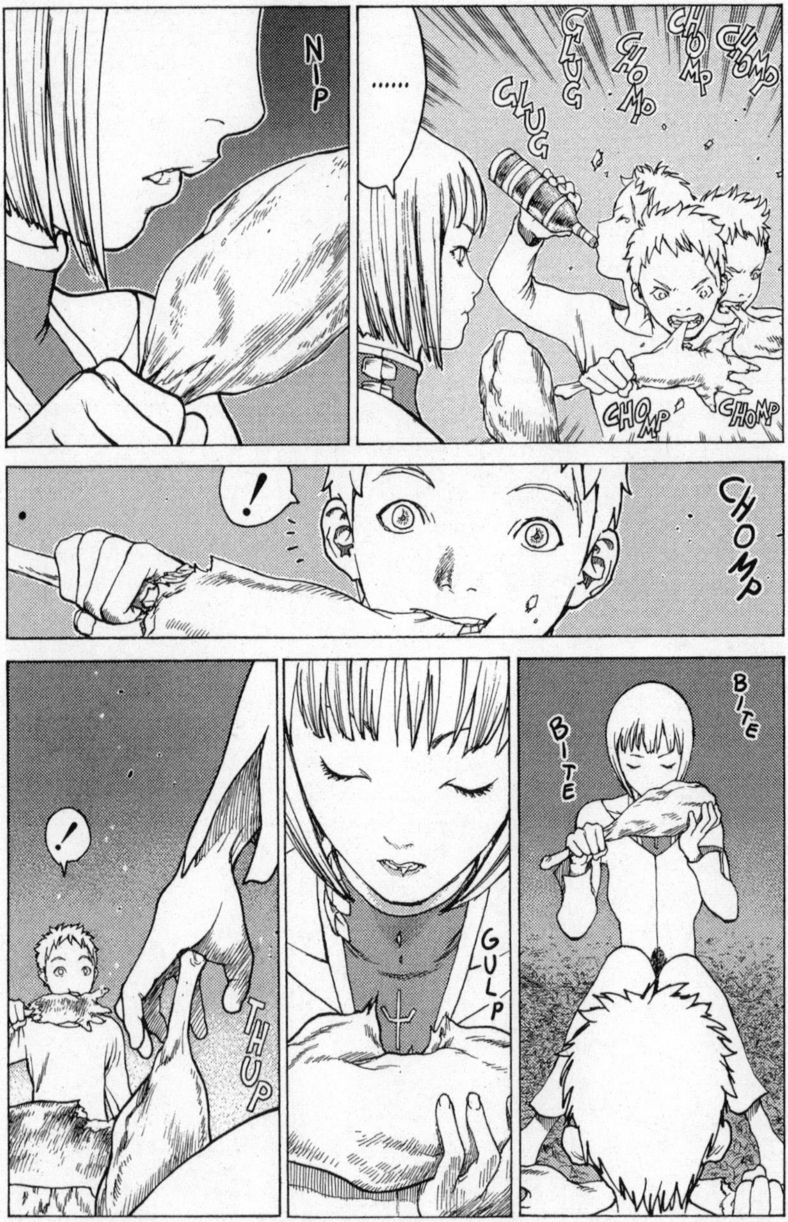
CHOMP
CHOMP
CHOMP
GLUG
GLUG
......
CHOMP
CHOMP
NIP
CHOMP
!
BITE
BITE
GULP
THUP
!

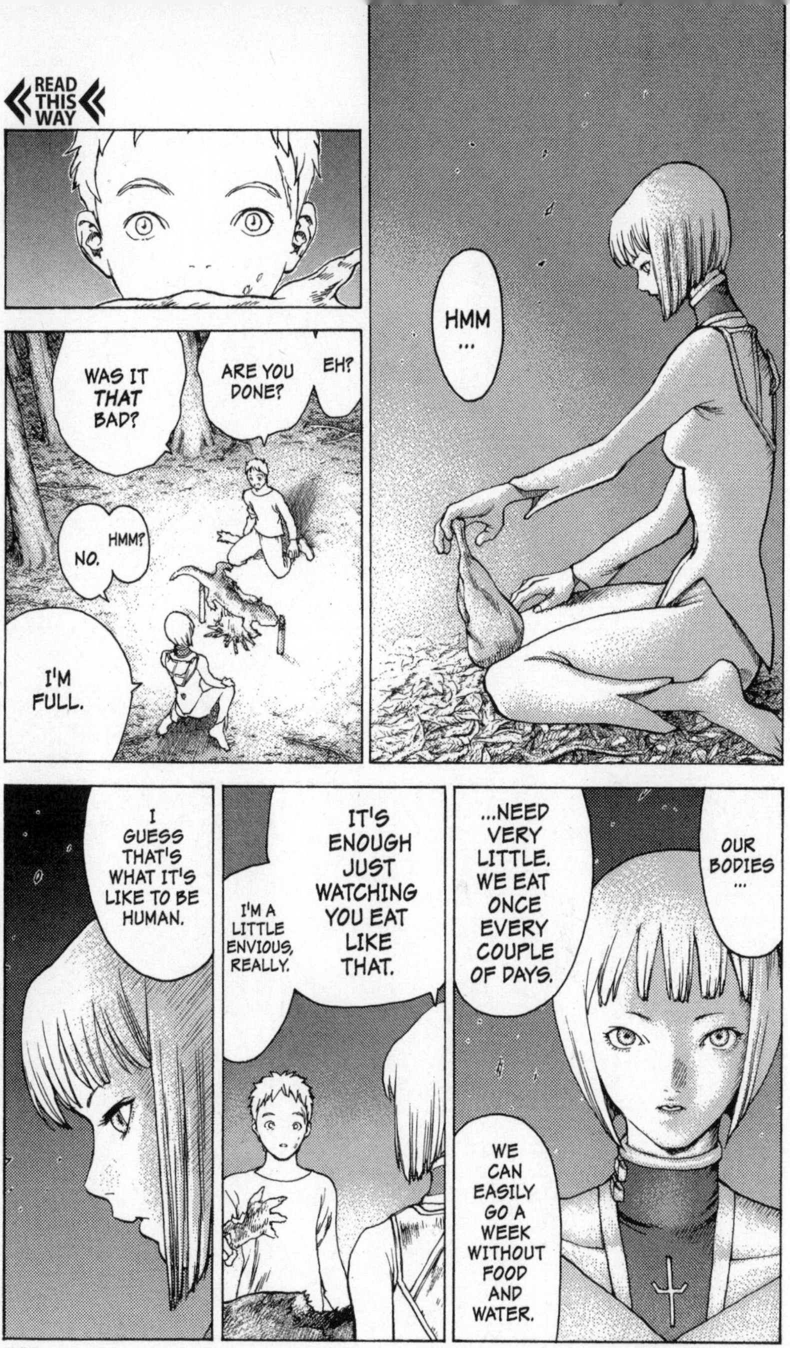
READ THIS WAY
HMM ...
EH?
ARE YOU DONE?
WAS IT THAT BAD?
HMM?
NO.
I'M FULL.
OUR BODIES ...
...NEED VERY LITTLE. WE EAT ONCE EVERY COUPLE OF DAYS.
WE CAN EASILY GO A WEEK WITHOUT FOOD AND WATER.
IT'S ENOUGH JUST WATCHING YOU EAT LIKE THAT.
I'M A LITTLE ENVIOUS, REALLY.
I GUESS THAT'S WHAT IT'S LIKE TO BE HUMAN.

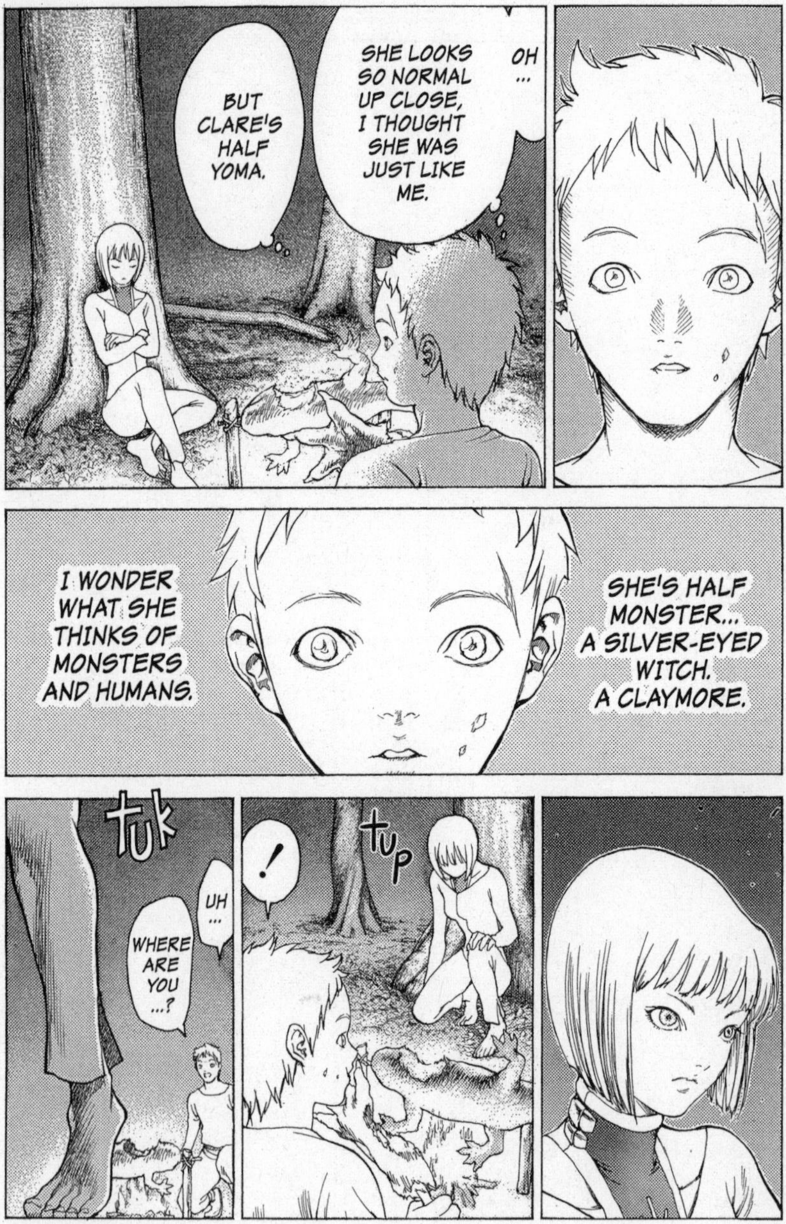
OH ...
SHE LOOKS SO NORMAL UP CLOSE, I THOUGHT SHE WAS JUST LIKE ME.
BUT CLARE'S HALF YOMA.
SHE'S HALF MONSTER... A SILVER-EYED WITCH. A CLAYMORE.
I WONDER WHAT SHE THINKS OF MONSTERS AND HUMANS.
TUP
!
TUK
UH ...
WHERE ARE YOU ...?

READ THIS WAY

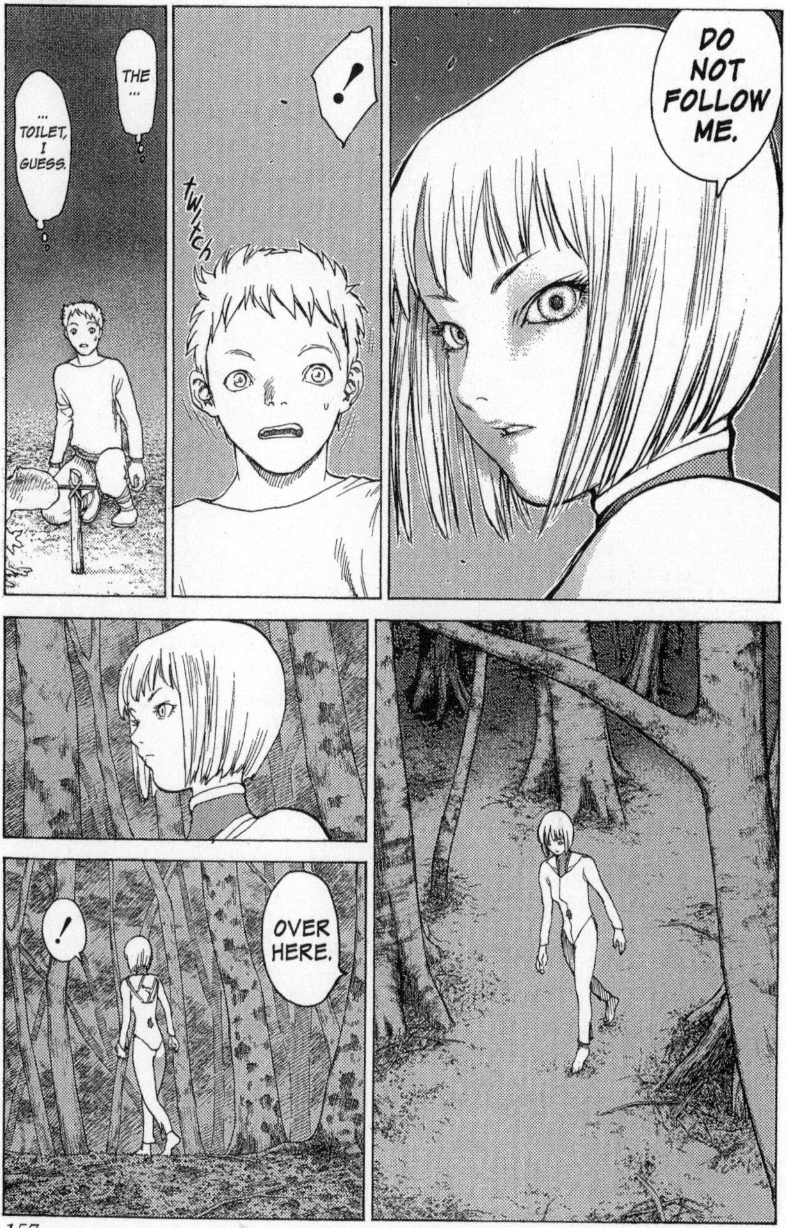

DO NOT FOLLOW ME.
!
TWITCH
THE ...
... TOILET, I GUESS.
OVER HERE.
!

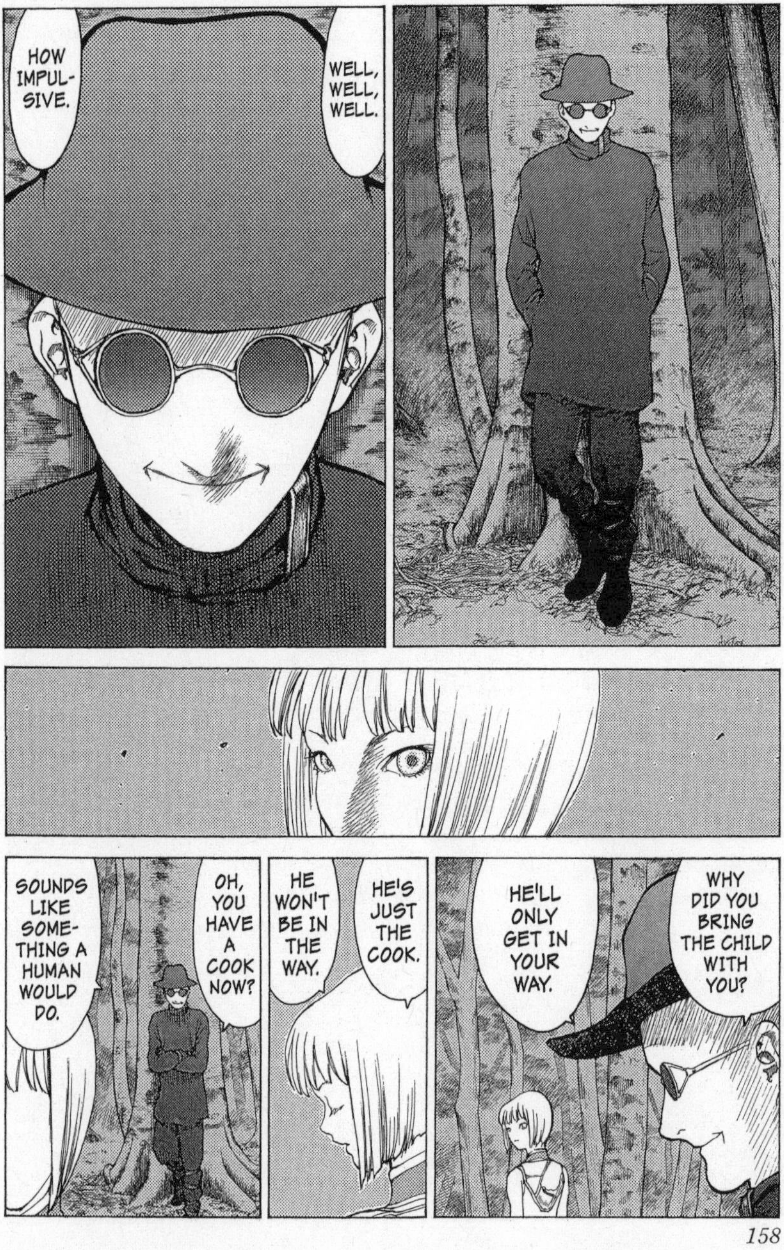
WELL, WELL, WELL.
HOW IMPUL-SIVE.
WHY DID YOU BRING THE CHILD WITH YOU?
HE'LL ONLY GET IN YOUR WAY.
HE'S JUST THE COOK.
HE WON'T BE IN THE WAY.
OH, YOU HAVE A COOK NOW?
SOUNDS LIKE SOME-THING A HUMAN WOULD DO.

READ THIS WAY

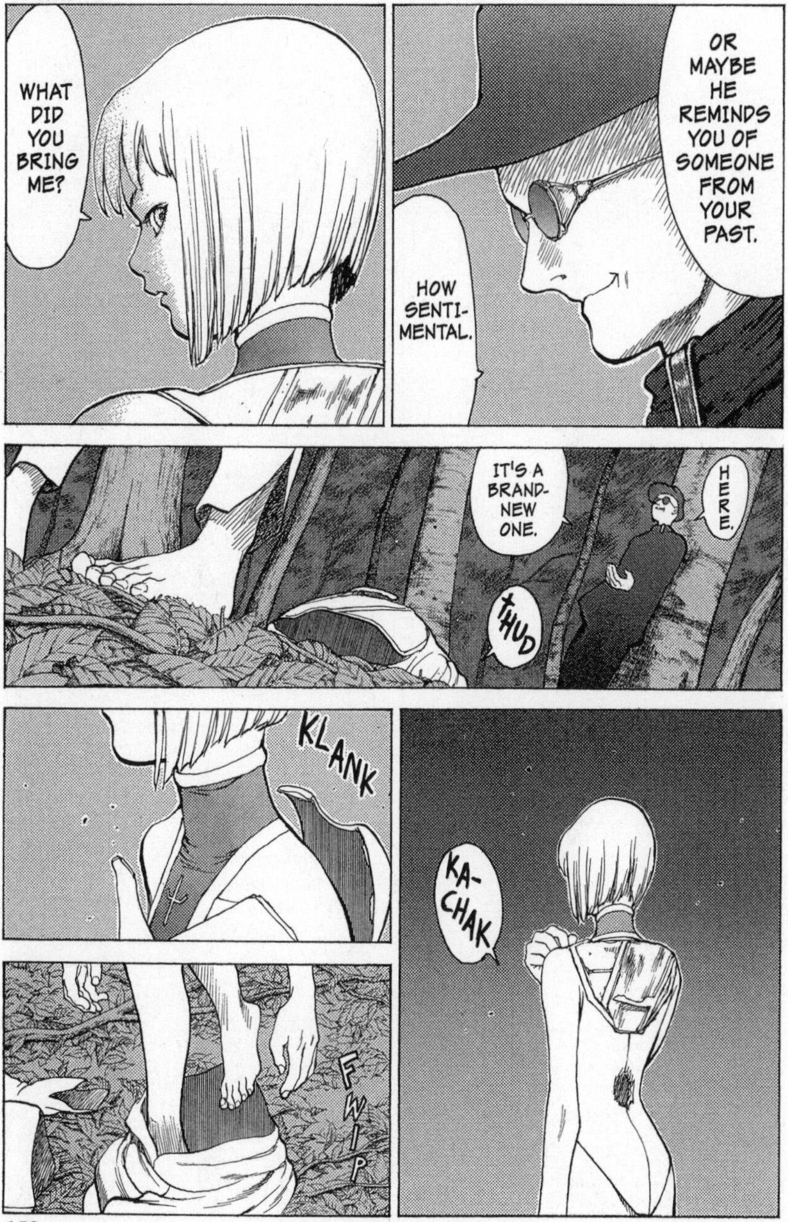
OR MAYBE HE REMINDS YOU OF SOMEONE FROM YOUR PAST.
HOW SENTI-MENTAL.
WHAT DID YOU BRING ME?
HERE.
IT'S A BRAND-NEW ONE.
THUD
KA-CHAK
KLANK
FWIP

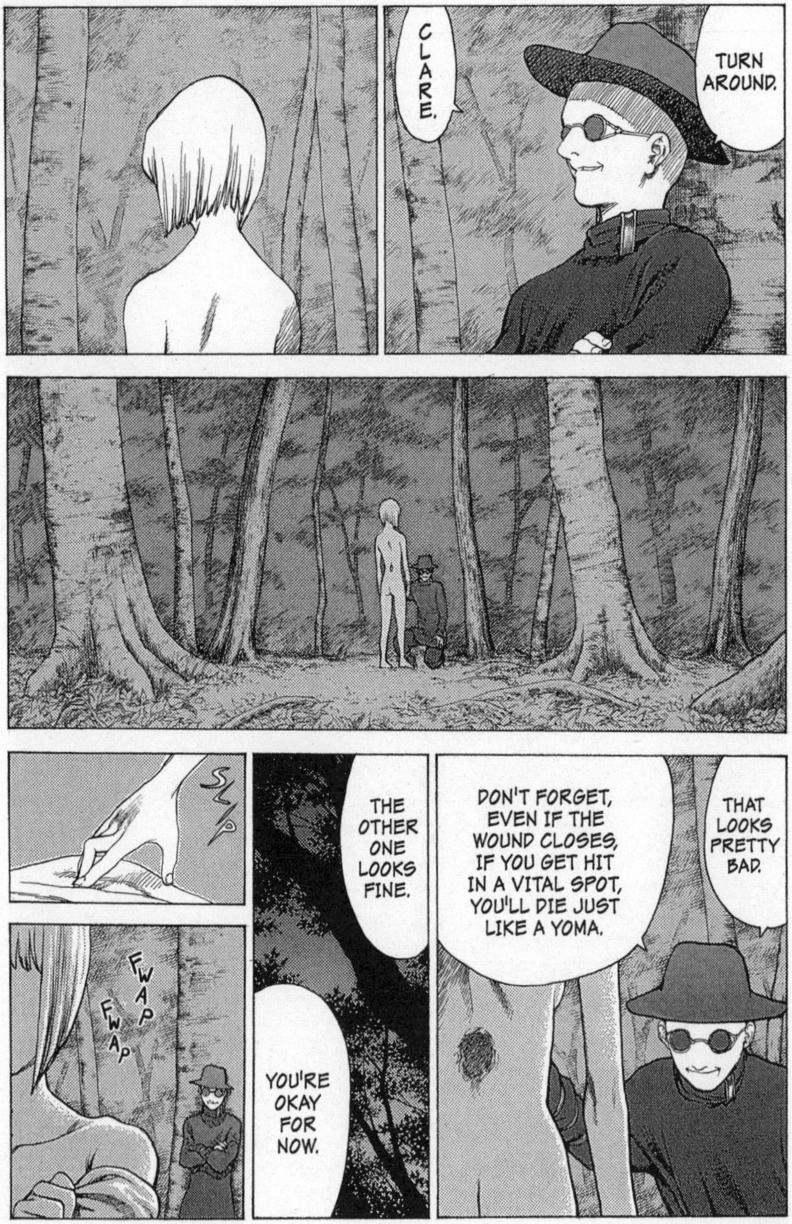
TURN AROUND.
CLARE.
THAT LOOKS PRETTY BAD.
DON'T FORGET, EVEN IF THE WOUND CLOSES, IF YOU GET HIT IN A VITAL SPOT, YOU'LL DIE JUST LIKE A YOMA.
THE OTHER ONE LOOKS FINE.
YOU'RE OKAY FOR NOW.
SLIP
FWAP
FWAP

READ THIS WAY

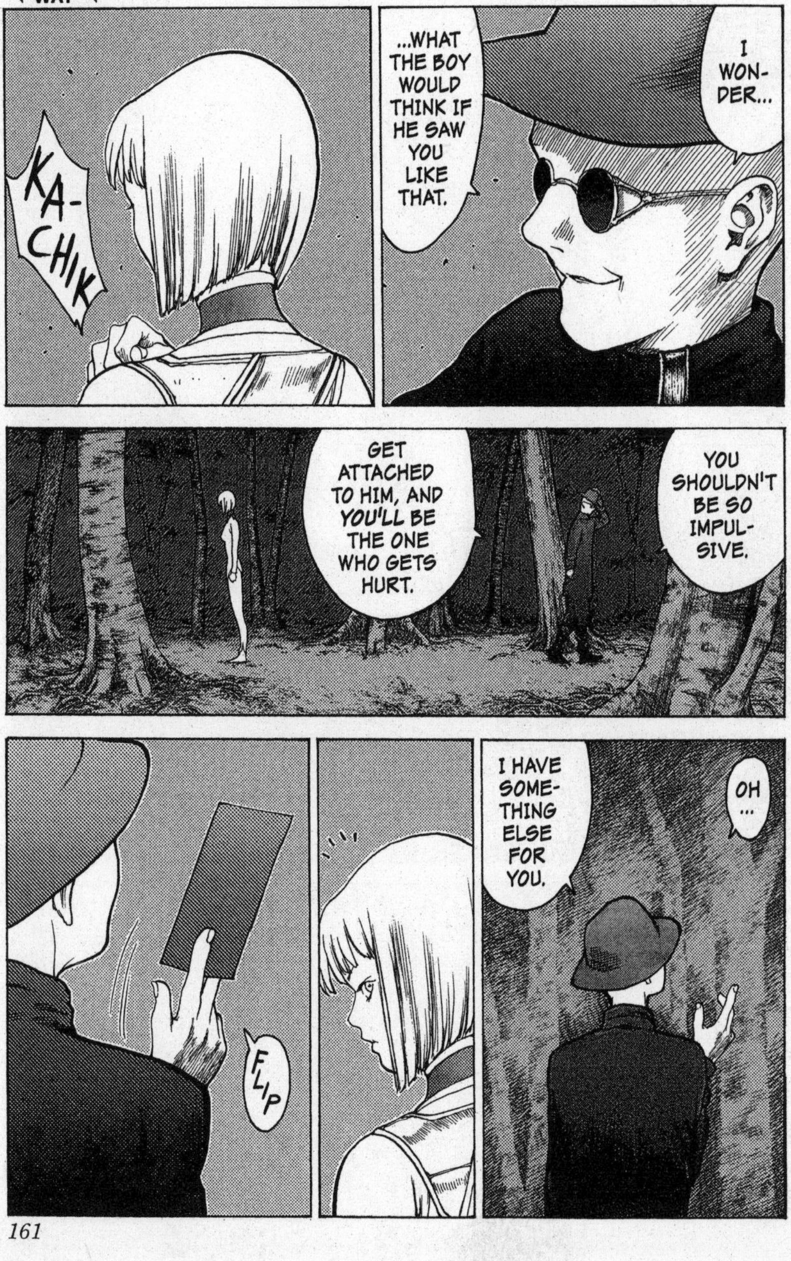
I WON-DER...
...WHAT THE BOY WOULD THINK IF HE SAW YOU LIKE THAT.
KA-CHIK
YOU SHOULDN'T BE SO IMPUL-SIVE.
GET ATTACHED TO HIM, AND *YOU'LL* BE THE ONE WHO GETS HURT.
OH ...
I HAVE SOME-THING ELSE FOR YOU.
FLIP

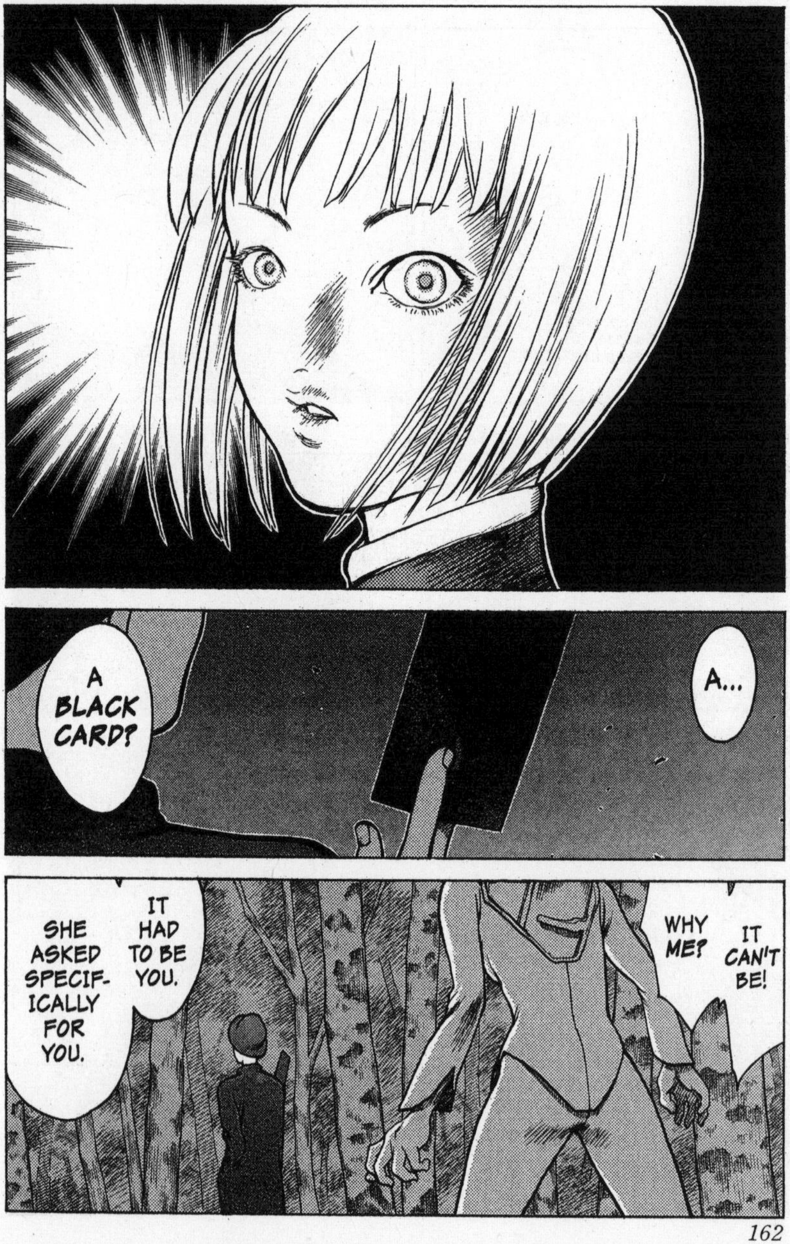
A...
A BLACK CARD?
IT CAN'T BE!
WHY ME?
IT HAD TO BE YOU.
SHE ASKED SPECIFICALLY FOR YOU.

READ THIS WAY

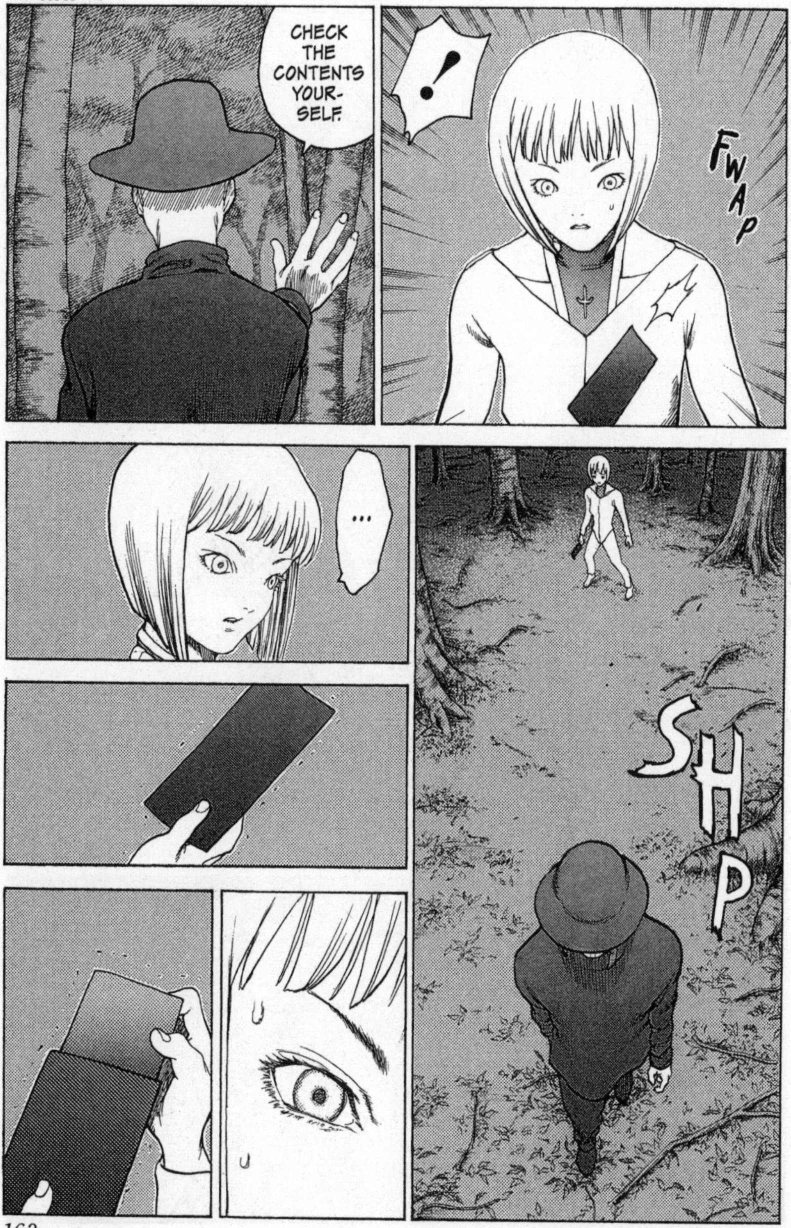
!
FWAP
CHECK THE CONTENTS YOUR-SELF.
SHP
...

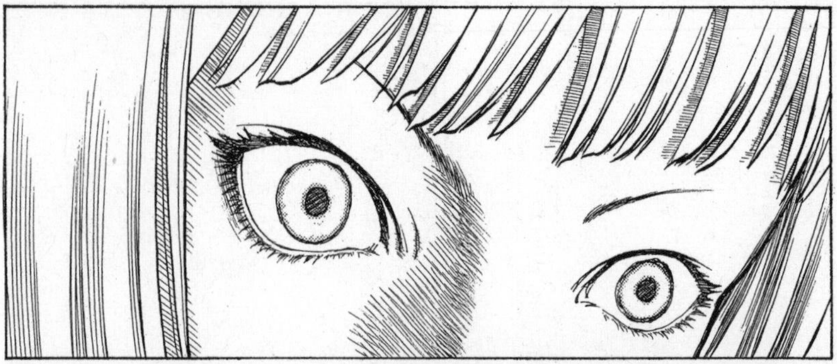
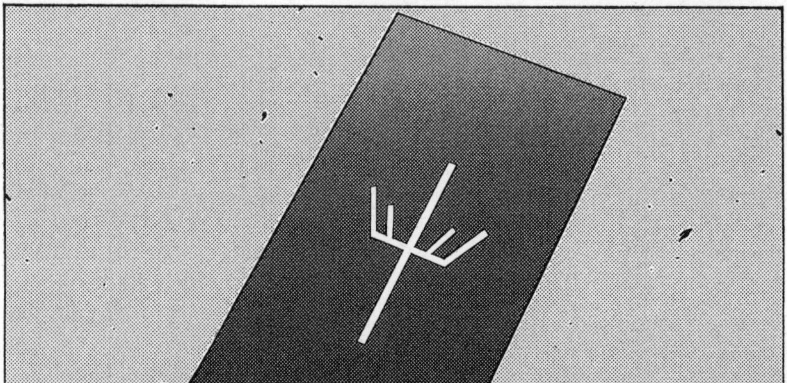
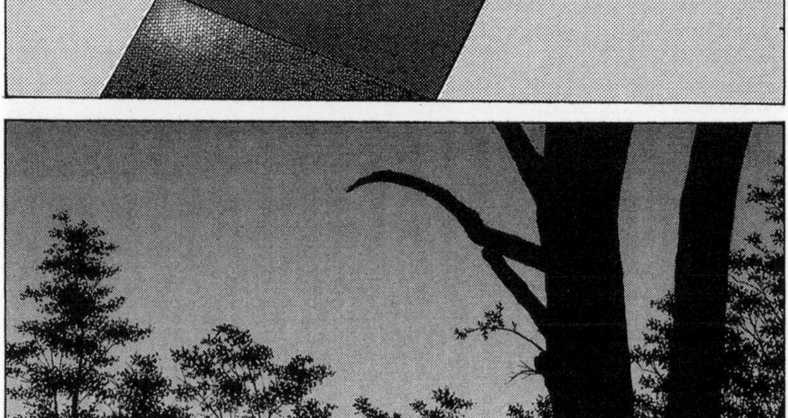

READ THIS WAY

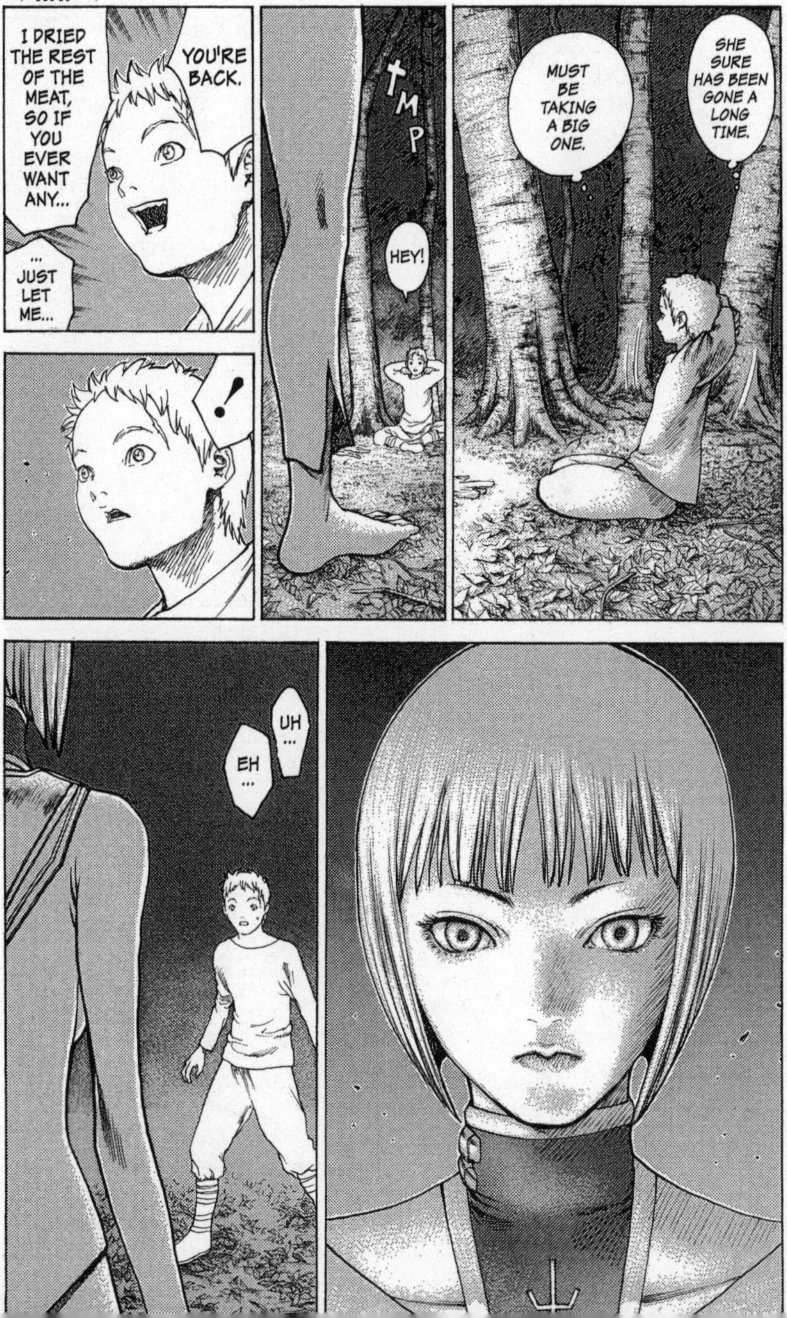

SHE SURE HAS BEEN GONE A LONG TIME.
MUST BE TAKING A BIG ONE.
TMP
HEY!
YOU'RE BACK.
I DRIED THE REST OF THE MEAT, SO IF YOU EVER WANT ANY...
... JUST LET ME...
!
UH...
EH...

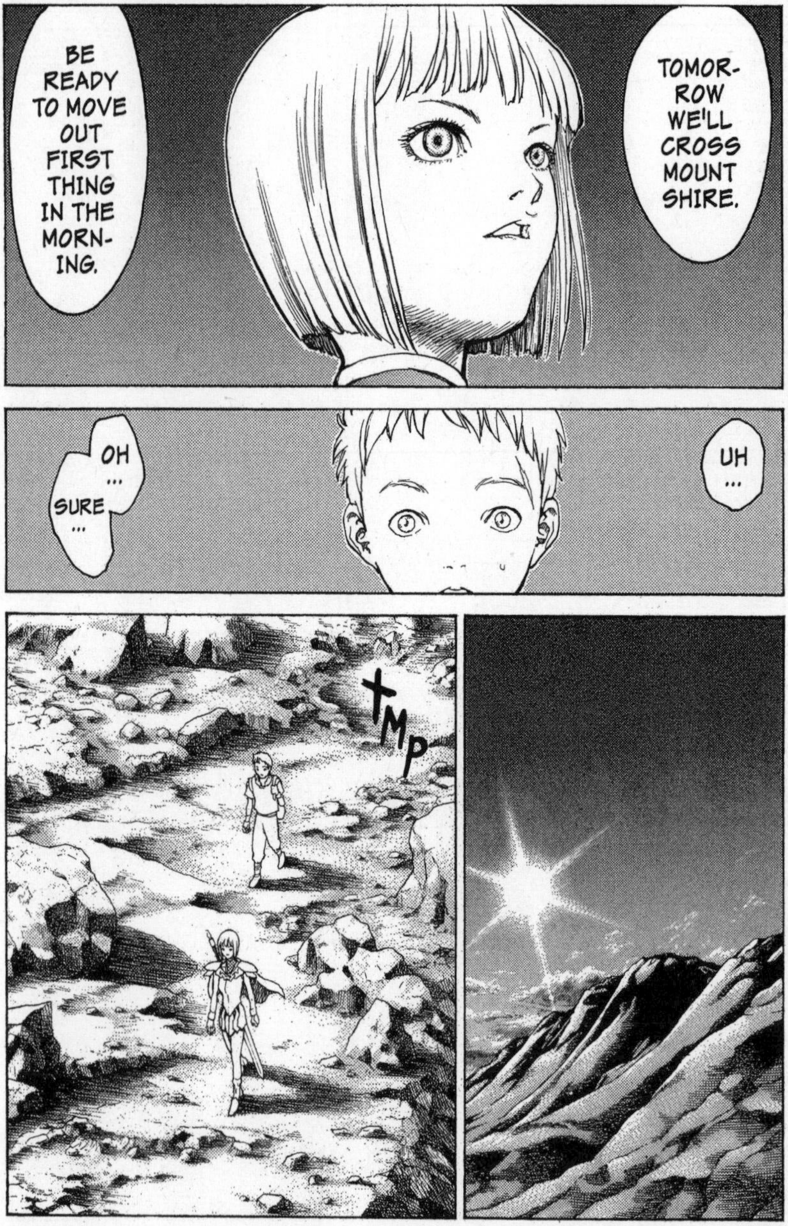
TOMOR-ROW WE'LL CROSS MOUNT SHIRE.
BE READY TO MOVE OUT FIRST THING IN THE MORN-ING.
UH ...
OH ... SURE ...
TMP

READ THIS WAY

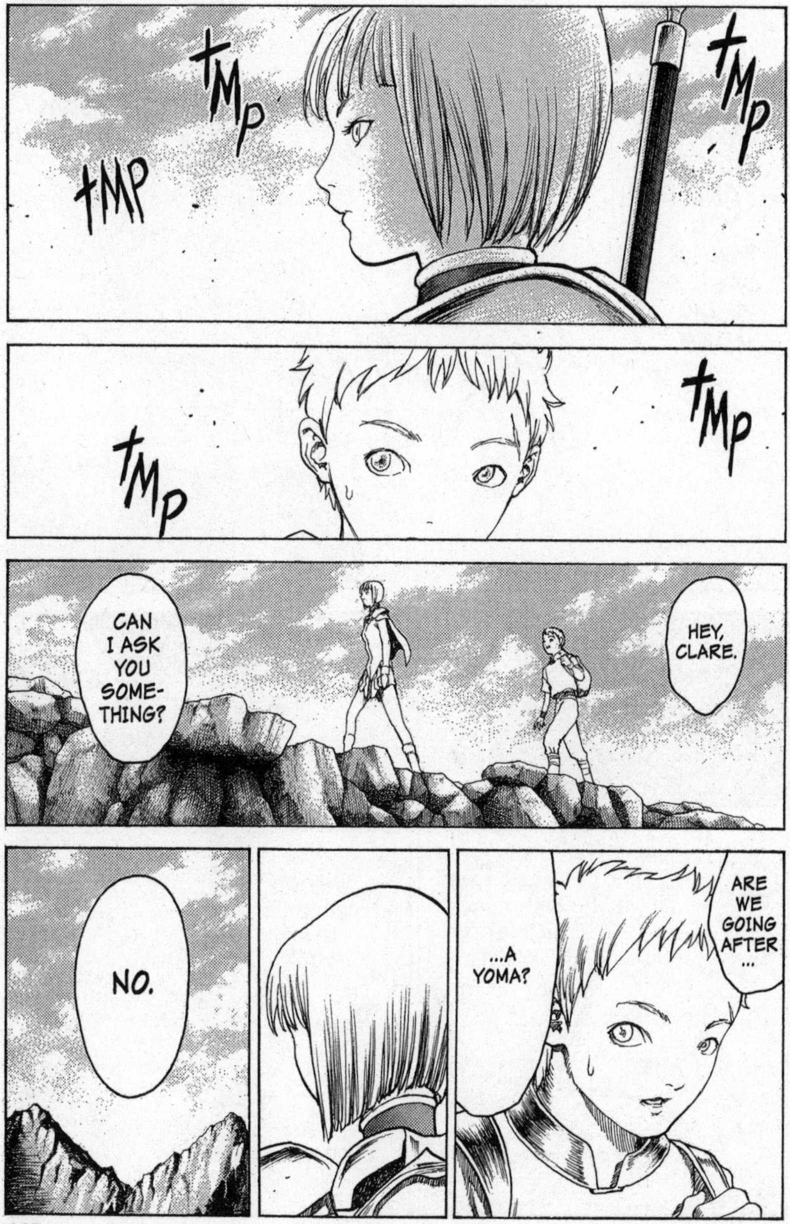

TMP
TMP
TMP
TMP
TMP
HEY, CLARE.
CAN I ASK YOU SOMETHING?
ARE WE GOING AFTER ...
...A YOMA?
NO.

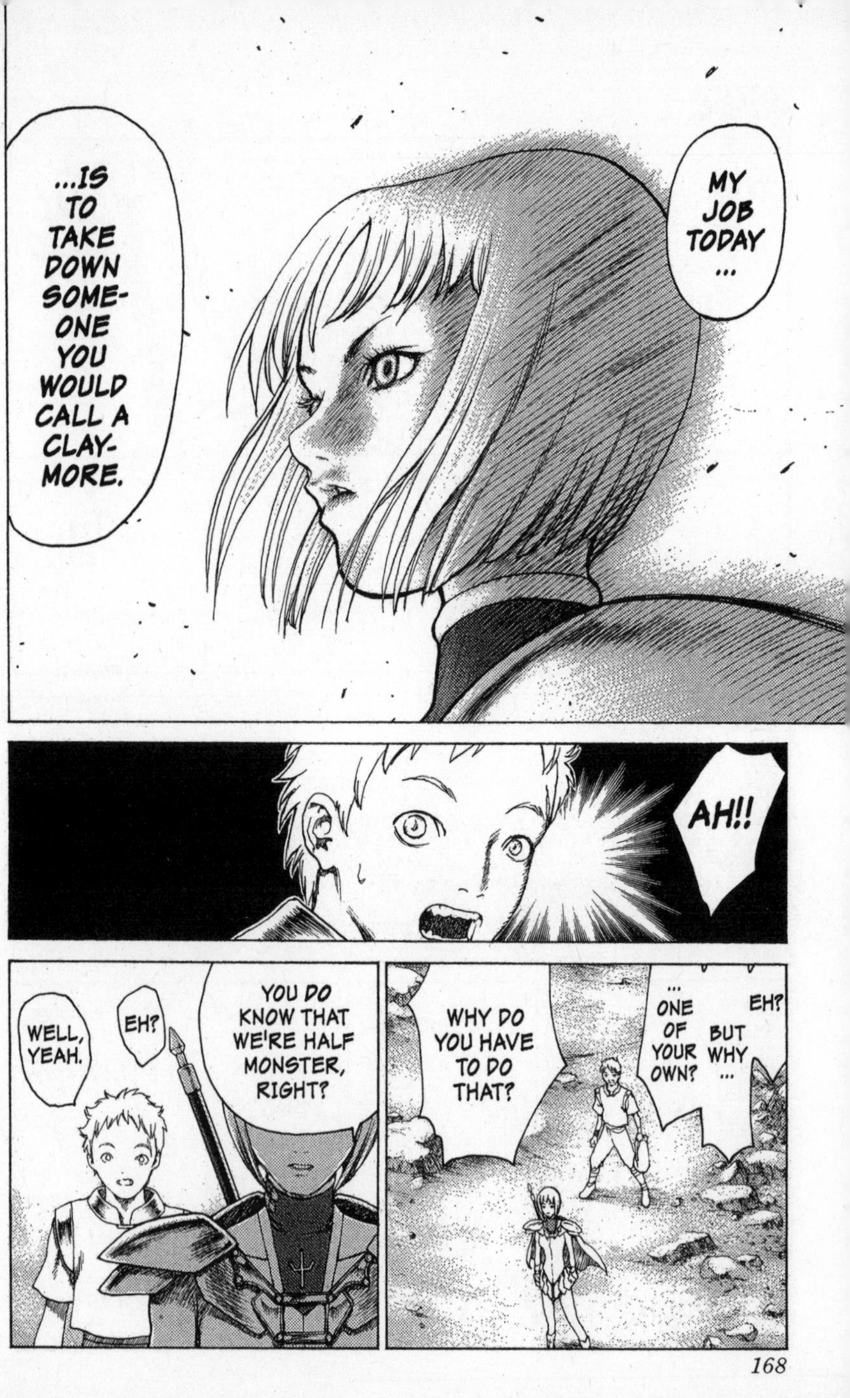
MY JOB TODAY ...
...IS TO TAKE DOWN SOME-ONE YOU WOULD CALL A CLAY-MORE.
AH!!
EH?
BUT WHY ...
... ONE OF YOUR OWN?
WHY DO YOU HAVE TO DO THAT?
YOU DO KNOW THAT WE'RE HALF MONSTER, RIGHT?
EH?
WELL, YEAH.

READ THIS WAY

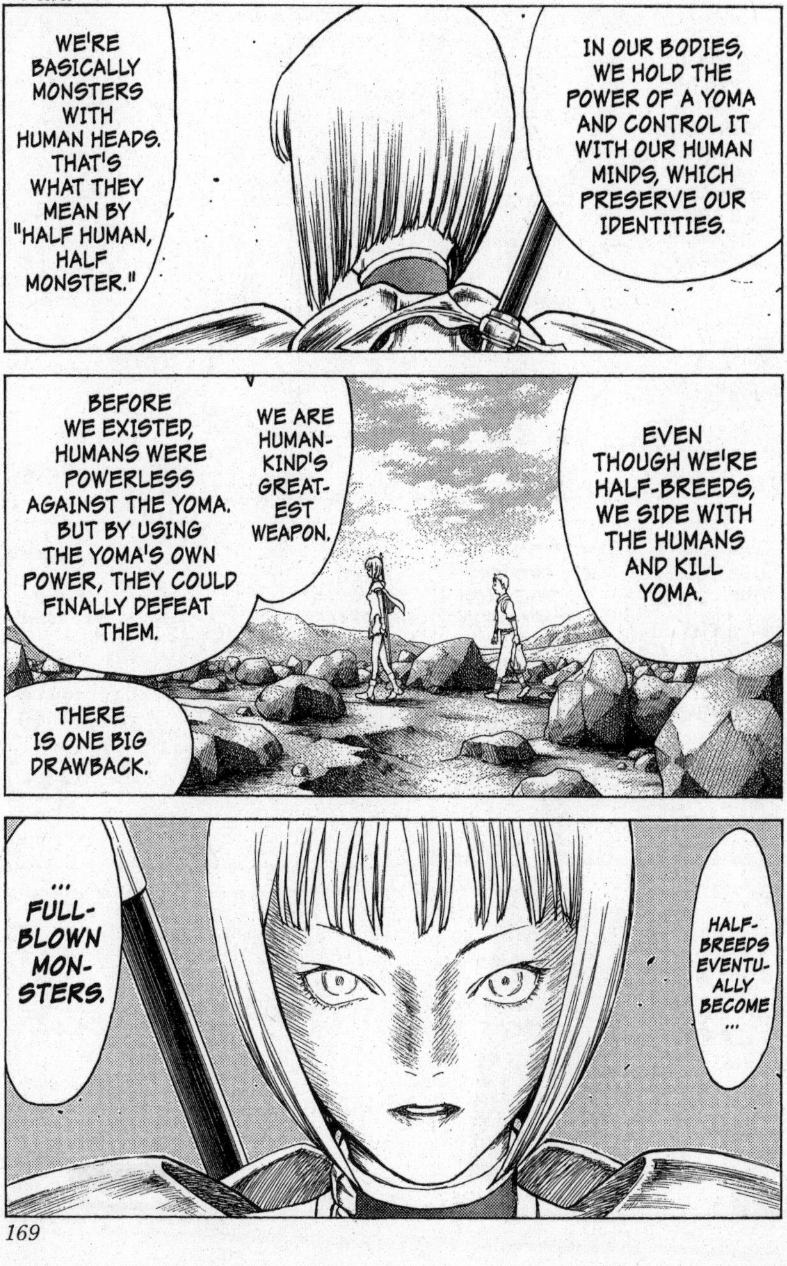
IN OUR BODIES, WE HOLD THE POWER OF A YOMA AND CONTROL IT WITH OUR HUMAN MINDS, WHICH PRESERVE OUR IDENTITIES.
WE'RE BASICALLY MONSTERS WITH HUMAN HEADS. THAT'S WHAT THEY MEAN BY "HALF HUMAN, HALF MONSTER."
EVEN THOUGH WE'RE HALF-BREEDS, WE SIDE WITH THE HUMANS AND KILL YOMA.
WE ARE HUMAN-KIND'S GREAT-EST WEAPON.
BEFORE WE EXISTED, HUMANS WERE POWERLESS AGAINST THE YOMA. BUT BY USING THE YOMA'S OWN POWER, THEY COULD FINALLY DEFEAT THEM.
THERE IS ONE BIG DRAWBACK.
HALF-BREEDS EVENTU-ALLY BECOME ...
... FULL-BLOWN MON-STERS.

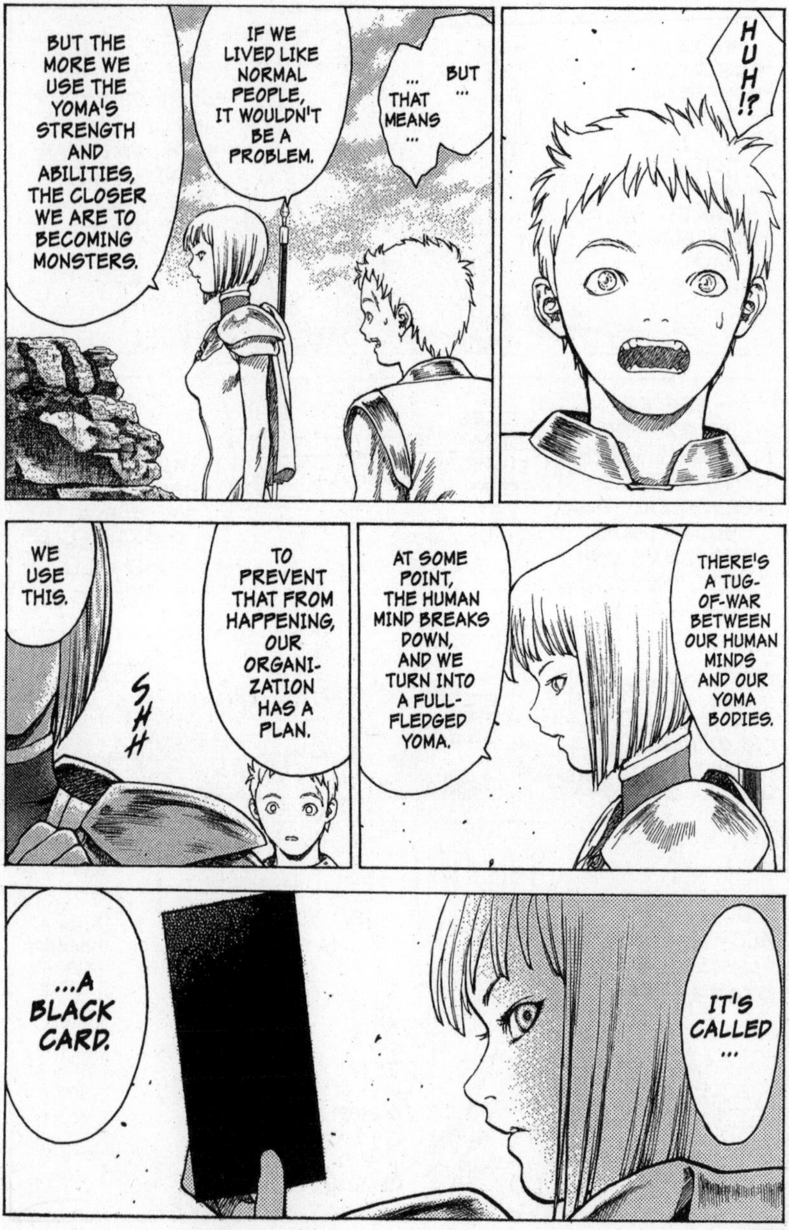
HUH!?
BUT ... ... THAT MEANS ...
IF WE LIVED LIKE NORMAL PEOPLE, IT WOULDN'T BE A PROBLEM.
BUT THE MORE WE USE THE YOMA'S STRENGTH AND ABILITIES, THE CLOSER WE ARE TO BECOMING MONSTERS.
THERE'S A TUG-OF-WAR BETWEEN OUR HUMAN MINDS AND OUR YOMA BODIES.
AT SOME POINT, THE HUMAN MIND BREAKS DOWN, AND WE TURN INTO A FULL-FLEDGED YOMA.
TO PREVENT THAT FROM HAPPENING, OUR ORGANI-ZATION HAS A PLAN.
SHH
WE USE THIS.
IT'S CALLED ...
...A BLACK CARD.

READ THIS WAY

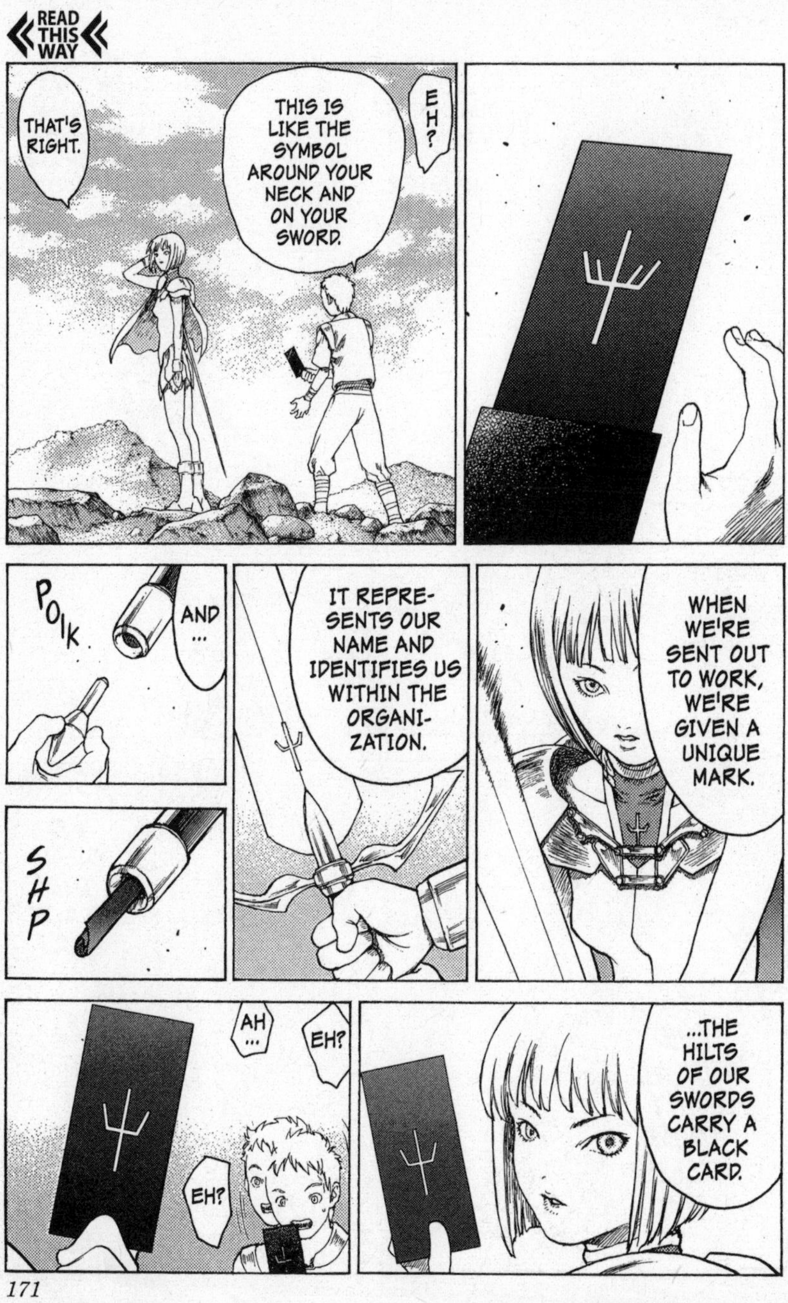
EH?
THIS IS LIKE THE SYMBOL AROUND YOUR NECK AND ON YOUR SWORD.
THAT'S RIGHT.
WHEN WE'RE SENT OUT TO WORK, WE'RE GIVEN A UNIQUE MARK.
IT REPRE- SENTS OUR NAME AND IDENTIFIES US WITHIN THE ORGANI- ZATION.
AND ...
POIK
SHP
...THE HILTS OF OUR SWORDS CARRY A BLACK CARD.
EH?
AH ...
EH?

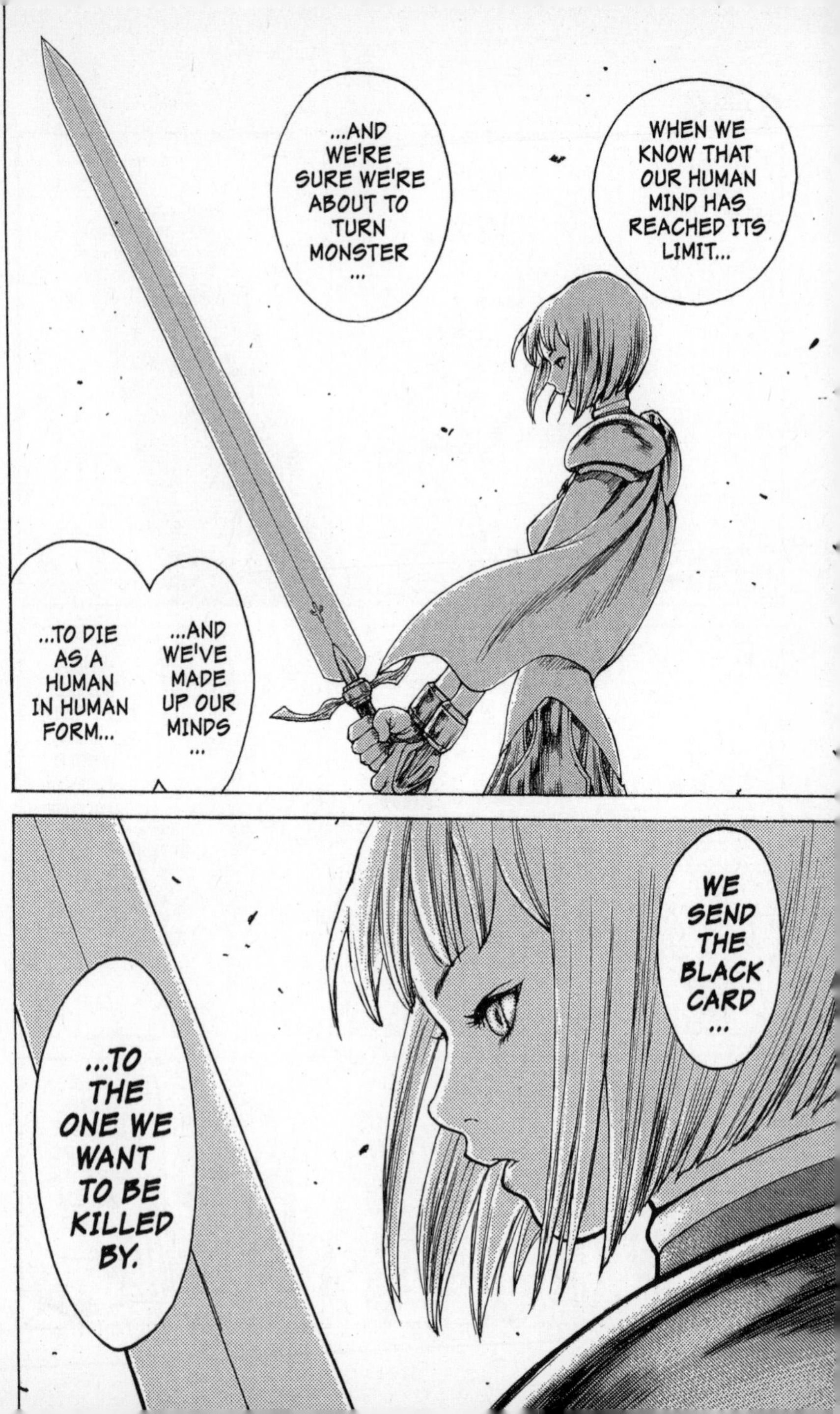
WHEN WE KNOW THAT OUR HUMAN MIND HAS REACHED ITS LIMIT...
...AND WE'RE SURE WE'RE ABOUT TO TURN MONSTER ...
...AND WE'VE MADE UP OUR MINDS ...
...TO DIE AS A HUMAN IN HUMAN FORM...
WE SEND THE BLACK CARD ...
...TO THE ONE WE WANT TO BE KILLED BY.

READ THIS WAY

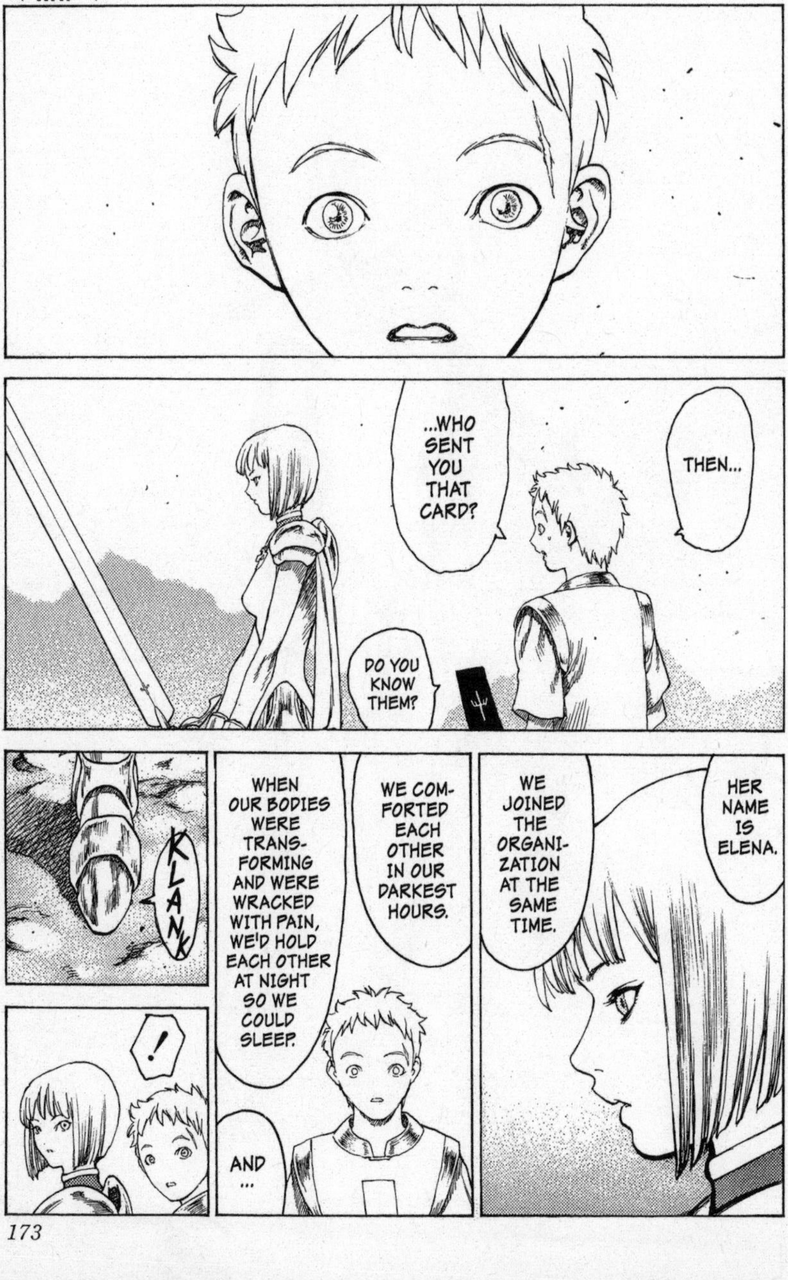
THEN...
...WHO SENT YOU THAT CARD?
DO YOU KNOW THEM?
HER NAME IS ELENA.
WE JOINED THE ORGANIZATION AT THE SAME TIME.
WE COMFORTED EACH OTHER IN OUR DARKEST HOURS.
WHEN OUR BODIES WERE TRANSFORMING AND WERE WRACKED WITH PAIN, WE'D HOLD EACH OTHER AT NIGHT SO WE COULD SLEEP.
AND ...
KLANK
!

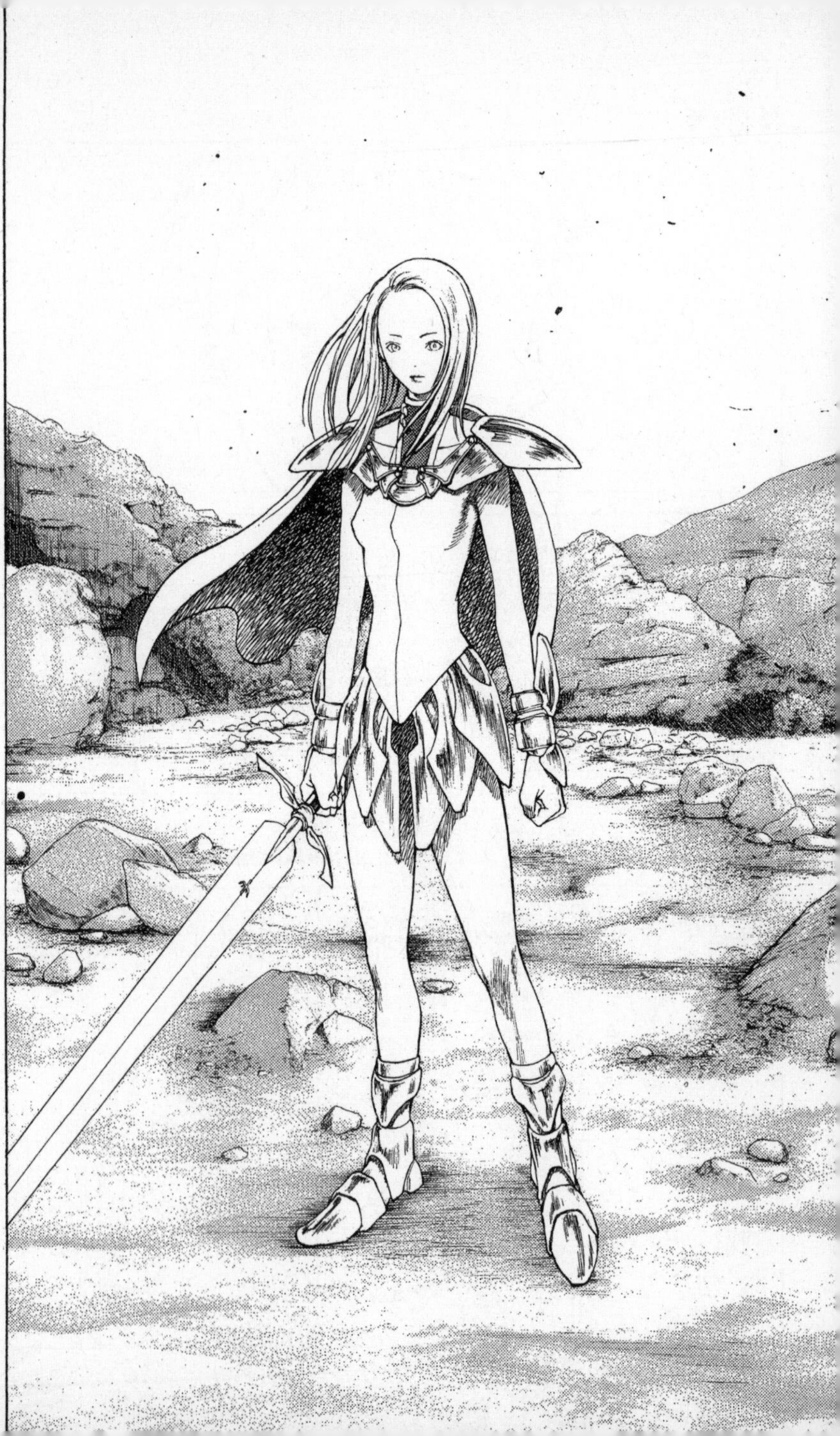

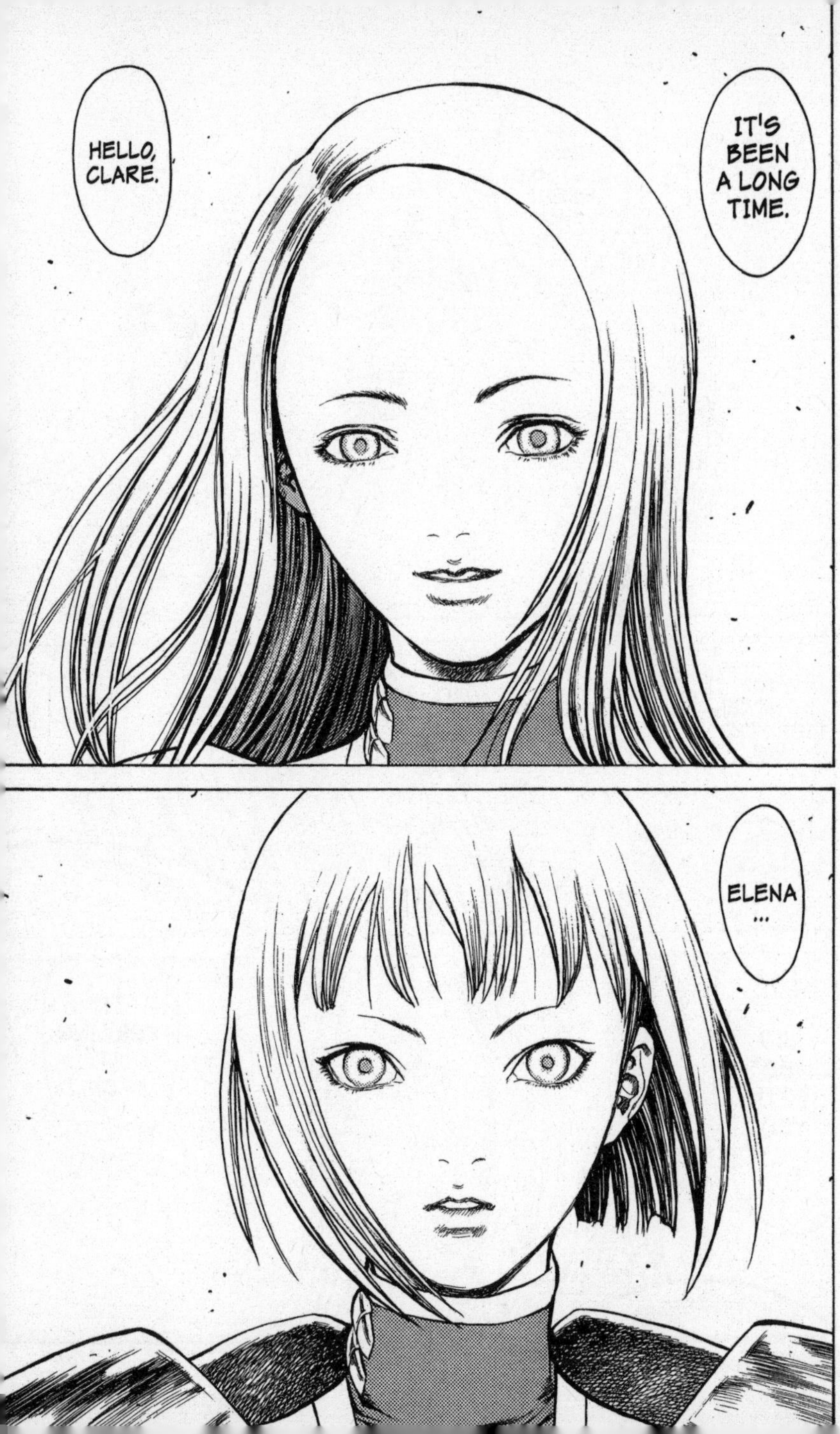
IT'S BEEN A LONG TIME.
HELLO, CLARE.
ELENA ...

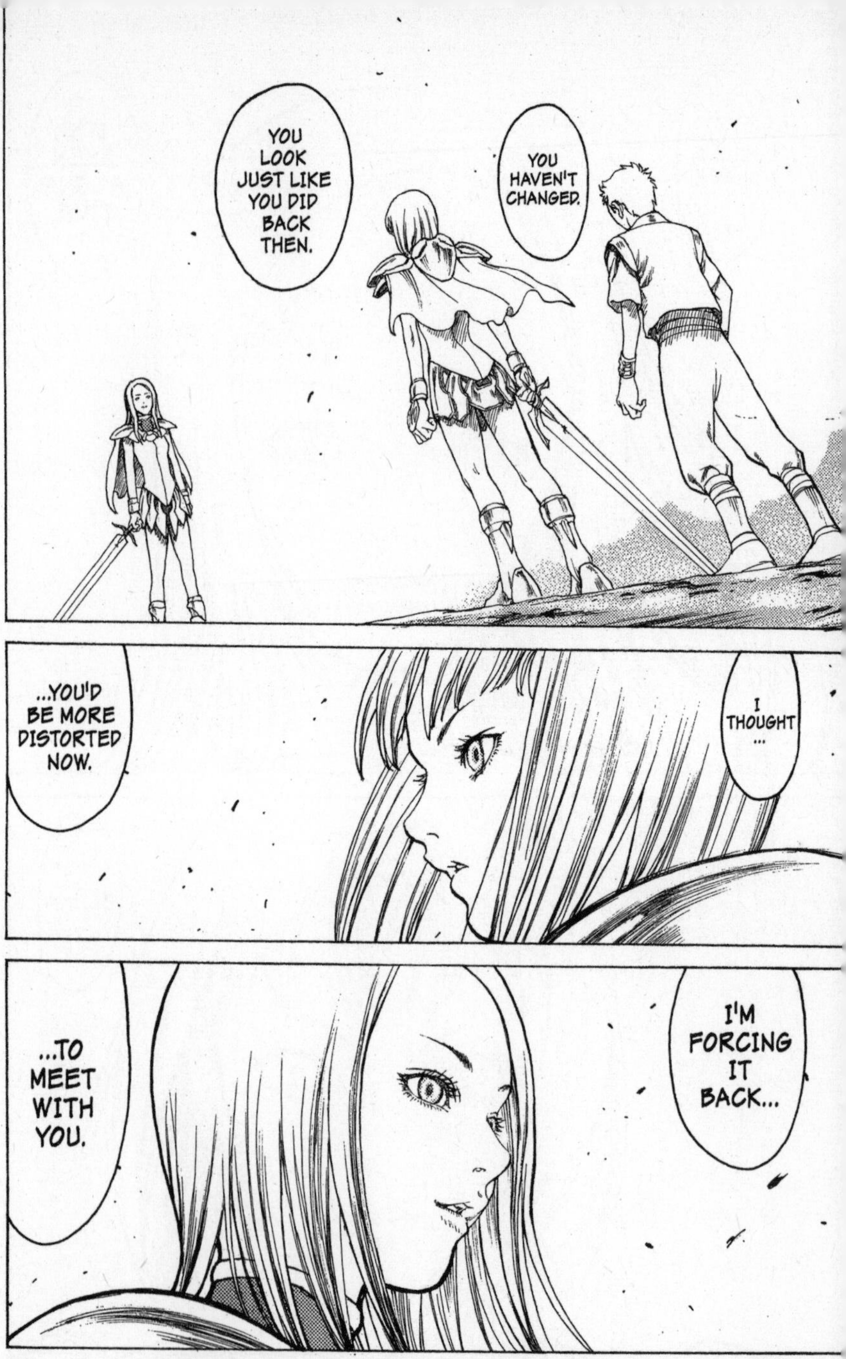
YOU HAVEN'T CHANGED.
YOU LOOK JUST LIKE YOU DID BACK THEN.
I THOUGHT...
...YOU'D BE MORE DISTORTED NOW.
I'M FORCING IT BACK...
...TO MEET WITH YOU.

READ THIS WAY

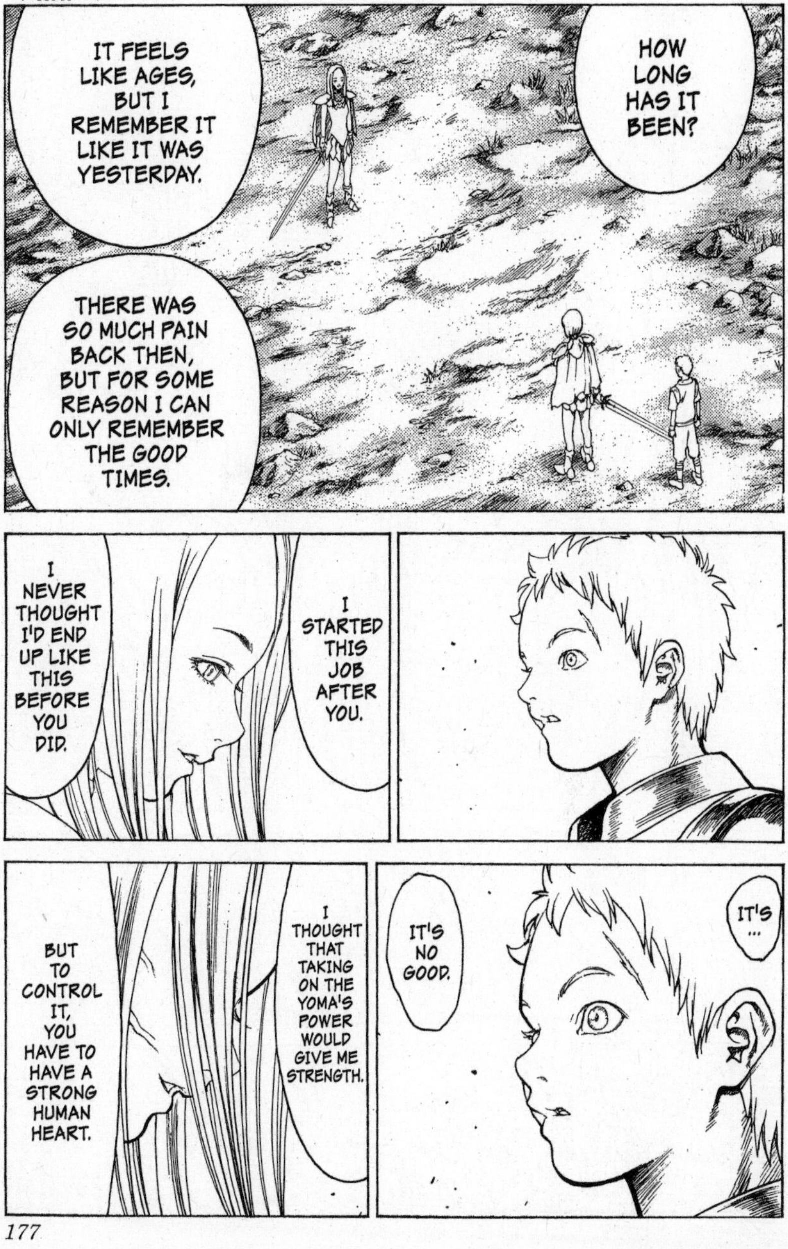
HOW LONG HAS IT BEEN?
IT FEELS LIKE AGES, BUT I REMEMBER IT LIKE IT WAS YESTERDAY.
THERE WAS SO MUCH PAIN BACK THEN, BUT FOR SOME REASON I CAN ONLY REMEMBER THE GOOD TIMES.
I STARTED THIS JOB AFTER YOU.
I NEVER THOUGHT I'D END UP LIKE THIS BEFORE YOU DID.
IT'S...
IT'S NO GOOD.
I THOUGHT THAT TAKING ON THE YOMA'S POWER WOULD GIVE ME STRENGTH.
BUT TO CONTROL IT, YOU HAVE TO HAVE A STRONG HUMAN HEART.

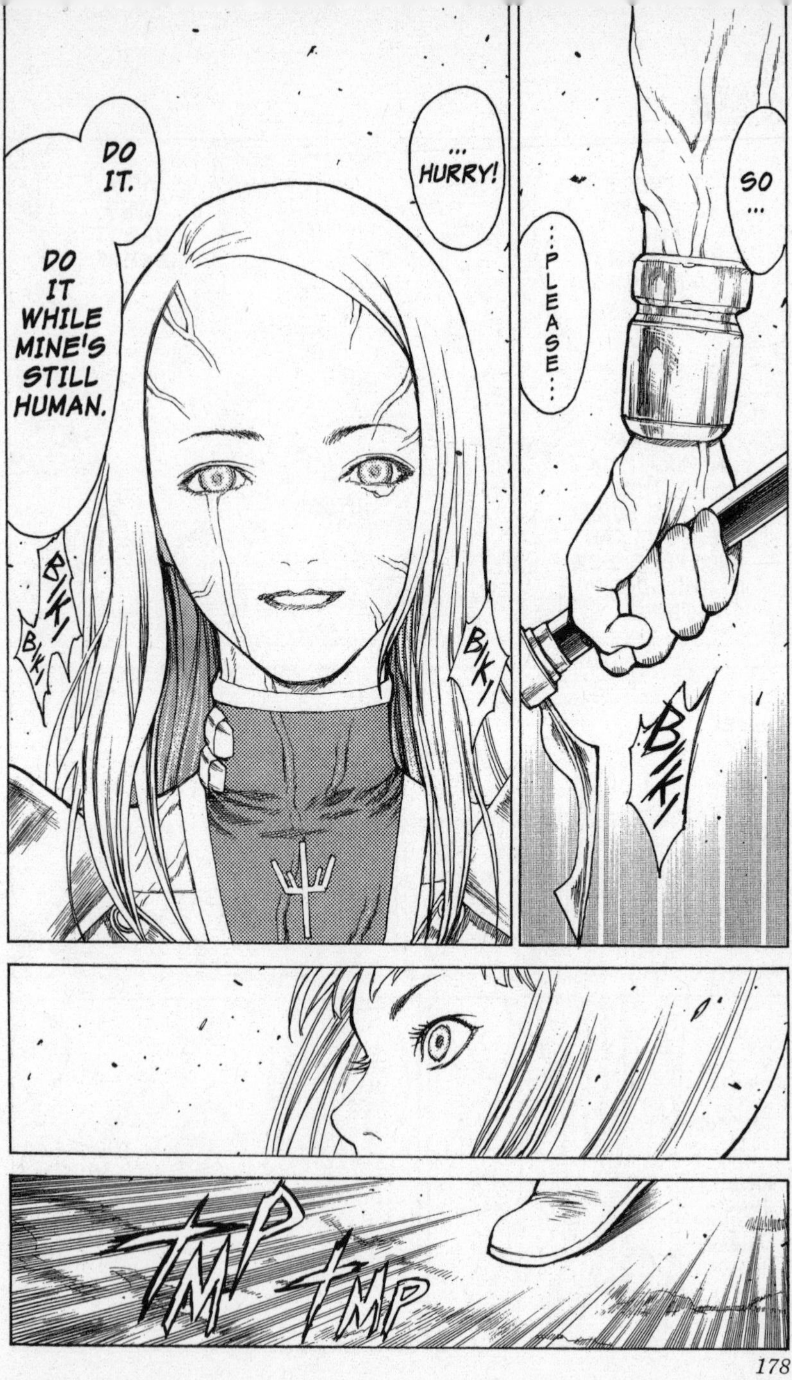
SO ...
...PLEASE...
BIKI
... HURRY!
DO IT.
DO IT WHILE MINE'S STILL HUMAN.
BIKI
BIKI BIKI
TMP TMP

READ THIS WAY

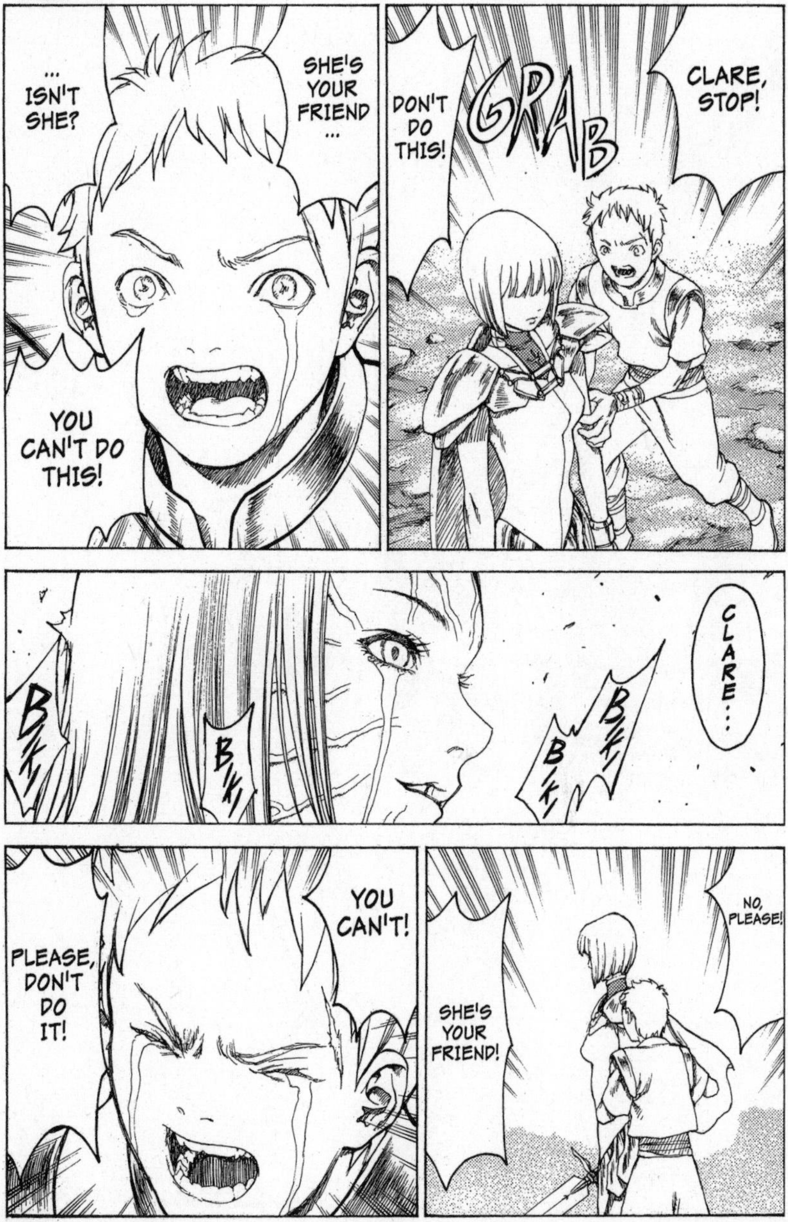
CLARE, STOP!
GRAB
DON'T DO THIS!
SHE'S YOUR FRIEND ...
... ISN'T SHE?
YOU CAN'T DO THIS!
CLARE...
BIKI
BIKI
BIKI
BIKI
NO, PLEASE!
SHE'S YOUR FRIEND!
YOU CAN'T!
PLEASE, DON'T DO IT!

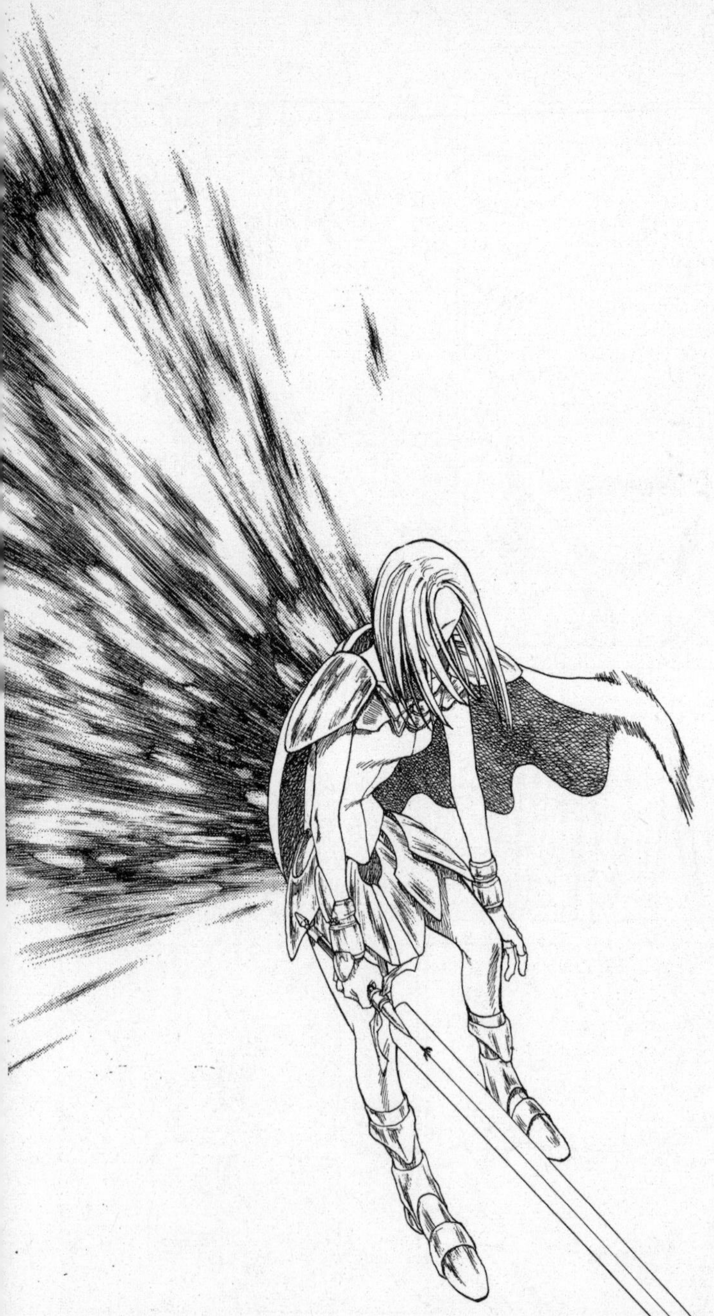

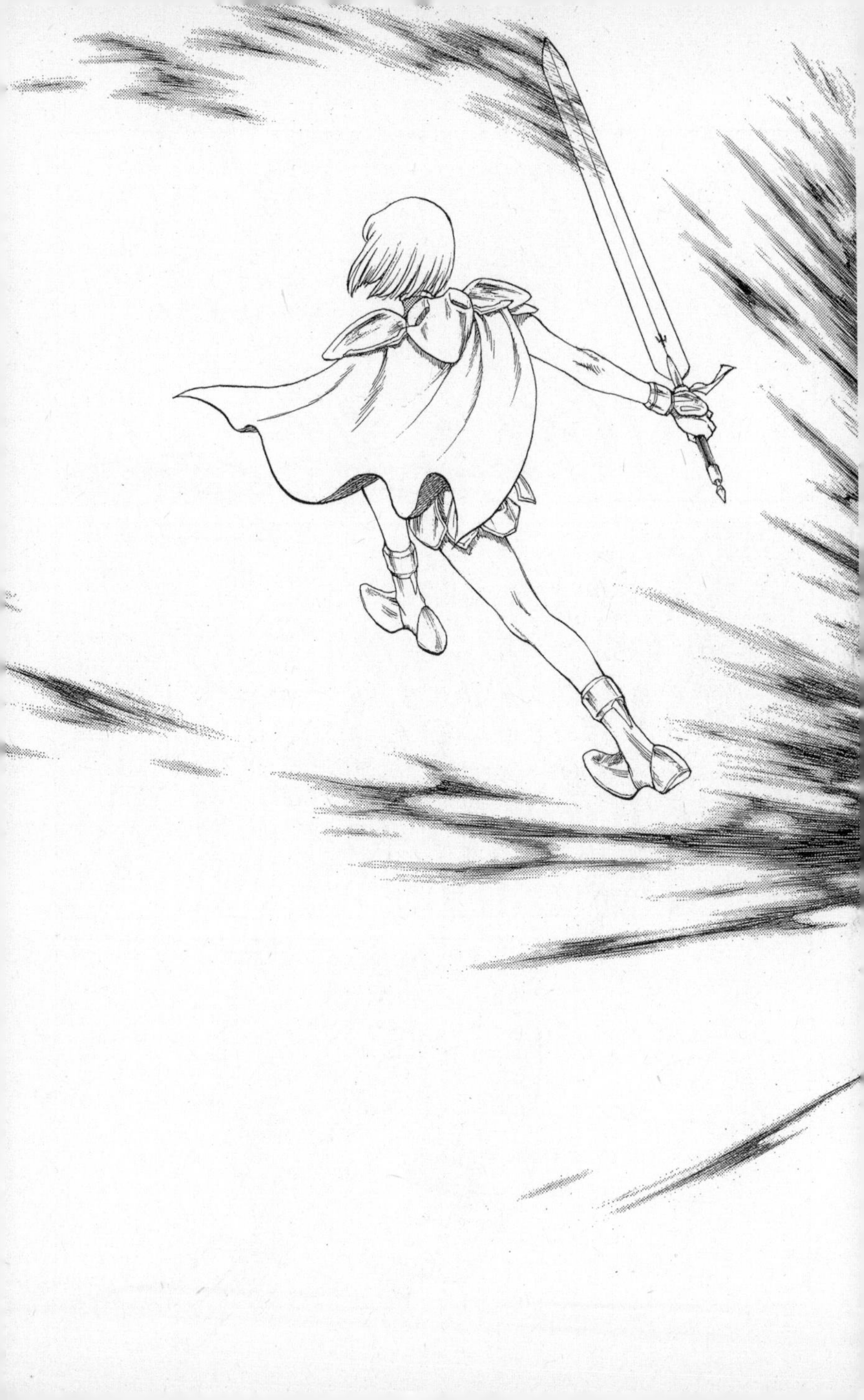

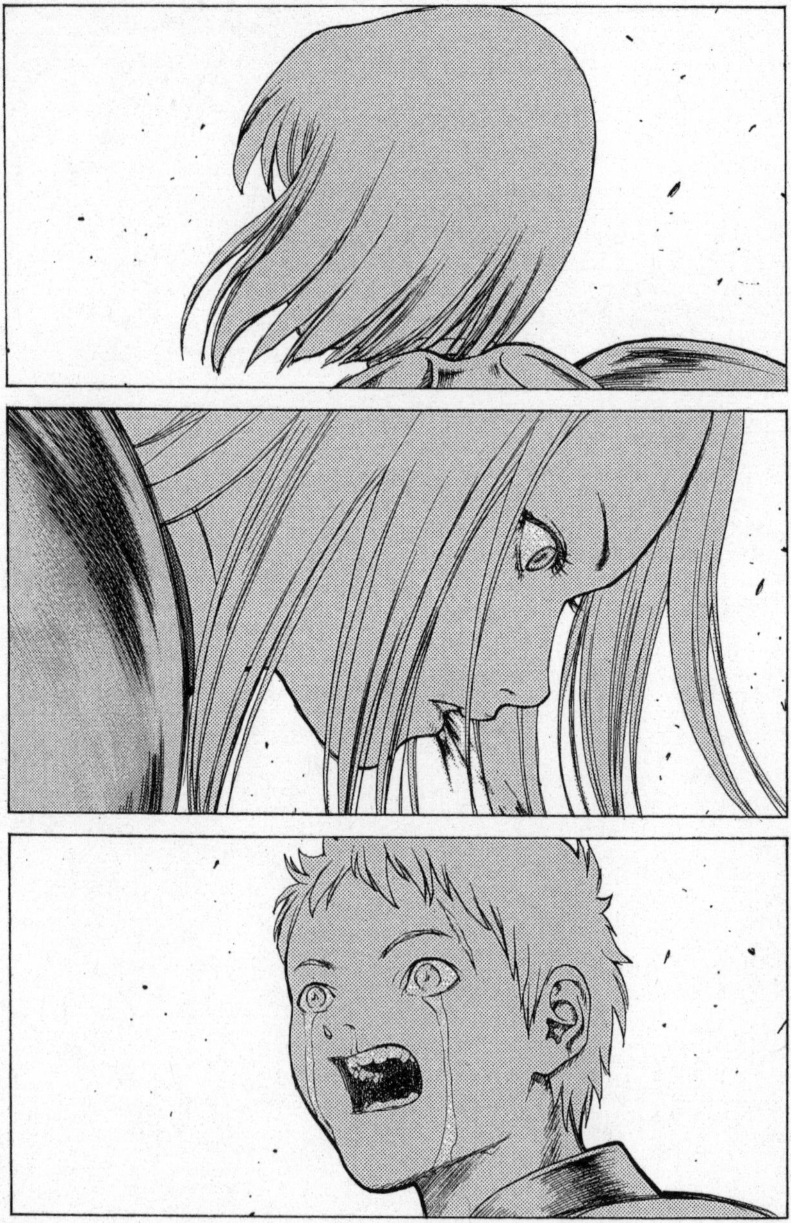

...I CAN DIE AS A HUMAN.

NOW...

THANK YOU...

CLARE...

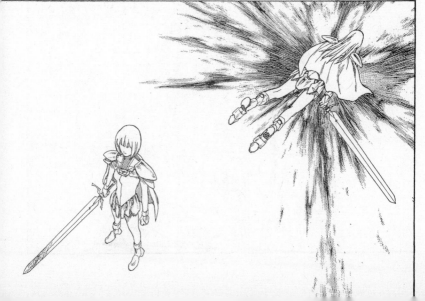

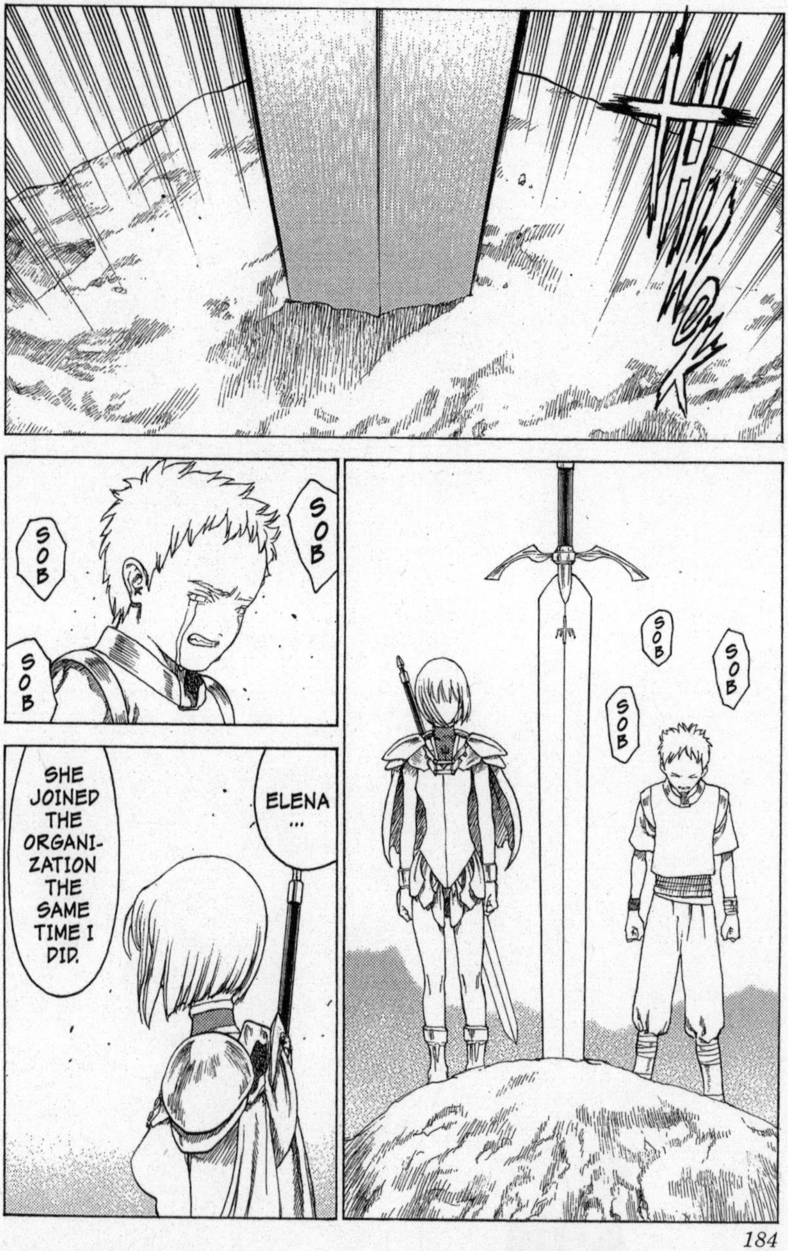
THWOCK
SOB
SOB
SOB
SOB
SOB
SOB
ELENA ...
SHE JOINED THE ORGANIZATION THE SAME TIME I DID.

READ THIS WAY

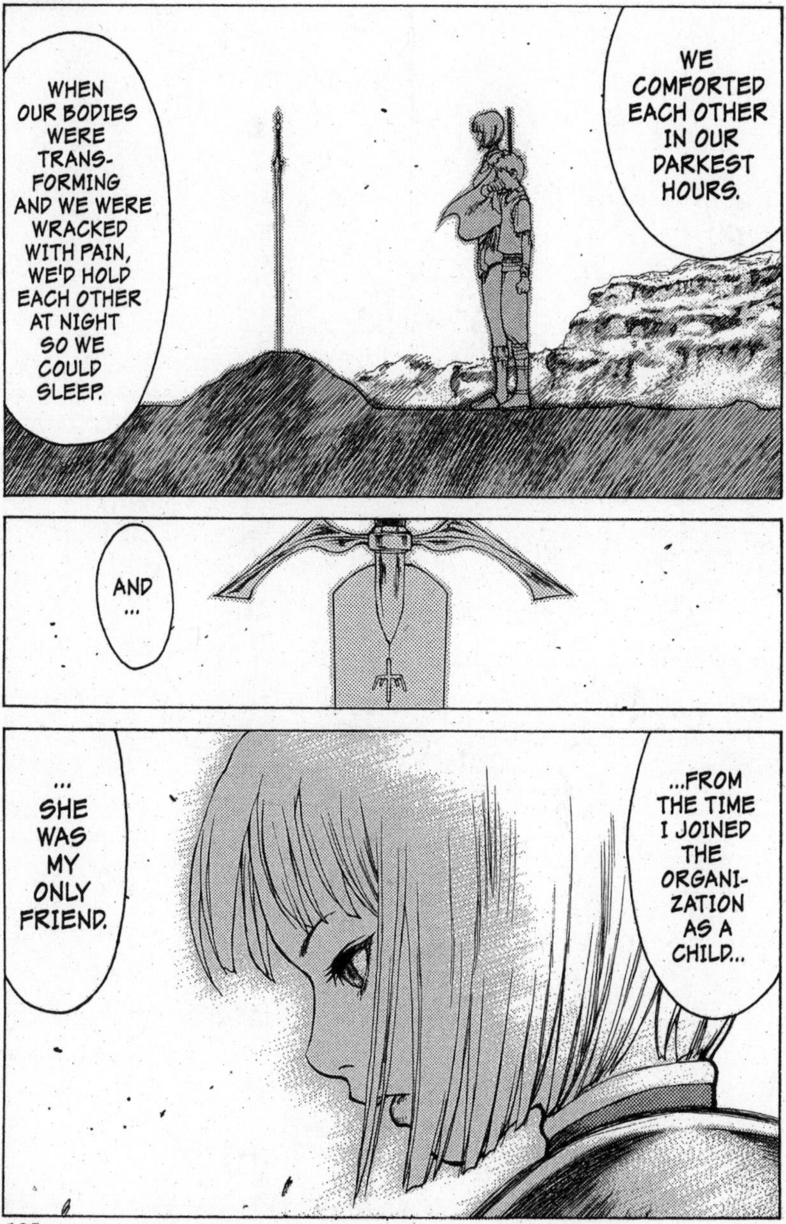
WE COMFORTED EACH OTHER IN OUR DARKEST HOURS.
WHEN OUR BODIES WERE TRANS-FORMING AND WE WERE WRACKED WITH PAIN, WE'D HOLD EACH OTHER AT NIGHT SO WE COULD SLEEP.
AND ...
...FROM THE TIME I JOINED THE ORGANI-ZATION AS A CHILD...
... SHE WAS MY ONLY FRIEND.

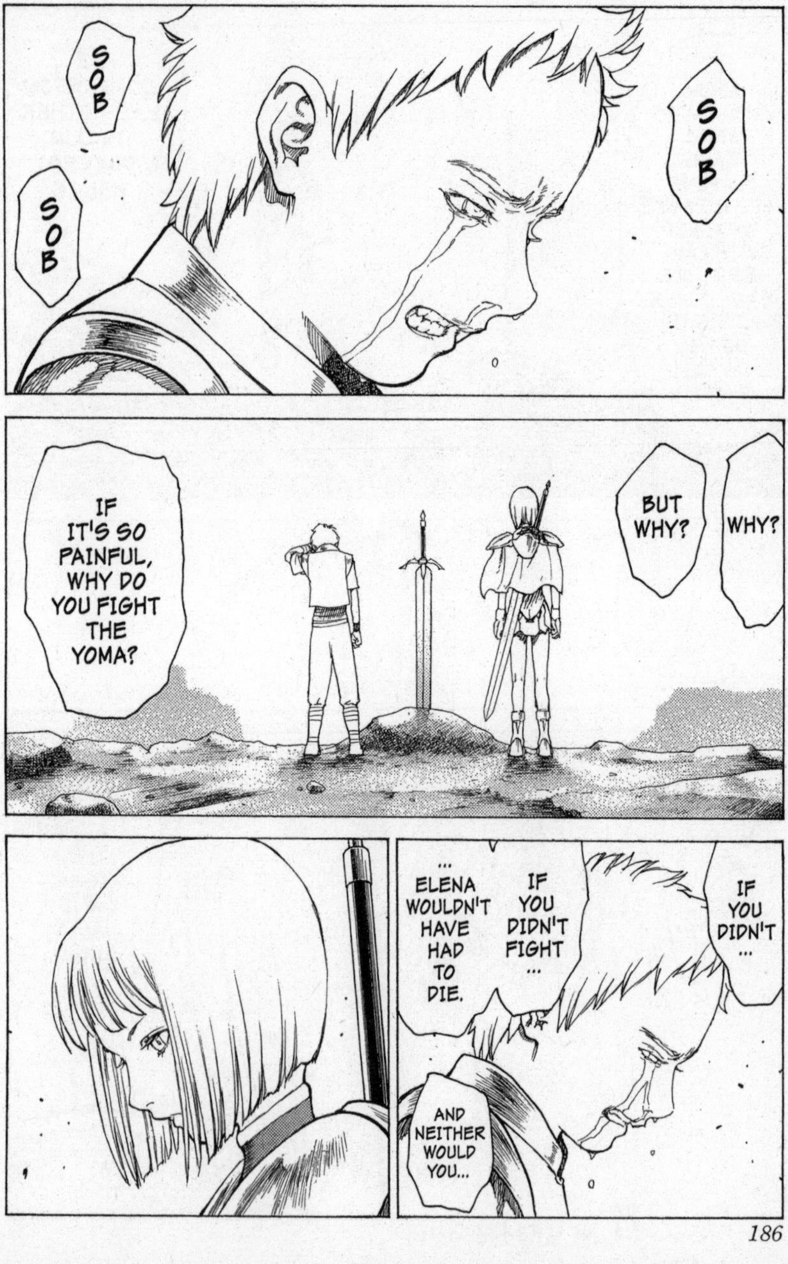
SOB
SOB
SOB
WHY?
BUT WHY?
IF IT'S SO PAINFUL, WHY DO YOU FIGHT THE YOMA?
IF YOU DIDN'T ...
IF YOU DIDN'T FIGHT ...
... ELENA WOULDN'T HAVE HAD TO DIE.
AND NEITHER WOULD YOU...

READ THIS WAY

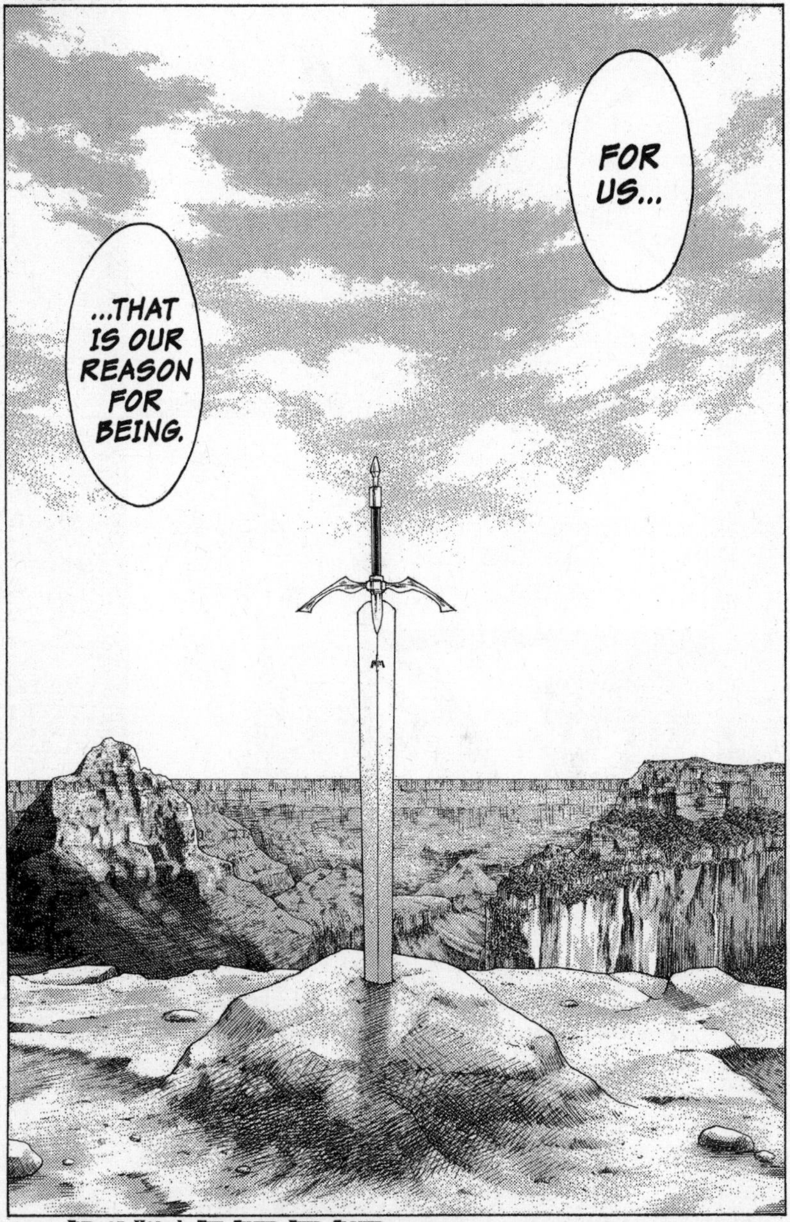
FOR US...
...THAT IS OUR REASON FOR BEING.

 END OF VOL. 1: THE SILVER-EYED SLAYER

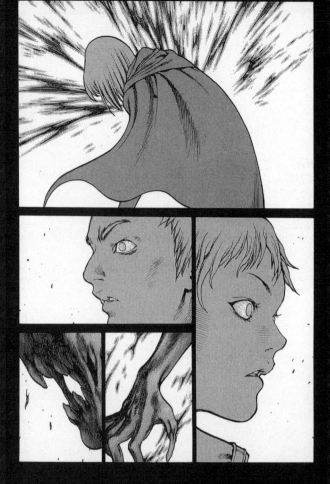

IN THE NEXT VOLUME

Clare and her companion, Raki, travel to a town where the
local priesthood is being stalked by a Yoma. But tracking down
the cunning creature proves to be no easy task. How has the
Yoma managed to escape detection? And how many more lives
will be lost before it's found?

Available Now!

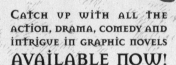